Type in Use

M

Alex White

Type in Use
*Effective typography for electronic publishing*

*Design Press*

First Edition, First Printing
Copyright © 1992 by Alex White
Printed in the United States of America
Designed by Alex White

Library of Congress
Cataloging-in-Publication Data
*White, Alex.*
    *Type in Use / Alex White*
        *p.   cm.*
    *Includes bibliographical references and index.*
    ISBN 0-8306-3796-6
    *1. Printing, Practical – Layout.*
    *2. Type and type-founding.*
*I. Title.*
*Z246.W57  1992*
*686.2'21 – dc20   91-25449*
                    *CIP*

Design Press offers posters and The Cropper, a device for cropping artwork, for sale. For information, contact Mail Order Department. Design Press books are available at special discounts for bulk purchases for sales promotions, fund raisers, or premiums. For details contact Special Sales Manager. Questions regarding the content of the book should be addressed to:
    Design Press
    11 West 19th Street
    New York, NY 10011

Design Press books are published by Design Press, an imprint of TAB BOOKS. TAB BOOKS is a Division of McGraw-Hill, Inc. The Design Press logo is a trademark of TAB BOOKS.

# ACKNOWLEDGMENTS

The most important people I'd like to thank are the 284 designers whose work is included in this book. Their efforts show that each of us in our unique circumstances can improve the quality and the presentation of our written communication.

None of the designers who created the examples shown in this book could have done so without the support and encouragement of their editors and publishers. My thanks to each of them for fostering the teamwork it takes to create the environment in which creativity flourishes and for granting me permission to include their publications here.

Thank you Barbara Love and Michael Garry at Folio: Magazine for asking me to write a series of articles that grew into this book. It is wonderful for an author to be given three blank pages every so often for more than two years to do with as he pleases. I am deeply indebted for their enthusiasm and confidence.

Thanks also to:

• all of you who have attended my seminars on typography and design. It is from my interaction with you that the idea for this book was formed.

• my good friends Dean Stuart Schar, who initiated release time from my classes at the Hartford Art School of the University of Hartford so I would have more time to devote to this work; Don Dyer, whose enjoyment of type is infectious and inspiring; and Mark Zust for researching some of the examples from his personal collection up there on the North Coast.

• Pasquale Temperio, Leon Appel, and Murray Tinkelman, from whom I have learned more than seems reasonable for the short time we worked together.

• Fen Winslow and Martin Madeux, whose print shop is always a friendly place in which to get work done.

• and Willow and Elizabeth, who are so helpful in the office every day.

Nancy Green, my editor, has made this project so much easier for me. She knows design and typography thoroughly, which makes her comments indispensable. But she knows editing is a people business and it is in this regard that she simply is in a class by herself.

*Type in Use* is dedicated to Abby, who invigorates my life with her humor and love.

*Alex White*
*Burlington, Connecticut*

# CONTENTS

# INTRODUCTION

**The music is** not in the violin. I can make an ugly document very easily. I own a computer and layout software. The problem is, so do many others. Consequently, in the last few years, the state of publication design has both deteriorated and improved (the hardware and software can, after all, make magnificent documents in the right hands). The gap between good and bad design has grown because, after investing fifteen or twenty grand in a system, the boss puts a visually untrained person at the wheel. Good, persuasive, communicative design is difficult enough for trained designers to achieve. What possibility of success has a neophyte, given the array of possible missteps the computer provides? It is too tempting to change text size, mix several display typefaces, alter the line spacing to stretch or compress type to fit the column, all done regularly because they *can* be done. Untrained designers are mistaken in thinking the music is in the violin.

Newly minted visual communicators do not understand that, as designers, we are agents for the reader. Our job is to compose elements to make them maximally interesting and comprehensible. "Maximally interesting" does not mean *Hey! Wow! Pow! Zoom!* It means revealing the content of the story instantly and efficiently. I do not read the publications to which I subscribe to get *Hey! Wow! Pow! Zoom!* I read them to get content. I look elsewhere to get *Hey! Wow! Pow! Zoom!*

Our job as visual communicators is not to fill in all the space but to make sure our messages are read and absorbed.

## What is good design?

Good design is communicative design. Period. Communication is why design exists in the first place. So what is communicative design? It is the presentation of information in a clear, un-self-conscious way. The reader must not be aware of the act of reading. And this includes display type.

To produce good, communicative design, you must put yourself in your readers' shoes. What will make them want to read? One thing is telling them clearly what is in the text. That means having well-written, informative headlines and subheads. It means selecting the pictures that tell the story, not the ones that are the prettiest. It means not going overboard with typefaces to make the page look more interesting (in this regard, self-discipline is vital).

Good design requires sharply defined visual relationships. It requires the self-discipline to make similar elements consistently similar; after all, you cannot make something pop out with importance if the surroundings are all popping out, being special. Good design requires breaking long items into smaller, friendly, nonthreatening, bite-size pieces. It requires a sufficiency of entrances into the copy, not just the headline on the first page. Good design requires a clear page structure. Scanning a page to find new beginnings must be effortless. The hierarchy of information must be neon bright. This requires that the designer understand the material being designed! But much design is done without the designer simply having read the material, I suppose because thinking and understanding is harder than just creating prettiness. Few of your readers, however, read for the prettiness of the page; readers read to glean some information from the page.

Design by listening to the material you have to work with. This is called "organic design," where shape grows out of and corresponds to the content. It is a way of organizing elements by attending to their inherent characteristics. Developing sufficient sensitivity to do this well requires a great deal of experience in handling type and imagery. But the learning process is what makes design as a career so rewarding and so much fun.

## Design with a capital D

Designers create hierarchies. Designers align elements. Designers differentiate components based on true differences. Designers select images based on their expository content.

It is the designer's job to prepare publications that convey their messages effectively, requiring minimal exertion by the reader. This goal is accomplished by making design decisions that result in a bal-

---

*TYPOGRAPHY IS A MEANS TO AN END, AND NOT AN END IN ITSELF, AND IT IS SUBJECT TO CERTAIN RESTRAINTS.*
*HERBERT SPENCER*

anced, ordered page. Each decision is not mightily significant by itself. But if, of ten decisions made for a single page, two or three are bad decisions – for example, too many text characters per line and non-alignment of headline and subhead and too narrow an outside margin – the page will be sufficiently disturbed to repel readers. The designer must focus on the *cumulative* effect.

Space is undefined until it is articulated by positioning at least one element in it. But a single element in space creates problems. You cannot tell whether the element is big or small, near or far, high or low, because it is merely floating in space. The perimeter of the space helps, but a second element must be added to provide scale. Design elements are viewed in relation to their surroundings. To be an effective designer, you must pay as much attention to the surroundings as to the elements with which you are working.

The human eye looks for similarities and differences. Similarities and differences, or relationships and contrasts, are flip sides of the same coin. A relationship is a visible connection or association. A contrast shows or emphasizes difference, or lack of association. To create a relationship, all you must do is have two or more elements in agreement. They may be the same size, shape, color, or position, but their shared characteristics cause them to be perceived as related. A designer who fully understands the importance of this

*It is interesting to discover typographic rules containing inconsistencies in logic, which are in use only because of tradition. It is also interesting to ponder the origin of these errors, the practical reasons for their perpetuation, and to suggest remedies.*

*Bradbury Thompson*

idea will be able to make *any* group of elements function as effective visual communication. This is true whether the elements are typographic, photographic, or illustrative.

Relationships require that tough decisions be made so that almost similar elements appear to be similar. A simplified page is a scannable page. Relationships require that alignments be true: half a pica between friends makes a big difference.

Contrasts require one element to dominate another. Good design organizes information in a hierarchical fashion. Elements are organized to be seen in a specific order. The element that is seen first, called a focal point, dominates the page. A very basic contrast exists between type and imagery. Because type and imagery and, of course, space are the elements at a designer's disposal, designs are said to be either type dominant or image dominant. You must decide which of these two is more important to your message as you begin your preliminary sketches. The subject matter will most often suggest its own treatment. Great visual material lends itself to an image-dominant layout; a great headline or pull quote or a lot of copy suggests a type-dominant layout.

## About typography

Type holds a publication together. The one thing every page in your publication has is type. It is the constant, the thread leading from spread to spread. It is vital to the life of your publication that the type be presented consistently and in a way that makes sense to the reader (that is, keep it simple!). Groups of similarly designed typefaces are known as *families* and, when used throughout a publication, unify the pages. Develop a system that works for your particular needs and stick to it. You will tire of your typographic system long before your readers do.

Restrict your typeface use. Use the least possible number of typefaces, sizes, and weights, while still allowing for flexibility as unusual circumstances warrant. When in doubt, do *not* make a special change. Your readers are well served if you err on

the side of typographic consistency. If your system is well conceived initially, the variations in your regular typographic arsenal will cover any situation. Making special changes or experimenting from page to page or issue to issue confuses and severely weakens the unity of your product. Minor typographic variations confuse and distract the reader from the content. Besides, they take a lot of time to produce.

Standardize columns and type specifications. The column structure and text type are pervasive in a publication. Together, they create its personality. Uninformed design is taking a standard three-column format and shoving "interesting" display type at the tops of the columns; it is no wonder that it still looks familiar. Informed design is fundamentally altering the column structure so that all type looks special to this publication, so that readers can scan the page and be informed and enticed to get into the text. A Rule Of Thumb That Should Never Be Broken: The wider the column, the larger the type size and the greater the necessary line spacing. When type is set for a two-column format, it should always be set bigger with more line spacing than when it is set for a three-column format. Catalog all the necessary typographic treatments for the past year's worth of issues of your publication, and develop a system of text settings and column placements that can accommodate all those circumstances. It is extremely likely that future stories can be

*Type well-used is invisible as type. The mental eye focuses through type and not upon it, so that any type which has excess in design, anything that gets in the way of the mental picture to be conveyed, is bad type.*

*Beatrice Ward*

made to behave like one of those past articles, that there is some similarity in importance and content that would allow them to be treated in the same way.

Standardize type placement. After you have decided on type specifications, determine exactly where every element will be placed, how far from the trim, how far from other type elements. Also decide how much space will occur from picture to caption, from headline to subhead, from subhead to text. This space management is what will make your publication look clear and well organized. It will make readers trust the content.

*In typography, function is of major importance, form is secondary, and fashion almost meaningless.*
*Aaron Burns*

Flush-left/ragged-right type is an all-purpose setting. Word spacing in flush-left/ragged-right type is always consistent, regardless of the column width. Justified type, on the other hand, achieves two smooth edges at the expense of even word spacing: each line of type is sucked out to or shoved into the full measure, and word spacing is inserted or deleted as needed. This is a minor distraction in lines of type that contain sufficient characters (about forty), but shorter justified lines create horrible word spaces. Avoid the problem by setting all type flush left/ragged right, allowing hyphenation. The idea that such a setting looks more casual, or that justified type looks more dignified, is nonsense. What is far more important is how the display type is handled and how it relates to the text.

**How do I make it work?**
The choices made while designing are too often based on a narrow horizon of possibilities. They grow from past decisions, what others involved with the project will allow or like, our self-confidence in taking a chance on doing something new and

risky, and perhaps most important, our knowledge of what is possible.

*Type in Use* is intended to widen the horizon of typographic possibility, to take off the designer's blinders. Inspiration for interesting typography can be found in other places too. But don't just look at type for ideas. Look at other objects and visual relationships as well. Be imaginative. Experiment. Galleries and museums are useful resources. Read as much as you can about design.

There are many typographic ideas, a lot of choices, in this book. It is not a good idea to wander through the pages, arbitrarily selecting a headline scheme or caption format and tossing them into your publication. You probably will not have compiled a coherent typographic system, so you won't be much better off for the effort.

Instead, determine the most important typographic element in your publication. It can be either the most problematical or the element that deserves to be made prominent because it is unique to your publication (like its name). Now, pencil and paper in hand, turn to the chapter describing that element, and look for a treatment that sparks an idea or seems to solve your problem. Look for the *idea* expressed in the examples, and reinterpret the idea, not the typographic execution itself. That is just a ripoff and no fun. Redraw it, making whatever changes are needed to satisfy your unique situation. As you flesh out your design by looking through the other chapters, find design solutions that are harmonious with the initial treatment. Every treatment can be altered to fit with other elements.

Even when following this technique, developing an initial, unified design by lifting various treatments from a book is very risky. Computers allow quick and relatively easy changes. Create several variations of an idea, print them out, and pin them on the wall. Live with them for a few days before making a final decision.

If a treatment is amusing merely for amusement's sake, your readers will quickly tire of it. If you use a novel treatment that helps convey content, that is, if

you solve a real problem in an effective, communicative way, you will cement a bond with your readers.

There are many books available that discuss the principles and theories of good typography. Two of the best are Carl Dair's *Design with Type* and Erik Spiekermann's *Rhyme & Reason: A Typographic Novel.* I recommend them as the brilliantly thorough, entertainingly presented classics they are recognized as being.

*Typography is the efficient means to an essentially utilitarian and only accidentally aesthetic end, for enjoyment of patterns is rarely the reader's chief aim.*
*Stanley Morison*

*Type in Use* is a type primer and guide to effective editorial typography. The book is broken into chapters describing the essential elements of publication design, with an additional chapter at the end on typographic development, which puts the present standards in perspective.

This book shows examples from a variety of publications – famous, high-profile, high-volume magazines and small, limited-run publications. Good typography is available to everyone. A big budget is not necessary. The only resources you need are thought and imagination.

# 1

1.01

You have used all the tricks at your disposal to entice the reader into the text: provocatively written, dynamic display typography, intriguing imagery, visible captions, and well-placed white space. Once there, the reader too often finds the text handled as blocks of grayness, as though a 50 percent screen tint is equivalent to words and sentences that actually contain *thoughts.*

Text is all the little type, the stuff that so often looks gray and uninteresting. But text is the most important part of your message because it contains the greatest amount of information per square pica on the page.

Text contrasts with display type, which is any area of typography meant to attract the reader's attention. The elements of display typography are: headlines, subheads, department heads, breakouts (brief sections of the text reset large and surrounded by regular text), folios (page numbers), and picture captions or legends.

Text and the page's underlying grid fundamentally affect the look of visual communication. The treatment of text type and its underlying grid cannot be separated. Josef Müller-Brockmann, the noted Swiss designer, wrote in his book *The Graphic Designer and His Design Problems*: "Each problem calls for a grid suited especially to itself. It must enable the designer to arrange the [text], captions, and [imagery] so that they are as visually ef-

fective as their importance warrants and yet form an ordered whole."

It is vital that all typographic elements work well with the two other primary page ingredients: white space and imagery. Because of the hand-in-glove relationship of text and its environment, it is wise to take a brief look at page layout basics at the beginning of this discussion of text typography.

**White space** is the empty area to which type and imagery are added. It is the "ground" in a figure-ground relationship (fig. 1.01). It is perceived as background and goes unnoticed until we place elements in it, at which point it becomes defined by the positive shapes. White space appears around paragraphs, between columns and lines and words and letters. It defines the perimeter shape of individual characters and words. Naturally, the treatment of white space greatly affects a document's legibility and attractiveness. The intelligent and informed management of white space will do more to improve your visual communication than any other design decision.

It is important to realize that the spacing rules we follow today evolved over thousands of years, each development a response to speed the process of writing

1.02

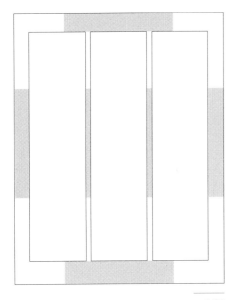

1.03

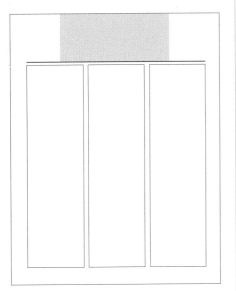

1.04

All the world's a stage and all the men and women merely players. They have their exits and their entrances, and one man in his time plays many parts,

*+2pt line space*

1.05

All the world's a stage and all the men and women merely players. They have

*solid*

All the world's a stage and all the men and women merely players. They have

*-2pt line space*

1.06

and to ease the transmission of written communication. Word spaces, for example, were not developed until around A.D. 400 by the Romans as a way to separate word symbols (fig. 1.02).

Consistent spacing throughout is crucial to making typography both attractive and easy to read. The ultimate goal of letter, word, and line spacing is to make it invisible, to avoid self-consciousness, allowing the reader to absorb the meaning and content of the type effortlessly.

White space infiltrates every element on the page. Let's look at each of these locations in turn.

**Margins** are the four areas surrounding the live area of a page (head, foot, and two sides), and the vertical spaces between columns of type (fig. 1.03). Generous margins make a document more appealing by reducing the daunting quantity of text on a page. Unequal margins give a publication a unique appearance. A deep and consistently applied head margin is called **sinkage** (fig. 1.04).

**Line spacing** (also known as **leading**, though the days of lead slugs separating lines of type are long gone) is the space that appears between the descenders and ascenders of lines of type (fig. 1.05). Line spacing is added to separate lines of type from one another, making the reading process easier. Proper line spacing prevents skipping or rereading lines of type. Additional line spacing is recommended for long line widths (over about forty characters), type styles with large x-heights (the lower-case letter excluding ascenders and descenders), and for readers with reading deficiencies (the very young, the very old, and poor readers). Well-proportioned line spacing improves the legibility of a document.

Line spacing is often added when a story is short and must be stretched to fill the space. While a logical method for filling space, it usually looks out of place and draws undue attention to itself. Better ways to fill the space are to enlarge an image or run a breakout.

When no additional line spacing is included, the type is said to be **set solid**. Reducing line spacing so that ascenders and

descenders actually overlap is called **minus leading** (fig. 1.06), a practice that should be used – and, indeed is actually recommended – only for display-size type.

A new printed thought is signaled by **paragraphing**. Indention is one method of indicating paragraphs. The other is skipping a line space or adding several points of space between paragraphs, without indenting (fig. 1.07). Paragraphs that are separated by additional space should not also be indented, because it is a redundant signal. Whether you choose indention or adding space between paragraphs, do not indent the very first paragraph, as doing so spoils the attractive upper left corner of the text. There is always another signal at work, telling the reader that a new idea is beginning. The change in type size or weight from that of the preceding headline or deck is sufficient.

**Word spacing** is the space that separates words on a line. Word space should only be sufficient to separate one word thought from the next. Too much word space slows the eye down. For optimum legibility, word spacing should remain consistent from line to line. It also should be set in proportion to letterspacing, that is, open letterspacing complements open word spacing.

A **flush-left/ragged-right** setting is the best way to achieve even word spacing because the spaces stay exactly the same while the ends of the lines flex – some lines are a little shorter than others. Allowing hyphenation creates a "soft rag," or gently curving right edge (fig. 1.08). The text in this book is set with a soft rag. Prohibiting hyphenation causes a "hard rag," or strongly uneven right edge, because entire words that do not fit on a line are dragged down to the next line, leaving a big gap on the right side of the column (fig. 1.09). The ideal rag is called a sawtooth because it has alternating long and short lines, thereby avoiding inadvertent bulges or gaps. A sawtooth edge is more easily achieved if you specify all lines that are within a few points from the full measure be set justified, thereby defining the column's maximum width. These few justified lines will not have badly compromised word spacing. A hard rag is considered poor typography because the zigzag of the right edge is distracting and because achieving a sawtooth is practically impossible. Occasionally ragged-right copy becomes too ragged – numerical copy is one example. Specifying a minimum measure often solves the problem.

**Justification** is setting lines of type to the same exact width, altering word spaces to achieve the equal measures. Justified type looks fine as long as the line length, or measure, is sufficient to absorb the word-spacing fluctuations. A measure of forty characters (equal to an average of eight words) per line is essential for reasonably even justified word spacing. Justified type always produces poor word spacing when the type is set without hyphenation: the extra white space is inserted within the line, between words and between characters, to make up for the exaggerated shortage of letters (fig. 1.10).

If several consecutive lines of poor word spacing occur, "rivers" of white appear vertically in the text, creating a distraction and giving the reader a convenient – if subconscious – reason to stop reading.

**Letterspacing** is the space between letters in a word. By completely surrounding individual characters, it defines their shapes. It is proportional to the width of the letterforms and should be visually consistent from letter to letter and from word to word.

Letterspacing and word spacing are controlled on typesetting equipment by setting the **tracking**. Ordinarily, letter and word spacing are directly related, but it is possible to set them independently, that is, to have increased letterspacing and decreased word spacing, for example. Each software and equipment manufacturer has its own system, so check the User Manual or speak with your supplier to get the codes needed to adjust the tracking of your type.

Irregular, arbitrary letterspacing decreases the eye's ability to perceive famil-

iar word shapes and significantly slows reading speed and comprehension.

**Kerning** smooths out letterspacing between specific character combinations by reducing letterspacing for optical consistency (fig. 1.11).

**Typographic color** is the relative lightness or darkness of an element on the page. A variety of tones on the page tells the reader straight away what is most important and what is less so. Along with relative positioning on the page, grayness denotes the hierarchy of the elements (fig. 1.12). This example of a newsletter page shows three distinct grays. Each suggests a level of importance because the eye naturally focuses on the area of greatest color concentration (that's why headlines are bolder type). Using three typographic colors gives the page depth and creates visual movement: darkest for masthead, medium for headlines and visuals, lightest for text.

## The
## examples

The text examples shown in the balance of this chapter generally break typographic conventions such as "use forty characters per line" or "always add two points of line spacing," but do so carefully, without compromising legibility. Just as it is necessary for a lawyer to understand the law to best serve his or her clients, so one who works with type must understand text setting "laws" to know when they are being broken and to know what to do to compensate for the violations.

Adhering to the nine type conventions that follow will provide clear, communicative typography. If you follow them and make a few well-placed and highly visible customized adjustments, you will have good, clear, readable type that has its own distinctive personality.

• **CONVENTION 1:** Text type is sized in relation to the width of the column. The wider the column, the larger the type must be.

Text works best in columns of about forty characters per line. The eye can scan

All the world's a stage and all the men and women merely players.
They have their exits and their entrances, and one man in his time plays many parts, his acts being seven ages.
At first the infant, mewling and puking in the nurse's arms. And then the whining schoolboy, with his satchel and shining morning face, creep

All the world's a stage and all the men and women merely players.
They have their exits and their entrances, and one man in his time plays many parts, his acts being seven ages.
At first the infant, mewling and puking in the nurse's arms. And then the whining schoolboy, with his satchel and shining

1.07

bearded like the pard, jealous in honour, sudden and quick in quarrel, seeking the bubble reputation even in the cannon's mouth. And then the justice, in fair

1.08

bearded like the pard, jealous in honour, sudden and quick in quarrel, seeking the bubble reputation even in the cannon's mouth. And then the justice, in

1.09

bearded like the pard, jealous in honour, sudden and quick in quarrel, seeking the bubble reputation even in the cannon's mouth. And then the justice, in fair round

1.10

All the v

*unkerned*

All the wo

*kerned*

1.11

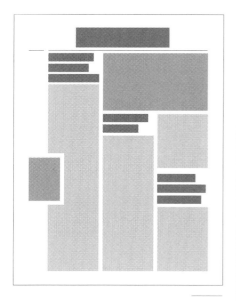

1.12

All the world's a stage and all
the men and women merely
players. They have their exits
and their entrances, and one

All the world's a stage and all
the men and women merely
players. They have their exits
and their entrances, and one

1.13

## A LL THE WORLD'S A STAGE AND ALL ARE PLAYERS

*An exploration of humankind
and life's passing*

They have their exits and their entrances, and one
man in his time plays many parts, his acts being
seven ages. At first the infant, mewling and
puking in the nurse's arms. And then the
whining schoolboy, with his satchel and shining morning face, creeping like snail unwill-
ingly to school. And then the lover, sighing like
furnace, with a woeful ballad have their exits

1.14

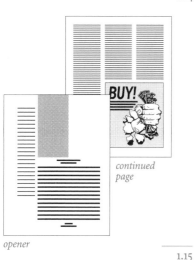

*continued
page*

*opener*

1.15

forty-character lines quickly and return to the left-hand, leading edge of the next line effortlessly. Setting text across a line of more than forty characters requires an increase in line spacing to provide a clear avenue for the eye's return path. Setting text across a substantially narrower measure causes problems with hyphenation and, if you are setting justified, will cause very uneven – and very unattractive – word spacing.

• **CONVENTION 2**: Word spacing is determined in proportion to letterspacing. If letters are set tightly, word spacing should be set tightly as well.

• **CONVENTION 3**: Sans serif type can be just as readable as serif type if you make a few adjustments. Sans serif typefaces lack the strong horizontal flow of a serif face, so shorten the line length and increase the line spacing to reduce eye fatigue (fig. 1.13).

• **CONVENTION 4**: Typographic variation is another way of saying typographic hierarchy. Our job as visual communicators is to understand the material and show it in scannable, easy-to-perceive segments. Differentiating elements on the page is helpful, but too many variations are counterproductive and confuse the reader. Keep your typography simple. Develop a system of defining kinds of information and stick to it. Consistency is perceived as quality. Inconsistencies, even minor ones "just this once," are perceived as disorderly and incoherent.

• **CONVENTION 5**: A simple spacing system for headlines, subheads, and text imparts a regular and clear hierarchy to typographic elements, easing the reading process and enhancing the appeal of your printed piece by suggesting logic and order (fig. 1.14).

• **CONVENTION 6**: An 8 - by 11-inch magazine page is chopped into the familiar, and dull, three-column format to accept standard ad sizes. If your publication does not run ads, you can develop a more unusual column structure. If your publication does require standard ad sizes, develop a system that allows greater flexibility on story openers, then reverts to ordinary three-column layouts on continued pages (fig. 1.15). The examples in this

chapter include many unusual story openers. In nearly every instance, the interestingness of the example disappears when the page is turned to the story's continuation: the exigencies of selling ad space requires a more traditional format.

• **CONVENTION 7**: When designing with type, consider the audience. Selecting a typeface is much like selecting clothing: you neither want to look too peculiar nor exactly like everyone else. Who is the intended reader? Under what conditions will the publication be read? From how far away will it be read? Is it to be scanned for tidbits, or is it to be read from start to finish, like a novel? These factors will help determine the typeface, type size, column width, and line-space configurations. Author and design consultant Jan V. White calls this "considerate typography."

• **CONVENTION 8**: Solutions to typographic problems are built in if you pay attention to communicating clearly. Typography becomes confusing and actually interferes with the message when it is manipulated for its own sake as a self-conscious art form.

• **CONVENTION 9**: Type is meant to be *read*. Use your own common sense and clear thinking to make your type as readable as possible.

Text can be made more appealing by manipulating six components:
• line spacing
• position on the page
• columnar structure
• shape
• relationship with imagery
• contrasting typeface
The following examples illustrate each of these ideas. They are offered as starting points. Once you begin thinking about unusual text settings, you will invent solutions that uniquely satisfy your particular needs, while still serving the needs of readers with clear, easy-to-read typography.

1.16

**1.16**

Open line spacing has an informal look, which is exploited by beginning and ending the columns at different heights. These casual starting points are balanced with a clear underlying structure, giving the spread great beauty. Note that the left-hand edge of each of the text columns, the caption, and even the byline each align with an initial at the top of the spread. *UC Santa Cruz Review*

**1.17**

This left half of a spread opener has an open (10/16) text setting; subsequent pages use tighter, more expected half-point (10/10 ) line spacings. Open line spacing hooks a casual browser into the story because it makes the text appear brief and quick to read. *The Washington Post Magazine*

**1.18**

This column is almost exactly twice as wide as it "should" be – about forty characters is recommended – but look at all that line spacing. It is set in 9/25 type, supplying more line spacing than a reader could possibly need to get from one end of a line back to the beginning of the next. This, then, is pure aesthetics, and a very handsome blend of typographic "flavors." The deck is red, the byline purple, and the initial green and tan. *Memphis*

**1.19**

Dropping text out of a background requires bold type. It is also a good idea to open up the line spacing if the background changes, as in this example, which is a four-color detail of the opening spread's illustration. The background colors vary from dark red to rust, black, and mustard. *Caring*

1.17

1.18

1.19

## Position
## on the page

**1.20**

This opener breaks its magazine's standard three-column format by floating centered in a lot of white space. The rigid structure of the justified column is contrasted with the huge *w*, which matches the width of the headline and unites all the elements on the page. *Pacific Northwest*

**1.21**

Following its standard three-column format, this publication has left the first column open on the feature story's opening spread. The opposite page on the right has a full-page photo of the article's subject.. This open column is an excellent cue that a major new article is beginning. *New England Business*

**1.22**

This publication has also left the lead column empty on feature openers. However, it runs the first line of text all the way across the first two columns, an impressive hanging indent. The initial cap helps the reader find the unusual starting point of the text. *Brake & Front End*

1.20

1.21

1.22

1.23

1.24

1.25

1.23

Attract attention by doing something very unexpected with the text. This article on cars as art objects is likely to engross true enthusiasts, who are probably more willing to read despite the angled baselines and reverse type. Note that the line spacing is greatly increased to compensate in part for the other liberties taken. *Automobile Magazine*

1.24

The wider text beneath WHERE THE MONEY GOES explains and serves as an umbrella for the twin columns of organization names and addresses. Together, the three elements act as a sidebar to the main article. *Psychology Today*

**Column
structure**

1.25

The format of this publication calls for two 16-pica-wide columns and one 9-pica column per page. The 11/12 text is always placed in the wide columns. Captions, pull quotes, and postage-stamp-sized photos are run in the narrow column, creating a natural content division for the reader. The structure is wonderfully adaptable: the narrow column can be placed in the center as shown, or to the left or right of the twin text columns, keeping this publication's pages exciting and fresh. *The Diamond*

**1.26**

When doubling the width of a column, enlarge the type and add line spacing, as in this example. Readers are willing to read that first paragraph – it looks so short – and then subconsciously decide whether to continue as they begin the normal text setting. The initial cap is printed in a rose red color, pulled from a detail in the color picture of the editor. *European Travel & Life*

**1.27**

This example also has increased line spacing to accommodate the particularly wide column treatment. The editorial never contains visuals, but this single extra-wide column treatment manages to convey some typographic personality nevertheless. *Textile Rental*

**1.28**

Exaggerated margins between columns create this page's personality. The illustrations are printed in bright orange and black and the bullets between items are red. *San Francisco Focus*

EDITOR'S

# NOTE

*About This Issue*

**R**ECENTLY I HAD LUNCH with a British friend, and she happened to ask what was coming up in the magazine. The first thing I mentioned, since it was the story I was most excited about and because of my friend's nationality, was this month's profile of Sarah Ferguson, the duchess of York. "Really," she said in that way the British have, "well then, lovely." It wasn't very difficult to pick up that my friend obviously had

some opinions of Fergie. No surprise. Everyone, it seems, has some opinions of the royal family and lately about Fergie in particular. There's an almost limitless fascination with the royals, especially the young royals, and Fergie is now the most interesting of the group. She has brought an exuberant personal style and a sense of playfulness to a family that could certainly take themselves a little less seriously.

My friend's feeling about Fergie was, in a word, ambivalent. "I mean I *do* like the fact that she's so relaxed in the performance of her royal obligations, but I must say she is a certain ......... and I'm all ...............

But Fergie is a lot more than that. She has brought a down-to-earth, almost irreverent style to the royal household. She's hot to Diana's cool, strawberry to her vanilla. All of which has resulted in a good deal of controversy in England, centered mostly on whether Fergie's behavior is appropriate for someone in her regal position. Many Brits think it's not, while Americans wonder what all the fuss is about.

There is something more important, however, than behavioral questions or questions of royal style. And this is pointed out by Ingrid Seward, who covers the royals ........... who wrote the profile of the duc'......

1.26

**Editorial**

*A new decade,
a new century,
a new world*

By John J. Conroy

*John J. Conroy is TRSA's executive director*

**R**ecently, I read a copy of a speech from Congressman Mel Levine of California reprinted in the June 15 Congressional Record. He outlined the unprecedented changes and challenges which face the United States both at home and abroad. I'd like to share some of his thoughts with you.

Levine says we are moving toward becoming one global civilization more quickly than ever before in human history. He outlined three changes. First, the principal global struggle no longer centers on the Cold War; second, economic competition is the key battleground of our time; and, third, success requires we rebuild at home rather than blame others abroad.

Levine proposes solutions that closely parallel those presented by Dr. John G. Stoessinger at TRSA's 77th Annual Convention late March in Dallas. Levine's suggestions are:

☐ Lengthen the school year to allow more time for education.
☐ Increase civilian funding for research and development and technology commercialization.
☐ Form a think-tank called "Rebuild America" to rebuild at home in order to win abroad.
☐ Promote a new concept called "investment economics" (this could be developed by a team of eminent economists led by Nobel Laureate Robert Solow).
☐ Develop an industry-led policy to revitalize and strengthen America's strategic industries.
☐ Encourage making an investment in people, particularly by promoting new learning technologies that can increase students' desire to learn.
☐ Support global co-development and growth through economic cooperation rather than protectionism.

A number of Levine's comments should be heeded by our industry on both a national and global basis. First, many companies in the industry are operating on a global, not a national basis. Next, one of our major industry demands is and will be people—securing and keeping qualified people to run the automated systems being developed by our industry. And finally, the development of a capital base necessary to finance automation and equipment (including pollution control equipment and systems to meet environmental concerns) is crucial to profitable survival in the next decade.

The challenges are great. We hope TRSA's Strategic Analysis of the Industry for 1990 in this issue of *Textile Rental* is helpful to you in your corporate planning.

For copies of Levine's article in the *Congressional Record*, call me at 303/457-7555. ☐

*Textile Rental ∾ September 1989*                                                                  14

1.27

PULSE

"MY JOB IS FIGHTING HELL ON EARTH."

## What Fire Fighters Know

BY VIVIAN WALSH

SINCE THAT APRIL MORNING IN 1906, FIRE FIGHTERS in this town have earned and enjoyed a respect of almost mythic proportions. Their heroes, these children's role models, these—well, yes—sex symbols have been somewhat infrequent in the news of late, but they're still proud of—and have plenty to say about—the job they do.

"The fire fighters in San Francisco are supposed to be the best in the nation because the title is so compact. When a house catches in Los Angeles they fight it from the outside to make sure it doesn't spread. This is the only city where we have to fight fires from the inside out."

"About a third of the calls to the firehouse are for medical treatment. Recently, I helped deliver a breech baby. It was awful. The mother waited too long before she called an ambulance and so his image where was let into the focus case, because it was cut new."

"People should realize that, if they park in front of a fire hydrant, not only are they endangering lives and property, but we won't have time to protect their car. We're gonna string hoses right over it, and the car is gonna get wrecked."

"A few years back a fire fighter rescued a cat from a burning building. The cat was unconscious, so he revived it with mouth-to-mouth resuscitation. He became an in-house hero."

"I'm all for fair hiring practices, but I think people lose track of what bottom are supposed to do. If someone was burning, I sure wouldn't want anyone fighting it who was let into the force because it was cut new."

"The most frightening fire is the combination of burning old wood and brick walls, which is very common in San Francisco. We call it the barbecue effect."

"Morale has never been lower, and there is inhouse fighting, but all that goes out the window when a call comes in for a fire."

"I can understand women finding firemen very sexual. When I put on my hat, my big jacket, and get on the red fire truck to rush across town, that's exciting."

"This one woman wanted to burn her Christmas tree, so she lit a fire in her fireplace, picked up her tree, and thought she would feed it in as it burned. Of course, fire on a dried-up old pine isn't that accommodating. Her whole living room went up."

"At the airport, we used to have maintenance pull maintenance men out of burning planes, but now, because of air pollution, we just use smoke bombs."

"We've got six women on the force right now. There two have had a slightly easier physical test, but I've worked with them, and they're doing a real good job. They're perfectly capable."

"The discrimination is subtle. It comes out in who gets the overtime, who gets the knee in arguments, who gets promoted. Stuff like that."

"If that caveman had never rubbed those two sticks together I'd probably be an accountant right now."

38 ∾ SAN FRANCISCO FOCUS

1.28

1.29

1.30

### 1.29

Alternating narrow and wide columns are used to convey the idea of dieting in this spread. Four different column widths are used, with the text reading continuously from one column to the next. Note that all text is set with the same open line spacing, the most appropriate for the widest column. *Shape*

### 1.30

Doubling the column width makes one of three articles stand out because it is different – it has become an anomaly. A wider measure does not always require increased type size or line spacing. Here the text is readable because, though the line length is long, the copy is relatively short. The extra white space surrounding the copy block also helps. The margins between columns are 1 picas wide, and there is a great deal of space carefully and consistently inserted into the headline units. *New York Woman*

### Shape

### 1.31

This example illustrates the use of white space to maximum advantage. The text's shape acts as its own illustration. *Time*

**1.32**

The shape of the paper itself can affect the text treatment. This publication's elongated shape is made of several panels, accordion-folded to fit in an envelope with monthly electric bills. The format allows for as few as three panels or as many as six panels, determined by the quantity of material to be included. *Edison News*

**1.33**

Putting type in a box that is completely surrounded by image is called a mortise. This mortise is shaped to echo part of the background image and forces the text into an unusual shape. Each line is set justified across the same 28-pica measure and indented in increments of 8 points. The result can also be achieved simply by cutting the repro with a razor and sliding the text lines over. *Normal*

**1.34**

Allowing columns of text to hang loosely at the bottom provides a natural place for a series of photos. The one photo/one column relationship and repetition of size unifies this spread. *East West*

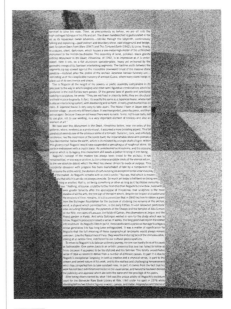

1.32     1.33

1.34

1.35

1.37

1.36

1.38

**1.35**

Text squeezed into a narrow vertical column almost becomes a long caption and therefore is very well read. This type had to be set flush left/ragged right because its measure is so narrow. Had it been set justified, it would have had awful letter and word spacing. Notice that the photos are as tightly cropped as the text, binding the elements on the page together. *Continental Profiles*

**1.36**

The slanting left edge of this text is a regular treatment in this employee publication. It is much easier to read than a ragged left edge because there is some degree of regularity here – the eye knows approximately where to begin the next line. The huge initial *s* and the text share the same angle of stress, and the initial slightly overlaps the photo, unifying the three elements into a single visual unit. *All About Us*

**Wrapping text around an image**

**1.37**

An intrusion into a column of justified type is highly visible. Ordinarily, a pica of space between the image and text provides the right amount of separation. In this case the text-free left-hand column's white space permits a more generous 2-pica space separation. *Hippocrates*

**1.38**

Wraparounds look best in a justified text setting. The eccentric column edge becomes more visible when contrasted with a clean vertical opposite edge. *Wigwag* regularly uses a wraparound, sometimes having more than one on a single page. This is not nearly as difficult as it once was, because desktop page-makeup programs can pour the text into predrawn shapes. Nevertheless, it is always necessary to go back and check word spacing for unattractive gaps on extremely short lines created by wraparounds. *Wigwag*

**1.39**

A more casual and easy way of wrapping text is to interrupt the copy and insert a visual, as with the SUPER CARD here. It looks like a wrap because the corners are tucked into naturally occurring gaps in the type and because the text is set flush left/ragged right. The visible grid and two large white spaces also help. Printed in several screen tints of two colors. *Connecticut Lifestyles*

**Contrasting typefaces**

**1.40**

Trade publications almost always have a page listing personnel changes. The secret to making such a page work is to have the names pop out of the surrounding text so the page can be easily scanned. This example works because there is sufficient weight contrast in the names. *Children's Business*

**1.41**

This page is from an article reprinting various quotes about AIDS. Each quote is given a different typographic treatment, helping the reader understand that each is an independent item. It also invites the reader to become involved. *Art New England*

1.39

1.40

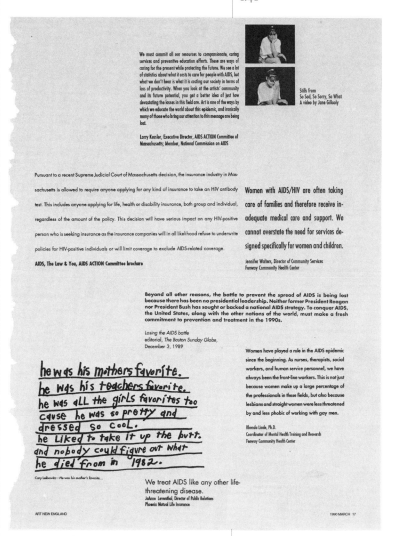

1.41

## Good Times, Bad Times

*Sometimes, even after you've made a fortune the size of Shepard Broad's, life can play tricks on you. Like slipping you the biggest securities fraud in history.*

by ALBERT STERN

At 83 years of age, Shepard Broad is reluctant to grant an interview. He says he already has had all the fame and glory he's interested in, and no desire to pursue any more. The will to make money, to do business, "well, that's kind of all out of me," he says. "I am retired. I am an old man."

1.42

1.43

1.44

1.42
Wider columns need bigger type and more line spacing. The text on the opening page of this article is 12/15 by 24 picas and converts to this publication's normal 9/11 by 13 picas on subsequent pages. The first page's enlarged text looks palatable and easily read. The hope is that by the time the reader turns the page he is too deeply involved to quit the article. *New Miami*

1.43
Begin reading this example at the bold lead-in. Continue down the left-hand column, which is printed in purple ink, and then move to the right-hand column, which is printed in black. This treatment offers an unusual reading experience, and it must have been used for that reason alone. *The Face*

1.44
Sitting amid longer stories set in serif type, the BRIEFLY segment is set in Futura Extra Bold and printed in purple ink. The one-two punch of subhead/story length and contrasting typeface demands that this be read before either of the other two stories. *Tampa Bay Life*

**1.45**

The text at the top of the pages details business developments of this corporation; the text at the bottom reviews marketing decisions. They are differentiated by column width and typeface. Such typographic differences help the reader understand that there are different kinds of information on the same page. *Bandwagon*

**1.46**

Clear typographic contrast separates this sidebar article from its partner. Pulling part of the article out and creating a sidebar shortens the main text and gives the browser one more opportunity to enter into the copy. Breaking the copy into three short segments delivers on the headline's promise. *Psychology Today*

**1.47**

A marvelous way of drawing the reader into a story or breaking up text is to begin large and reduce the type size in successive steps. This technique also eliminates the need for heads, though the first few words must be well chosen. The initial cap signals the starting point to the reader. These two examples, taken from different sections of this magazine, show how the technique helps define its personality. *Brake & Front End*

1.45

1.46

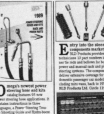

1.47

# HEADLINES

# 2

**The best way to improve** the look of your publication is to redefine the structure of its columns. That gets at the root of the "sameness" problem. But if making a structural overhaul is too ambitious, the next best way to upgrade your publication's appearance is to develop more compelling, more involving primary display typography.

Headlines create the *apparent* personality of printed material (the underlying structure, or grid, actually does most of the work). As primary typography, headlines are intended to stop the reader and persuade him or her to look at the secondary (subheads, breakouts, and captions) and tertiary (text) levels of typography.

There are over twenty thousand typefaces available, some several hundred years old and still used because their proportions are so magnificent (fig. 2.01), many more recently designed (fig. 2.02). Selecting the right typeface for your needs is indeed one of the most important decisions you will make. Remember, however, that *how* you use a typeface is at least as important as *what* typeface is being used. You must consider both legibility and character when selecting a typeface.

*Legibility* is the ease and speed with which the reader can decipher each letterform and word. Tops of letters are easier to read than bottoms (fig. 2.03), lower-case easier than caps because the word shapes are more varied (fig. 2.04). Letterspacing and word spacing that are too tight or too loose make reading considerably more difficult. Legibility is also affected by the choice of ink and paper colors. It is easiest to read black on white because that has the greatest contrast (fig. 2.05). Any departure from that combination must be carefully considered. Any severe reduction in contrast must be sampled beforehand to check whether creativity and expression are impeding communication.

*Character* is the type's personality. Some typefaces look **plain** or *Classic* or **strong** or *gentle* or ꜰ ꜰ ᴀ ᴀ s s ᴛ ᴛ or **solid**. Some are quite elaborate or are designed to resemble various objects (fig. 2.06). These can be very useful in limited and specific applications, but they are not very legible, as each letter must be individually read. Appropriate uses of such typefaces include short two- or three-word headlines or initial caps set into text.

When selecting a typeface, consider the image you want to project. Match the typeface to the message. A typeface's character will be helpful, harmful, or unimportant to your message. Use special typography that conveys character sparingly, only on pages that will be improved by such treatment, as on openers for feature stories, for example. The rest of a

Fish not, with this
*Janson, 1470*

Fish not, with thi
*Garamond, 1540*

Fish not, with this
*Caslon, 1740*

2.01

Fish not, with this
*Futura, 1927*

Fish not, with this
*Times, 1932*

Fish not, with this
*Optima, 1958*

2.02

Wilt thou be
it is not yet

2.03

Wilt thou be gone? it is not yet near day; it was the nightingale, and not the lark pierc'd the fearful hollow of thine

WILT THOU BE GONE? IT IS NOT YET NEAR DAY; IT WAS THE NIGHTINGALE, AND NOT

2.04

Wilt thou be gone? it is not yet near day; it was the nightingale, and not the lark pierc'd the fearful hollow of thine ear, nightly

Wilt thou be gone? it is not yet near day; it was the nightingale, and not the lark pierc'd the fearful hollow of thine ear, nightly

2.05

2.06

What's in a name? that which we call a rose woul
*8pt text*

What's in a name? that which we call a rose
*9pt text*

What's in a name? that which we call a r
*10pt text*

What's in a name? that which we call
*11pt text*

What's in a name? that which we c
*12pt text*

What's in a name? that which
*14pt display*

What's in a name? that w
*18pt display*

What's in a name? t
*24pt display*

What's in a n:
*36pt display*

What's in
*48pt display*

What's i
*60pt display*

What's
*72pt display*

2.07

For the flowers now that frighted thou let'st fall from Dia's wagon! Daffodils that come before the swallow dares, and take the winds of March with beauty. Violets dim but sweeter than the lids of Juno's eyes or those of Dia's fairest dream

2.08

publication must be designed with unity foremost in mind.

Some of the more elaborate display faces are not designed to be set in all caps. The letters do not fit together, and reading speed is slowed.

Display type is used to draw attention to itself and to lead the reader to the next level of typographic importance, usually the subhead or deck. Most text typefaces make excellent headline faces when set in larger, bolder form. Legible text faces run from a minimum of 8 points to a maximum of 12 points; display type ranges from a minimum of 14 points to an infinitely large size (fig. 2.07). Indeed, enormous letterforms cropped by the edge of a page can serve as a very effective visual attractant (fig. 2.08).

Selecting and using visual signals in a logical way that illuminates the relative importance of the typographic treatments will convey the message memorably while requiring little effort from the reader. Arbitrary emphasis and signal selection, however, will significantly hinder the absorption of the content by the reader – though it may look quite attractive.

Display type sends visual signals that should *demand* attention. It must have sufficient contrast to stand out from the surrounding material. Rarely does a message suffer from too much contrast (except when the designer selects too many typefaces or introduces too many slight variations that the reader perceives as confusing). But it is impossible to make a headline too much larger than text or too much bolder than the subhead. Contrast clarifies a message by making it easy to distinguish one element from another.

As a general rule, do not use more than two typefaces on one project, and do not use more than two weights of each typeface. Add italic versions of each weight, and you have eight typographic "voices," which should certainly be enough to convey any message. If you need more than eight voices, you are definitely overdefining the kinds of information you want to convey.

Attention can be caught by increasing typographic contrast using the following visual signals:

- **size**
- **weight**
- **color**
- **stress**
- **format**
- **character shape**
- **character width**
- **density**
- **position on the page**

If you mix these means of contrast, be aware that you may confuse the reader with unclear symbols or an unclear system.

**Size**: Small/large; big = important; small = less important; big = read first; small = read second.

**Weight**: Thick/thin; **the eye naturally goes to the darkest area first**, so the most important type is made bolder.

**Color**: Dark/light or black/contrasting color.

**Stress**: Vertical/angled; the letterform's *stress* determines whether it is roman or angled. Angled type comes in two varieties: italic, which has a complementary roman typeface, and oblique, which is a roman typeface that has been pushed sideways. Oblique type has the same letterforms as its roman counterpart. Italic type has different letterforms in its roman version (fig. 2.09). Angled type is used for emphasis within an area of roman type. Italic type suggests the touch of a human hand and is often used for pull quotes, which are direct thoughts of an individual and thus more human.

**Format**: CAPS/lower-case; CAPS/SMALL CAPS.

**Character shape**: Hard/soft; serif/sans serif, shape of letterforms, and position on the page.

**Character width**: Narrow/wide; expanded/condensed.

**Density**: Solid/outline; positive/negative; tight/loose.

**Position on the page**: vertical/horizontal; top/bottom.

No matter which typographic contrast variation you use, it is necessary to maintain a condition of clear "normalcy" so that the unusual element really stands out. If, for example, about half a page is set in regular and half in italic type, which of the two is asking to be recognized first? Neither is in the majority, and so neither is special, and the reader is simply confused. A very wise artist named Leon Appel told me years ago about the 75 Percent Rule he followed to maintain maximum visual interest (fig. 2.10). The 75 Percent Rule is simply making sure one element is about three times bigger than any other element. It is a good way to remember to have one dominant element.

The effectiveness of display typography is not dependent on the black letterforms, but on the management of the white space between and around the letterforms. Because display type is always brief (to grab the reader's fickle attention), letterspacing, word spacing, and line breaks become very important.

The speed at which words are comprehended is dictated by their typographic presentation. Except in gross instances, the space between individual letters is only noticed when the type is larger than about 18 points. So letterspacing becomes very important in display typography and is somewhat less so in text typography. The optimum letterspacing is invisible. It is un-self-conscious. You are not even aware that letterspacing exists when it is done well.

Words are strung together to form lines of type. Word spacing is the glue that holds lines of type together. The secret to good word spacing is also invisibility. The reader should not be aware of the type that is being read but should be concentrating only on its meaning. Display word spacing is often too large, the eye leaping across too-great spaces to get to the next word. This significantly slows the eye and eventually makes the reader acutely aware

of the process of reading, at which time he stops reading and finds something less effortful to do.

How a line is broken becomes important in type that is 14 points or larger. The aim is to break for sense. A phrase attributed to Danny Kaye illustrates the point:

*I'm so tired I could sleep for a week who would care to join me*
*In saluting the glorious members of our crew.*

Words have a rhythm, and the rhythm must be followed for maximum comprehension. Read the words in a headline out loud to find the natural breaks. Try not to break a headline to follow a design; rather break a headline so that it makes the most sense to the reader. It is the designer's job to communicate and present and enhance the content without losing the author's thought.

Display type (headlines and department headings) should relate in some way to the flag (logo) on the cover. For your publication to achieve visual unity, the editorial – or non-advertising – pages must be consistent in some way or ways. It is easy to develop a typographic system that uses a few variations of a single typeface. Display type is the most visible type and therefore makes the biggest impact, so typographic consistency is particularly necessary among the logo, department headings, and headlines. For example, in figure 2.11 *The Treasury Pro* uses Palatino Bold on the cover and for its headlines and subheads throughout the publication. This consistency gives a feeling of cohesiveness and unity to the product and reinforces the singular personality of the publication, traits that endear a magazine to its loyal readers and make it more popular with advertisers.

It can be a good idea to change typefaces for a specific feature story, to give it more emphasis in the magazine, which is a correct treatment for a true "feature," or special event. But the headline typography should then remain consistent throughout that one story.

Make headlines smaller and blacker than you might at first think they should be. If the story requires a short headline, add a lengthy blurb describing the article to supply darkness and attract the reader's

2.09

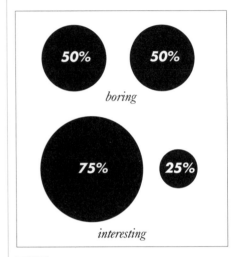

2.10

2.11

*My* bounty
is as boundless
as the sea,
my love as deep

*18/20*

*My* bounty
is as boundless
as the sea,
my love as deep

*18/16*

2.12

*My* BOUNTY
IS AS BOUNDLESS
AS THE SEA,
MY LOVE AS DEEP

*18/20*

*My* BOUNTY
IS AS BOUNDLESS
AS THE SEA,
MY LOVE AS DEEP

*18/17*

2.13

My only love sprung from my only
hate! Too early seen unknown, and
known too late!

My only love
sprung from
my only hate!
Too early seen
unknown, and
known too late!

2.14

the flowers now that
frighted thou let'st fall from
Dia's wagon.

### A sad tale's best for winter

Daffodils that come before
the swallow dares, and take
the winds of March with
beauty. Violets dim but
sweeter than the lids of
Juno's eyes or those of Dia's

trerea's breath
pale prim rose
that died unm:
ried, ere they ;
can behold an
bright Phoebu
in his strength
A malady mos
incident to the
maids. Bold a:
oxlips and the
crown imperia

2.15

eye. Reduce the line spacing in headlines to make them darker. Ordinarily, the rule for line spacing in display type is: "Descenders and ascenders should never touch" – unless it looks better when they do. When ascenders and descenders touch, they create a visual spot on the page that cannot be avoided (fig. 2.12). All-cap headlines in particular should have no extra line spacing because there are no descenders to fill in the space between lines. Minus leading, or removing line space, makes a headline darker and more visible (fig. 2.13).

Headlines can be structured to contrast with the text, to stand out on the page. For example, a headline can be stacked in several short lines, as in figure 2.12. Type should reflect different tones of voice. The same words presented in three lines "sound" different than when they are presented in six lines (fig. 2.14).

In two-line headlines, the second line should be shorter than the first (fig. 2.15). The short second line encourages the reader to continue on to the text because the end of one element is closer to the beginning of the next.

Headline treatments fall into three broad categories: alignment and position, contrasting type styles, and the integration of type and imagery. These three areas are illustrated by the examples in this chapter. But whatever the treatment, the best headlines are provocatively written and have a point to make. A good headline must be more than just visually attractive; it must be written to *say* something. It must be meaningful.

2.16

2.17

2.18

Alignment/
position

**2.16**

A hanging indent pokes the leading line of type into the left margin, increasing its visibility dramatically. This headline hangs into a 2 -pica margin. *The Treasury Pro*

**2.17**

In addition to sharp typographic contrast, this example makes use of eye-catching white space by aligning both the headline and deck flush left with the second column. *Sales & Marketing Management*

**2.18**

Headlines do not require horizontal base lines. The word TOP is dropped out of a solid red field, making it more visible. *Dimensions*

**2.19**

This article is about a legendary skier, so the reader is led into the type by a line of dots suggesting a perfectly carved turn in deep powder. The primary words, STEIN AT SIXTY, evoke the hands of a clock and are printed in red and orange. The white space on this page is left intact. *Lodestar*

**2.20**

This headline and department heading combination is repeated at the top of every product review in this magazine. Each review begins on a left-hand page, but because there are as many as twenty-five pages between reviews, this very powerful treatment was developed to help the reader locate the next review quickly amid the intervening advertising. *Audio*

**2.21**

This headline at first appears to have been haphazardly placed, but it in fact follows its own internal structure. It is set flush left, except for the word REFLECTION, which pokes out to the left edge of the live area for emphasis. Notice also the excellent blend of type sizes and weights on this page: each variation helps the reader perceive a difference in the kind of information being expressed. *Golden Years*

2.19

2.20

2.21

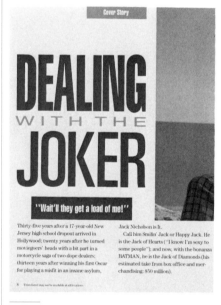

2.22

2.23

2.24

**2.22**

This is a very interesting combination of centered, flush-left, and justified type. The centered NETWORKING FOR POWER bisects the page, separating the headline above from the text and subhead below. The headline is the same typeface as and aligned flush left with the initial cap in the text. *Personal Computing*

**2.23**

What a magnificent study in verticality! The H and II of HAWAII are enlarged and mirror each other. The AWA is palindromic (the same forward and backward) for more symmetry. SUBTLE SECRETS has been heavily kerned to match the visual width of HAWAII, and the subhead has been set centered. *American Way*

**2.24**

Creating a headline column by carefully filling each line to full measure is a much used and never boring treatment. This headline is sized and the typefaces chosen so that each line comes to full measure, in this case 30 picas. DEALING and JOKER, printed solid purple, are condensed variations of the same sans serif type family as the expanded and letter spaced WITH THE, printed in lime green. *Blockbuster*

**2.25**

These mini-headlines introduce separate segments of the editor's message. Printed in Columbia blue, the all-cap, bold, sans serif setting contrasts admirably with the text. The flush-right setting binds each headline clearly to its text. *Columbia*

**2.26**

This simple yet very strong headline works because each line is sized to the same width, creating an effective alignment and increasing the visual impact by creating a recognizable shape. Heavy, sans serif type defines each line clearly. Printed in two shades of tan on black with full-color photos. *Lodestar*

**2.27**

*MAKING A STATEMENT* wraps around the bottom left corner of the photo, with the subhead aligned flush left with the spine of the *E* and the vertical edge of the photo. Such clear relationships separate real typography from mere type use. Printed in deep red and black with the photo as a duotone. *GP Growth*

# N O T E S

## *Getting Out the Word*

With this issue, we renew our acquaintance with 70,000 readers who may not have heard from us since June of 1988, the last time we mailed *Columbia Magazine* to the entire alumni body. We're delighted to add such a large contingent of discerning readers to our mailing list for this and future issues.

Some history: *Columbia* was established in 1977 by the Office of University Development and Alumni Relations. We began as a quarterly mailed to 30,000 alumni donors and friends. That number grew steadily as the percentage of donors increased, and the frequency of the magazine went up, too, to six times a year.

Last summer, with the support of Peter Buchanan, vice president for University Development and Alumni Relations, and our other colleagues at UDAR, we developed a plan to send

THE PEOPLE WHO BRING YOU COLUMBIA — keeps you informed about Alma Mater.

Thanks to the people who keep our alumni records tidy we have some idea of who you are. Let me reciprocate and tell you about us. New to our masthead as publisher of *Columbia Magazine*, though not new to our operation, is Peter McE. Buchanan. A graduate of the Business School and Teachers College, Peter has been vice president since 1982, his second stint in the University administration (he was here as vice president in the 1970s before leaving for a similar post at Wellesley College).

Also new to our masthead, though again not to our operation, is Bill Oliver, listed among the members of our advisory committee. Many of you know Bill from his long service to the

Florence Keller, art director, has been with the magazine since its founding 13 years ago (for two years before that she was a senior designer in the Office of University Publications). She's overseen several redesigns as well as some technological transitions, most recently the switch to computer publishing.

THE BEST JOB IN THE WORLD — I've been with *Columbia* since 1979, loving a job that has taken me on a tugboat ride up the Hudson River, to the laboratories of world-renowned geneticists, to operating rooms at Columbia-Presbyterian Medical Center, to speeches and seminars by the likes of Leon Lederman, the Dalai Lama, Eudora Welty, Vaclav Havel, and hundreds of others. My husband, Peter, a lawyer who slaves daily over securities regulations, says I have the best job in the world.

2.25

2.26

2.27

2.28

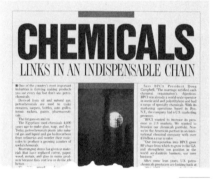

2.29

2.30

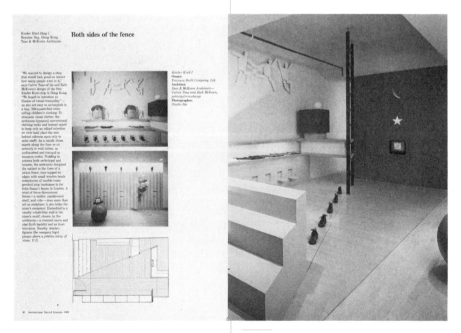

2.31

2.28

Headlines can be bound to a curved base line, which is highly visible here. This great green snake of a headline continues throughout the twelve pages of this issue, propelling the reader from spread to spread. It is an effective way of ensuring each page is seen. *Interface*

**Contrasting type styles**

2.29

Contrasting typefaces, in addition to width alignment, are used here to great effect. Notice that the overscore's width matches the photo's. *BP America Scene*

2.30

This headline/subhead combination uses vastly different members of the same type family, and the all-cap treatment contrasts with upper- and lower-case. The -point rules and flush-left/ragged-right setting give the type a simple, clean environment. *Medical Economics*

2.31

Headlines need not be huge to be noticeable. This magazine uses a consistent sinkage of 13 picas at the head margin, giving the relatively small 18-point headlines visibility in a great deal of white space. *Architectural Record*

**2.32**

Like the previous example, this headline is not set in very large type, but it is made quite visible by leaving generous white space all around. *Caring*

**2.33**

The headlines reside in a 15-pica-wide column to the left of the wider text column. This formula never varies, making a quick scan of headlines easy (but this requires very sharp and appealing headline writing). *USCEA Info*

**2.34**

The extreme verticality of the all-cap headline contrasts with the horizontal flow of the very bold text. The vertical/horizontal playfulness extends to the use of rules (printed in red). *UCLA Magazine*

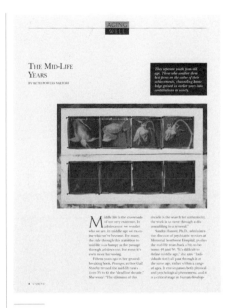

2.32

2.33

2.34

2.35

2.36

2.37

There is an obvious contrast (which is the best kind!) between the headline and subhead typefaces in this example. But also at work is the magnificent contrast in column width between the display type's narrow area and the over-twice-as-wide text columns. *Personnel Journal*

2.36
Hand lettering is appropriately used on this opening spread for an article on the occult. The same "typeface" is used for the initial caps in the text. VOODOO is printed red, and the deck and byline are dropped out of the full-bleed photo. *New York Woman*

2.37
Here the contrast is between occupied and unoccupied space on the page. These headlines pop off the page because they are bold, they are bigger than the text, and because a system has been created whereby white space is guaranteed to surround them. The rules are printed in pale purple. Such clear segmentation of the page makes it easy to scan and immediately informs the reader of the length of each item. A consistent headline treatment also makes the job of putting the publication together much easier: the editor can concentrate on writing rather than inventing typographic systems. *AT&T Focus*

2.38

Bigger and bolder headline type makes itself visible, but this page is further helped by having a 10 percent black screen tint behind the type only, which makes the photos seem to pop out because their lightest areas are lighter than the field on which they appear. The horizontal rules are printed in whatever second color is chosen for that month's issue. *InterView*

2.39

The all-cap, roman inline type printed in light brown contrasts with *AND*, printed in black over a pink shape. *BODY* and *SOUL* are letterspaced to match the width of the subhead and all type is centered above the text, making a formal presentation. The opposite page of this spread is a full-page color photo. *Caring*

2.40

The *w* was chosen to echo the scalloped ruffles of the wedding gown shown on the facing page of this opening spread. The initial is well-placed and integrated with the entire headline, not only with the expected last line. Strong typographic arrangements such as this can and should be used on subsequent pages of an article to bind the story together. Unusual initials can be found in clip books or bought as transfer type. *Pacific Northwest*

2.38

2.39

2.40

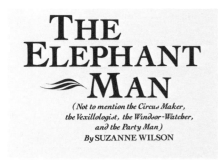

2.41

2.42

2.43

Type and
image integration

2.41

The asymmetrically set headline is complemented nicely by the leafy flourish, which is run in red. The subhead is centered in contrasting italic type. *New England Monthly*

2.42

One way of integrating headline and imagery is to alternate them in a rhythmic pattern. Each of these eight square halftones is shown in full and discussed on subsequent pages of the article. *KCET Magazine*

2.43

Type can be used as imagery. This and similar effects can be created with a stat camera, with special equipment that some typesetters have, with software programs on a Macintosh, and even with an ordinary photocopy machine. Use typographic gimmicks with discretion and only when the effect is directly related to the point being made, as it is here. *Children's Business*

**2.44**
Another example of type as imagery: the type treatment reflects the meaning of the words. This headline was printed in blue with black text and rules in the original. *Fleet Norstar Directions*

**2.45**
This elaborate and carefully crafted headline becomes artwork with its handsome letterform relationships and use of screen tints (red, yellow, and various shades of gray add depth to the original). The headline treatment is repeated atop every page as a story header, an excellent mnemonic device for a long series of pages filled with charts, as in this article. *Florida Business Southwest*

**2.46**
This headline is augmented by a simple form of a grand piano, which immediately telegraphs the subject of the article. The piano shape is then repeated with every initial cap. *American Way*

2.44

2.45

2.46

2.47

2.48

2.49

2.47
Placing the headline inside a shape effectively conveys its message if the shape buttresses the meaning of the words. This shape, printed in red with black type, is well chosen because it is bannerlike and suggests festivity. *Life Association News*

2.48
Another headline in a shape, this time printed black on 40 percent black screen tint. Once again, the shape supports the idea conveyed in the headline. *Fleet Norstar Directions*

2.49
Transforming the headline into artwork can be very creative. This headline was produced on a computer's color printer, and the various copies were torn and placed on top of one another. The final is red, green, blue, and black, with a full-color illustration of the boxing glove. *Wigwag*

**2.50**

It is ordinarily not a good idea to drop type out of a photo – or to surprint it – because the type may become difficult to read and tends to spoil the believability of the image. Nevertheless, if type is to be placed on a photo, be sure to put it in a relatively empty area, as in this example. And if the copy concerns rain, put the type in the sky! *Hamilton Spirit*

**2.51**

It is much more convincing to put an image in front of the type, being careful not to so obscure the letters that they cannot be read. This treatment makes the objects appear more real: things cover other things in reality. The headline is dropped out of a blue box to allow the foot to cover it without obscuring the type. *PassWord*

**2.52**

Type can relate directly to an illustrative element without touching the art. This is a very gentle wraparound, formal piece of typography made very handsome by using shades of umber and green found in the color photo that jumps the gutter. *New York*

2.50

2.51

2.52

# 3

If headlines are the enticing worms that persuade the casual browser to stop by, subheads are the hooks that ensure the reader risks valuable time by reading the first paragraph of the text. Subheads are important tools that can convince the reader to continue by expanding upon and explaining the headline. Headlines,

being brief, may convey enough to stop a reader but often do not contain enough information to give the reader a reason to start the text. A well-written subhead explains its headline and intrigues the reader into continuing on into the text. Headlines that lead to subheads that lead to text are more effective than headlines that lead directly to text; the reader wants sufficient information before committing himself to a sampling of the text, which takes time and is work.

Because subheads are considered secondary typographic elements, they are read after the headline but before the text and captions. They must therefore be set in a typeface that is bigger or bolder than the text. Good typography enables the reader to understand clearly the order of typographic elements. Copy should be broken into three levels: primary information should be in the headlines, secondary – or clarifying and illuminating – information should be in subheads or decks, and tertiary (third-level) information should be in the text (fig. 3.01).

This basic structure can be varied somewhat. For example, subheads can be replaced by pull quotes or breakouts, or captions can be intended as the primary typography since they are often read im-

mediately after the photos are scanned. Generally, however, the headline/subhead/text hierarchy is the norm because it serves the reader well with its familiarity based on sound logic. The unending visual variety of subheads can be classified into two basic forms: subheads that appear outside the text area and subheads that appear within it.

External subheads are primarily **decks**, which appear immediately below the headline (fig. 3.02) and further explain the content of the story. Another type of external subhead is the **floating subhead** (fig. 3.03), so named because it is placed alongside the text in the margin and requires some degree of surrounding space and clear typographic contrast in size or weight to be visible.

Internal subheads are usually breaker heads, which appear periodically in the text to break it into bite-size pieces (fig. 3.04). Breaker heads are brief synopses of the following paragraphs of text and, as such, should be provocatively written to catch the eye of the casual browser who managed to avoid being drawn in by the lead headline. Editorially, write breaker heads like the five-second news teasers that run during the commercial breaks in your favorite prime-time television show:

## Headlines are primary typography

*Subheads are secondary typographic elements*

Speak the speech, I pray you, as I pronounced it to you, trippingly on the tongue. But if you mouth it, as many of your players do, I had as lief the town crier speak

3.01

## Headlines are primary typography

*Decks are subheads that are placed directly beneath headlines*

Speak the speech, I pray you, as I pronounced it to you, trippingly on the tongue. But if you mouth it, as many of your players do, I had as lief the town crier speak my lines. Nor do not saw the air awfully much with your hand, so thus. But use all gently for in the very torrent, tempest, and as I may say, whirlwind of passion, you must acquire and beget a temperance that may give it so much smoothness.

Oh, it offends me to the soul to hear a robustious periwag-pated fellow tear a passion to tatters, to very rags, to split the ears of the groundlings, who for the most part are capable of nothing but inexplicable dumb shows and noise. I would have such a fellow whipped for o'erdoing Termagant. It out-herods Herod. Be not too tame either.

3.02

**Floating subheads live beside the text...**

Speak the speech, I pray it to you, trippingly on the tongue. But if you mouth it, as many of your players do, I had as lief the town crier speak my lines. Nor do not saw the air awfully much with your hand, so thus. But use all gently for in the very torrent, tempest, and as I may say, whirlwind of passion, you must acquire and beget a temperance that may give it so much smoothness.

Oh, it offends me to the soul to hear a robustious periwag pated fellow tear a passion to

**which requires dedicated white space**

tatters, to very rags, to split the ears of the groundlings, who for the most part are capable of nothing but inexplicable dumb shows and noise.

I would have such a fellow whipped for o'er doing Termagant. It out-herods Herod. Be not too tame either. Pray you, avoid it at any cost to your for in the very torrent, tempest, and as I may say, whirlwind of passion, you must acquire and beget a temperance that must to you, trippingly on the tongue. But if you mouth it, as many of you must passion, you must acquire and beget

3.03

tongue. But if you mouth it, as many of your players do, I had as lief the town crier speak my lines.

***Breaker heads are inserted into running text***

Do not saw the air awfully much with your hand, so thus. But use all gently for in the very torrent, tempest, and as I may say, whirlwind of passion, you must acquire and beget a temperance

3.04

smile and say, "This is no flattery."

**Flush left, no indent**
Hath not old custom made this life more sweet than that of painted pomp? Are not these woods more free from

**Bold lead in** Hath not old custom made this life more sweet than that of painted pomp? Are not these woods

### Deep indent with text
Hath not old custom made this life more sweet than that of painted pomp? Are not these woods more free from peril than

**Hanging indent**
Hath not old custom made this life more sweet than that of painted pomp? Are not these woods more free from peril than

**Hanging indent lead in** Hath not old custom made this life more sweet than that of painted pomp? Are not these woods more free from peril than the en-

**❚ Breaker with a rule**
Hath not old custom made this life more sweet than that of painted pomp? Are not these woods more free from peril than

**BREAKER HEAD
IN A BOX**

Hath not old custom made this life more sweet than that of painted pomp? Are not these woods more free from peril than

**This flush left breaker head pokes into the text** Hath not old custom made this life more sweet than that of painted pomp? Are not these woods more free from peril than the envious court? Here feel we safe from the

**THIS CENTERED SUBHEAD POKES HALF IN AND HANGS HALF OUT** Hath not old custom made this life more sweet than that of painted pomp? Are not these woods more free from peril than the en-vious court? Here feel we

3.05

thick upon him. The third day here comes a frost, a killing frost.

**❚ Breaker heads that run longer than one line interrupt the text's flow**
When he thinks, good easy man, full surely his greatness is aripening, nips his root, and then he falls, as I do. I have ventur'd like little wanting child

3.06

thick upon him. The third day here comes a frost, a killing frost.
**USE 2nd COLOR
IN BREAKER HEADS**
When he thinks, good easy man, full surely his greatness is aripening, nips his root, and then he falls, as I do. I have ventur'd like little wanting child

3.07

thick upon him. The third day here comes a frost, a killing frost.
**Lead ins
are entrances** into the text. When he thinks, good easy man, full surely his greatness is aripening, nips his root, and then he falls, as I do. I have ven-

3.08

thick upon him. The third day comes a frost, a killing frost.

12pts
18pts

**Add half a linespace**
When he thinks, good easy man, full surely his greatness is aripening, nips his root, and then he falls, as I do. I have ventur'd like little wanting child

3.09

thick upon him. The third day here comes a frost, a killing frost.

**Position a breaker head closer to the copy that follows than to the preceding text**

When he thinks, good easy man, full surely his greatness is aripening, nips his root, and then he falls, as I do. I have ventur'd like little wanting child

3.10

they provide just enough information to intrigue and make you want to stay tuned to hear the rest of the story.

Breaker heads offer myriad typographic possibilities. Shown in figure 3.05 are several fundamental styles that can be applied to your publication. Be sure your subheads and headlines agree in style.

Here are a few observations about breaker heads:

• Using punctuation at the ends of breaker heads creates a tiny pause in the reader's mind, giving a reason not to continue into the text. Do not punctuate!

• Because breaker heads that are longer than one line can interrupt the flow of the text column, they should be used judiciously (fig. 3.06).

• Contrasting color will make breaker heads more visible (fig. 3.07).

• Lead-ins are breaker heads in that they interrupt the text and give the casual browser an entrance into the article (fig. 3.08). Choose provocative wording for a lead-in, or the result will be the same as an inherently meaningless initial cap: a mere focal point on which the eye may land (which is still better than endless uninterrupted grayness confronting the reader).

• Do not indent the text immediately after a breaker head. The typographic difference between subhead and text supplies sufficient contrast to signal a new idea.

• A breaker head should generally have a half a line space added above it, not a full line space. A full line space looks too big, chopping the column into segments (fig. 3.09).

• Breaker heads describe the copy they precede. They should therefore be positioned closer to the text they describe – the text that follows – than to the text before them (fig. 3.10). That proximity signals to the reader that the breaker head describes the following text.

Like headlines, their typographic cousins, subheads have great potential for effective communication. Their important function as the secondary level of typography helps convert a browser into a reader.

# VW and Motorsports

Volkswagen's involvement in motorsports spawns product, personnel, and engineering development.

3.11

# Vintage Alumni

*In ancient Greece, the god Dionysus was revered as an expert on wine. But even he might find the technical expertise required to produce wine today beyond his powers. As the Santa Cruz alumni featured in this story have discovered, in 1989 there's a lot more to making wine than rolling up your pants and stomping grapes.*

## By Susan Chollar

3.12

NEW ENGLAND
MONTHLY

# The Lives of a House

*In the story of one home
in the Dorchester section of Boston,
you can see the history of
urban New England*

IT'S A BIG, GRAY, WEATHER-BEATEN house that you can't help but call rambling, set high on a hill in one of Boston's toughest neighborhoods. When it was last offered for sale three years ago, the house's cedar shingles had gone unpainted for half a century. The garage was filled with trash, rusted tools, and an old wooden icebox. The nearest commercial street featured almost as many vacant lots as stores. Around Mount Bowdoin — the hill that gives its name to this part of Dorchester — it was easier to buy drugs than groceries.

But Gerard Hurley and his wife, Iris DuPont, were willing to overlook a lot. As soon as they drove up to 7 Bowdoin Avenue in July of 1986, they knew they wanted to buy it. There was nowhere else in Boston that an airport skycap and his wife could get a renovated eighteen-room house for $150,000. Hurley and DuPont soon learned that rents from its two apartments would help to pay the mortgage. And they knew that the house held the promise of a different kind of life, where two people who had grown up in housing projects could live in a mansion on top of a hill. "I'd never had a patch of grass," says Gerard Hurley.

Most of the old Victorian mansions around 7 Bowdoin Avenue had long since declined or been torn down. Where mowed grass had once lain like a carpet on the hill's little green, now there was nothing but an abandoned park and the shadows of old paths. Burglaries were frequent. One week after moving in, Hurley and DuPont were robbed. "We were told that it's part of the initiation process," Gerard remembered. Nonetheless, there was a sense of potential renewal in the air on Mount Bowdoin as well. Some realtors coveted the down-at-the-

BY HOWARD HUSOCK

NEW ENGLAND MONTHLY · **31**

3.13

## Subheads external to text: decks

3.11

A typically structured – though particularly handsome – deck appears immediately below the headline. Its purpose is to clarify the meaning of the head in such a way that the reader is compelled to begin reading the text. *Volkswagen World*

3.12

This wall-to-wall deck is so named because it extends fully across the live area of the page. It is positioned in the most natural place, between the headline and text, and it is sized to be read in that correct sequence. This 1-2-3 structure has been used for centuries because it works. *UC Santa Cruz Review*

3.13

A centered headline above a centered deck, whose centerline aligns with the right margin of the text. This works because of the empty space in the outer margin. *New England Monthly*

**3.14**

Another standard deck arrangement, centered below the centered headline, is personalized with fun type for the headline and caps with small caps in the deck. Printed in purple, lime green, and red. *Tampa Bay Life*

**3.15**

A deck can be placed above and still be read *after* the headline. Provide sufficient contrast between the two, and use an initial cap at the beginning of the text so the reader knows where to go next. *Outside*

**3.16**

This headline and subhead sandwich a heavily boxed photo. The Futura Extra Bold is used to create a clear hierarchy: the largest type, in all caps, is seen first; the smaller upper- and lower-case copy is seen second; and the smallest setting, the light text, is read third. This typical treatment is made distinctive by the well-spaced justification (note that the last line of the subhead fills the measure). *Children's Business*

3.14

3.15

3.16

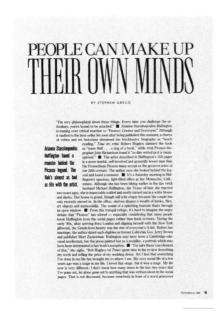

3.18

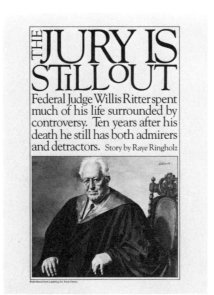

3.17

3.19

3.17

An effective way of uniting the head and subhead is to set them to the same width. The impact is strengthened by also matching the image's width, then surrounding the whole design with a box rule. *Lodestar*

3.18

This deck is set in very black contrasting type that is made even more visible by being set into crisp, square cut-ins in a justified text block. The black squares, called ballots, set into the text indicate paragraph breaks. *American Way*

3.19

This deck is also cut into the text but, being printed blue, is a more subtle treatment. Compare the densities of this and the previous example. The feeling of each is utterly different from the other. *Cleveland Magazine*

**3.20**

This subhead is as small as any you are likely to find. Its type size is, in fact, smaller than that for the text. But it is visible nonetheless, because of its boldness and its position in the wide outer margin. It is line-spaced to be visually the same depth as the headline, thereby creating a distinct design relationship and guiding the reader's eye. *USAir*

**3.21**

Everything lines up perfectly on this page. The byline is sized to match the width of the text column; the cap *B* ends at the base line of the first segment of text, and the subhead hangs into the left-hand margin the same visual distance the cap *B* rises above the headline's x-height. These relationships make the message clear and appealing. *Hippocrates*

**3.22**

This magazine leads off every story with a SUMMARY deck, giving each article a more serious feeling, whether the topic is Armenian protests or the three-point basketball shot. Readers get a very good idea of what to expect from each story and can decide whether to continue reading without having invested much time. *Insight*

3.20

3.21    3.22

3.23

3.24

3.25

3.23
This lengthy subhead acts exactly like a summary, without being so named. Its type size is considerably larger than that for the text, and at eight lines deep, it is close to the maximum length advisable for attracting readers. Printed green, it supports the idea of drinking liquefied grass. *Bestways*

3.24
Is this a subhead or a lead-in that works like a subhead? It doesn't matter, so long as the first few words illuminate the headline and keep you reading. *Public Relations Journal*

3.25
Deck and headline can be integrated into a single unit. The subhead lines are set justified to obtain the squared, even measures. Printed purple and black. *The Face*

**3.26**

This deck infiltrates the headline, but the two are clearly separate in the original: the subhead is printed bright red around the black headline. *Spy*

**3.27**

The subhead can be bisected by the headline, forcing the reader to make a visual leap to continue. *Rolling Stone*

**3.28**

This deck looks like a breakout because it is set to column width, in a clearly contrasting typeface, and it is written to be provocative and intriguing. Nonetheless, it is indeed a subhead because it is meant to be read immediately after the headline. *New York Woman*

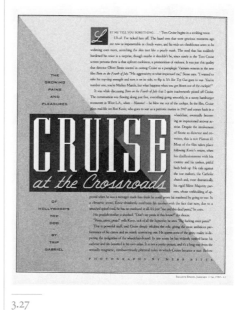

3.26

3.27

3.28

A Mine of Information

3.29

3.30

GUARD

*Ask any lifeguard: boredom and brats aside, they have the coolest job under the sun.*

DUTY

By Jon Bowermaster

Photography by Robb Kendrick

Is there a better job in the world than sitting atop a lifeguard's chair on a summer day, baking in the sun and generally goofing off before adulthood starts? A toot from your whistle stops wayward swimmers and gives pause to the opposite sex. Spring from the tower when duty calls, and all eyes are on you.

And the job comes with such great tools: pith helmet, bullhorn, sunglasses, tanning oil, swimsuit. No choking neckties, no high heels. No clogged freeways or shadowy

*Banner day: Karl Malmsheimer (left) loosens up before his shift at Sherwood Island State Park.*

3.31

3.29

This deck is sized and positioned to look like a caption, though the real caption is positioned at the bottom left corner of the photo. The subhead's white letters are dropped out of a solid blue background, and the caption is printed in blue, creating a positive/negative visual connection between the two elements. *Fleet Norstar Directions*

3.30

Top-of-column subheads may seem to overstep the fuzzy boundary between subhead and headline. In this case, a bona fide headline (*primary* typographic element) is on the facing page. The vertical rules, repetition, and imagery/text relationship combine to make this an easily absorbed cluster of information. The original is in full color, making the page even more dynamic than it looks here. *BP America Scene*

3.31

Subheads can be placed inside an image. In this case, the image has the headline superimposed on it, joining three elements. *Connecticut's Finest*

## Subheads external to text: floating subheads

**3.32**
A hanging or marginal subhead stands in the margin. Each subhead is three lines long, giving the page a rhythm. With an average of only seven words per subhead, the words used must be provocative and informative. *Medical Economics*

**3.33**
This magazine has a thin outer column used only for floating subheads and authors' biographies. The department heading joins the outer column to the body of the text area. *World Monitor*

**3.34**
These marginal subheads are also bold lead-ins. The first sentence of a long quote is enlarged and placed in a separate column, making it easy to scan the page vertically for a quote that appeals. *Chemical Processing*

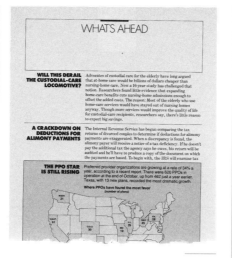

3.32

3.33

3.34

3·35

3·36

3.35
A floating subhead is positioned alongside the text in its own column. An excellent way to give a floating subhead visibility is to surround it with white space. The added line space makes these eight lines seem easier to scan than if they had been set with a more predictable couple of points of additional line spacing. *Electronic Musician*

3.36
This page is organized to guide you around the photo from top to bottom. Each of the five kinds of information is given a distinctly different typographic treatment, necessary to keep readers moving from one element to the next. The ultimate goal is to woo them into the text. *M*

3.37
This exuberant typography is a one-piece sample of contrast and how it – with the judicious use of white space – can make a page come to life. The centered deck juxtaposes with the asymmetrical design of the headline. *Syracuse University Magazine*

3·37

3.38

The floating subhead appears to become a caption as it jumps the gutter and is surprinted on the color photo. QUEEN NOOR is printed in the same pink as the dress. *Dossier*

**Subheads internal to text: breaker heads**

3.39

A breaker head is inserted into the text to divide it into sections and make it appear less of a chore to read. These breaker heads jump off the page because they contrast in nearly every conceivable way with the text: they are centered in a contrasting sans serif, all-cap, condensed bold typeface that has a slightly larger point size. *UCLA Magazine*

3.38

3.39

3.40

3.41

3.42

**3.40**

A single breaker head is used on each of the five pages in this article. Each is printed dark blue-green to unify it with a frieze running along the foot of each page. *Invention & Technology*

**3.41**

Here a run-in breaker head begins each new section. The bold all-cap treatment pops them out of the gray text. Always be sure breaker heads are immediately visible, so they will act as the flags they are meant to be. *Restaurant Business*

**3.42**

These breaker heads divide the copy by graduation year. The combination of boldness and extra line space above and below are sufficient to make them pop out on the page. *Notre Dame Magazine*

**3.43**

The question/answer format is common in nearly every publication. Questions must stand out, enabling readers to browse until their attention is arrested – graphically, they are identical to breaker heads. The difference between questions and answers is usually made clear by setting the questions italic or bold and the answers in regular type. This example shows unexpected ways of making the questions stand out. *L'Expansion*

**3.44**

A lead-in breaker evokes the Russian Cyrillic alphabet, relating to the content of the text. Note the simplicity of skipping a single line space and setting the breaker two lines deep. Breaker printed in light blue. *New England Monthly*

**3.45**

Pictures can work as well as words to break up an article. These "breaker heads" are illustrations. Printed black on 20 percent lavender. *Inside Albany*

3.43

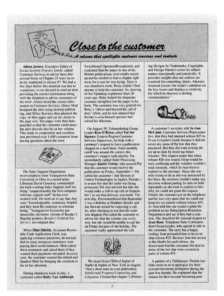

3.45

3.44

# 4

Breakouts, also known as pull quotes, callouts, or liftouts, should be thought of as verbal illustrations that draw the reader into a story. Editorially, they should be brief extracts of particularly provocative copy. Graphically, they should be highly visible – in strong contrast with their surroundings – and able to easily attract the reader's eye.

Breakouts were invented to solve a particular problem: how to slow or stop a casual reader who is not yet actively reading an article. The solution: enlarge a brief portion that is most likely to make the reader stop to read the article in its entirety.

Breakouts do more than trumpet the most salient or arresting segment of an article. Because they are meant to be read before the text, breakouts also provide an opportunity for typographic preening and experimentation. Their use leads to an over-all elevation of a publication's visual and typographic presentation.

To catch the reader's attention, the breakout must contrast strongly with the surrounding text. Contrast can be achieved in several ways:

• *Increase the type size.* Simple and effective: use the same font and weight as the text type but enlarge it (fig. 4.01). An enlarged breakout should be at least 18 points to stand out sufficiently. This size-only contrast can be enhanced by surrounding the breakout with a moat of white space.

• *Increase the type weight.* Make the breakout bolder than the text, or really pump it up by making it bigger and bolder (fig. 4.02). Experiment by making the text bold and the breakout lighter (fig. 4.03). Either will work, so long as sufficient contrast exists between areas of type.

• *Change the color.* Run the breakout in a second color or drop it out of a panel of the one available color to increase its visibility on the page (fig. 4.04).

• *Create an unusual column structure.* Breakouts can be positioned either within the text (fig. 4.05) or in dedicated white space, using consistent sinkage at the head margin (fig. 4.06) or in a narrow column at the outside margin (fig. 4.07) or between columns of text (fig. 4.08). Eccentric, or uneven, columns are a provocative means of separating kinds of information (fig. 4.09). If your publication can accommodate eccentric columns – on an opener or because it does not run ads – consider

were love-sick with them. The oars were silver which to the tune of flutes kept stroke, and made the water which they beat to flow faster, as amorous of their strokes. For her own person, it beggar'd all description. She did lie in her pavilion, cloth-of-gold of tissue, o'er picturing that Venus where we had been astride

**The nature of bad news infects the teller**

4.01

were love-sick with them. The oars were silver which to the tune of flutes kept stroke, and made the water which they beat to flow faster, as amorous of their strokes. For her own person, it beggar'd all description. She did lie in her pavilion, cloth-of-gold of tissue, o'er picturing that Venus where we had

**The nature of bad news infects the teller**

4.02

were love-sick with them. The oars were silver which to the tune of flutes kept stroke, and made the water which they beat to flow faster, as amorous of their strokes. For her own person, it beggar'd all description. She did lie in her pavilion, cloth-of-gold of tissue o'er picturing that Venus

The nature of bad news infects the teller

4.03

were love-sick with them. The oars were silver which to the tune of flutes kept stroke,

✿ ✿ ✿

*The nature of bad news infects the teller*

✿ ✿

and made the water which they beat to flow faster, as amorous of their strokes. For her own person, it beggar'd all description. She

4.04

**The nature
of bad news
infects
the teller**

4.05

---

**The nature of bad news
infects the teller**

4.06

---

**The nature of bad news infects the teller**

4.07

---

**The
nature
of bad
news
infects
the
teller**

4.08

---

*The nature

of bad news

infects

the teller*

perfumed that the winds were lovesick with them. The oars were silver which to the tune of flutes kept stroke, and made the water which they beat to flow faster, as amorous of their strokes. For her own person, it beggar'd all description. She

4.09

---

gold, purple the sails, and so perfumed that the winds were love-sick with them. The oars were silver which to the tune of flutes

*The    nature    of

bad    news

infects    the    teller*

kept stroke, and water which they beat to flow faster, as amorous of their strokes. For her own person, it beggar'd all description. She did lie in her pavilion, cloth-of-gold of

4.10

---

gold, purple the sails, and so perfumed that the winds were love-sick with them. The oars were silver which to the tune of flutes

**The nature of
BAD NEWS
infects
the teller**

kept stroke, and water which they beat to flow faster, as amorous of their strokes. For her own person, it beggar'd all description. She did lie in her pavilion, cloth-of-gold of tis-

4.11

---

using the narrower column or columns for breakouts. Clear rules for their use must be developed and followed. For example, text may be put in wider columns while breakouts, headlines, and captions go in narrower columns. When using narrow columns, allow the leftover white space to surround the breakout. It is not an extravagant use of paper, but an excellent way of creating a coherent hierarchy on the page.

• *Open the line spacing.* This will make a breakout look shorter and easier to read (fig. 4.10). To create sufficient contrast, add at least an additional half line space per line. This device is especially effective in conjunction with open letterspacing and italic type.

• *Use quotation marks if the breakout is a direct quotation.* Make the quotation marks illustrative by exaggerating their size – open with a 66, close with a 99 (fig. 4.11). Team the quote with its source by adding a photo of the source to the breakout configuration (fig. 4.12). Set the type in italics, which suggests handwriting and, to some extent, spoken thought.

• *Use a display initial.* The greater the contrast with the surrounding type, the better. It is almost impossible to overdo it. Found letterforms or objects (reproduced on a copier) make especially unusual, eye-catching initials (fig. 4.13) and can be chosen for their relationship to the subject of the story, thereby enhancing the communicative quality of the breakout.

• *Add rules.* Rules are visible because they are inherently directional and because they are usually darker than other elements on the page. If heavy enough, the rule creates a useful and unavoidable focal point. Add a rule when a light breakout does not pop off the page (fig. 4.14).

• *Use box rules.* These can be embellished to impart a unique character (fig. 4.15). Be careful not to overuse boxes: they tend to deaden a page and repel readers. To overcome this likelihood, avoid using ordinary boxes.

• *Surround the breakout with white space.* Any breakout will become more visible when it has more space around it. Particularly when placing a breakout in the text, leave sufficient white space on all four sides, or you run the risk of camouflaging it amid the textual underbrush. The rule of thumb is to leave from a half to a full line space above and below and a couple of characters of width on each side, but optical spacing is the ultimate determinant (fig. 4.16).

• *Put the breakout inside a shape.* Choose a shape that relates to the story's subject, or use a shape that echoes an element in one of the story's pictures.

Using any one of these techniques alone can give great results. A potent breakout will give the reader who is casually wandering through a reason to stop and become involved with the story. Adroitly combining two or more of these techniques will create highly visible, unique display type, bound to catch a browser's roving attention.

**More thoughts
on breakouts**

• Do not position a breakout too close to its appearance in the text. Readers are looking for the context of the extract. If they find it too easily, they may not read the rest of the piece.

• Insert a breakout in the middle – never at the end – of a paragraph (fig. 4.17). This helps the reader read past the breakout by indicating that the text continues.

• A breakout can be one of the most important typographic elements on a page. Do not bury it on the less visible bottom third of the page, where it is less likely to be seen.

• Combining a distinctive breakout and headline treatment for each feature story clearly tells the reader which pages belong together (fig. 4.18). It gives a consistency that should be instantly recognizable, especially if the story must be interrupted by advertising pages.

• Finally, it is *very important* to keep breakouts as short as possible – bite-sized, two brief sentences or less. They must seem scannable without effort to the reader. Long breakouts of three or more sentences dissuade the reader from nibbling. It's simply too big a taste test. Remember, the point is to interest, not necessarily to inform. The text carries the information, but the reader must be lured to it.

**The
examples**

The breakout examples on the following pages are grouped in the categories described in this chapter introduction. Classifying them is a bit tricky because they rarely exemplify just one technique. Though each example shows two or even three techniques combined, one usually predominates, and the example has thus been included under that heading.

gold, purple the sails, and so perfumed that the winds were love-sick with them. The

oars were silver which to the tune of flutes kept stroke, and water which they beat to flow faster, as amorous of their strokes. For

4.12

gold, purple the sails, and so perfumed that the winds were love-sick with them. The

**he nature
of bad news infects the teller**

oars were silver which to the tune of flutes kept stroke, and water which they beat to flow faster, as amorous of their strokes. For

4.13

gold, purple the sails, and so perfumed that the winds were love-sick with them. The

*The nature of bad news
infects the teller*

oars were silver which to the tune of flutes kept stroke, and water which they beat to flow faster, as amorous of their strokes. For

4.14

gold, purple the sails, and so perfumed that the winds were love-sick with them. The

*THE NATURE
OF BAD NEWS
INFECTS
THE TELLER*

oars were silver which to the tune of flutes kept stroke, and water which they beat to flow faster, as amorous of their strokes. For

4.15

music be    it came o'er my ear    odor. No
food of    like the sweet sod    more 'tis
e, play on.                          sweet nc
ve me ex-                            as it was k
ss of it that,                       fore. Oh s
r-feiting,   **The nature**          of love! Hc
e appetite   **of bad news**         quick ar
ly sicken    **infects the teller**  fresh art t
nd so die.                           that notw
at strain    that breathes upon    s t a n d i r
ain! It had  a bank of violets,    thy capac
ying fall. O, stealing and giving  receive th

4.16

the winds were love-    to the tune of flutes
sick with them. ○ *NO!*  kept stroke, and ○ *YES!*

**The nature of**       **The nature of**
**bad news**            **bad news**
**infects**             **infects**
**the teller**          **the teller**

The oars were          made the water
silver which to the    which they beat to
tune of flutes kept    flow faster, as amo-
stroke, and made       rous of their strokes

4.17

4.18

Older patients

**B**efore surgery, the surgeon drew George's wife aside to ask whether she thought this might be the time to let nature take its course. She thought not.

4.19

4.20

MEDICAL ECONOMICS MAY 25, 1989  141

## Increased type size

### 4.19

The biggest type signals the greatest importance and is read first. The photo is in color and the *B* is printed purple. *Medical Economics*

### 4.20

Large type enhanced by "printer's flowers" and handsome emptiness. A good breakout must be intriguingly written, as this example is. *Syracuse University Magazine*

### 4.21

This breakout is joined with a photo and caption, the three elements making a single concentrated unit. The initial *t* is light green, the caption is knocked out of deep blue. *New York*

MURDOCH TOASTING PETER AND MARY KALIKOW.

**T**he more people tell me not to do something," Peter Kalikow says, "or the more they say something is not going to work, the more I want to do it."

4.21

## Increased type weight

### 4.22

Increasing the type weight will make the breakout instantly visible. This type is printed 70 percent black so it will not completely overwhelm the color photo, which extends to the top of the page. *Tampa Bay Life*

### 4.23

A brief, one-sentence bold breakout is overprinted on a colored screen tint that bleeds off the bottom of the page on each department opener. The background colors change, but the size and position of the screen tint is always the same. *USAir*

### 4.24

Century Schoolbook Bold makes the breakout stand apart from the text – with some help from vertical and horizontal rules. The rules are printed green. *Pacific Tidings*

**Tere McLaughlin** won the battle of red tape and got a child out of Jamaica, only to lose custody of the boy to his father, her former husband.

4.22

## Orlando's Evolution

By Jacquelyn Denalli

Catch professional baseball action, a mile-long boardwalk, rides, and shows at Boardwalk and Baseball.

People are still friendly in this Florida city, but they're moving to a faster beat.

4.23

### Fraser River sockeye run best in years

They had returned to spawn in the millions and they were beautiful.

Sockeye returning to spawn in the Horsefly River came in the greatest numbers since the Hell's Gate slide in 1913.

**Chinook Conservation**
*Limited Edition Prints*

4.24

school.

Happily, he found a carpenter in Great Barrington who was willing to take on the job. When the carpenter was done, my father climbed in to make sure the box was big enough in case it should turn out to be his. I wish I'd been there to see the carpenter's reaction, but I'm sure Dad felt he was merely being practical. You don't buy a suit, after all, without trying it on first. The box was stored next to the cart in the barn by the house in Stockbridge, to await its occupant.

In 1971, my father calculated that the circles of the pie were increasing at such a rate that the family would run out of space by the year 2101. I can't imagine how he settled on that particular year. Far off as that time might seem, to my father the situation demanded action *now*. He immediately petitioned the board of selectmen for the right to buy an adjoining parcel. He put the matter rather plaintively in a letter to the selectmen: "If we rested content with our present land, we should be completely surrounded by graves and have nowhere to grow." It is uniquely Sedgwickian, I expect, to see death as expanding a family rather than contracting it. Nevertheless, at the selectmen's first meeting the question was quickly tabled as being "premature." It went down again at the second meeting, the shortest meeting, it was noted, "ever." But my father prevailed in the end; the pie's future is secure well into the twenty-second century.

My father died in 1976 when I was twenty-one. He had a stroke on Christmas Eve. He was incapacitated, and, difficult as it was for everyone in the family, we observed his wishes and asked the doctors not to intervene to prolong his life in that condition. He died two weeks later. He, too, was cremated. (He had always planned to be, but it was nonetheless important to my father for the coffin to be "full size.") For some reason it fell to me to collect his ashes; they came packaged in a cardboard box, which seemed crude even by Sedgwick standards. This was in January, and the main street in Stockbridge was covered with slush as the horse-drawn cart led the funeral procession. I had been steeling myself for the moment when I would have to throw the loose soil onto my father's grave, but to my surprise that didn't affect me. Grief picks its own moment. Instead, I had choked up during the service when we sang the hymn. "A Mighty Fortress Is Our God," I think it was. Behind me, I could hear my older brothers singing so bravely — Sedgwicks always belt out the hymns — that I was overcome. Tears spilled down my cheeks. I tried to sing, but I could barely make a sound.

My father's stone is mottled and gray like all the others now. I hadn't realized he had been gone so long. He lies beside his first wife, Helen, whose stone is topped by the Groton School crest (she was the daughter of Groton's founder). It is always strange for me to come into the pie and see, in effect, my father's other life. Helen had died on a visit to Stockbridge seven years before I was born. Babbo, her father-in-law, wept at her grave

the engraver would inscribe the words on the back, as if Dad was *still* marching forward. But I think that's a joke my father would have liked. Death, you see, can't stop him.

THE SEDGWICK PIE is sufficiently quirky that it has attracted considerable attention over the years, and it's often said that the graves are arranged so that on Judgment Day the Sedgwicks will rise and see no one but Sedgwicks. I doubt it was a Sedgwick who first put it this way. (It reminds me of the other bon mot that Sedgwicks have been trying to live down for generations, one attributed to Thomas Appleton, that the Sedgwicks are so deeply rooted in Stockbridge that even the crickets chirp *Sedg-wick, Sedg-wick*.)

The Judgment Day business was in fact the first thing my wife heard about me, and it nearly ended our relationship before it began. She and I both happened to attend a get-together for English majors at Harvard's Eliot House when I found Alan Heimert, the Puritan scholar and Eliot House master, standing before me. I introduced myself. "A Sedgwick!" he roared. "You're not one of those Sedgwicks of the *pie*, are you?" I quietly admitted it was true. "You know what they say about the Sedgwicks, don't you?" he continued at full

> The Sedgwicks do not, like most people, go to their graves dressed in their Sunday best. We wear our pajamas.

blast. Of course I did, but I couldn't stop him. "On Judgment Day, they all rise up and see no one but *Sedgwicks!*" Then he laughed uproariously, while I did my best to smile. On the other side of the room, my future wife, a Californian, fumed about the horrible WASP-iness of it all and vowed to avoid this ridiculous Sedgwick person. Happily, she relented.

Actually, we Sedgwicks don't think much about Judgment Day, and so far as anyone knows the plan of the burial ground has nothing to do with it. What it *does* have to do with remains unclear. Growing up, I had always assumed the original scheme for the pie was hatched by the Judge himself. He was a man of no small ego, and I figured it would suit him perfectly to have his descendants arrayed at his feet. In truth, the Judge had developed no plans for his gravesite when he died in Boston, where he was living with his third wife, Penelope Russell, in 1813. He was buried in Boston after a funeral service led by William Ellery Channing and attended by the leading

NEW ENGLAND MONTHLY • 37

4.25

## Color

**4.25**

Printed in two shades of green, this breakout is made visible in a purposeful field of gray. Note the center-jumping initial *T* and the square cut-in's contrast with the ragged-right breakout. *New England Monthly*

**4.26**

Boldness and bright red ink combine with a hefty outer margin to make this pull quote zing the reader's eye. *SSR-tidningen*

**4.27**

An asymmetrical setting and empty column define this red breakout. The photos at the bottom of the page are also asymmetrically positioned. *Spy*

liga lönesystem med löneplan och tjänstebegreppet är ett hinder som måste bort (se ruta) bör vägen ligga öppen.

## I princip ja

SAV:s förhandlingschef vill inte spekulera kring hur det kommer att gå i denna fråga, och svaret på frågan om vi till sommaren på frågan om vi till sommaren har tagit rejäla kliv blir försiktigt.

> Det är ju absurt att förhandla med SF om professorslöner."

delar av SAV:s område.

— Men stora systemförändringar, som det här är fråga om, går inte att tvinga igenom. Parterna måste komma överens.

"Styrkorna är formerade i två läger redan innan några realförhandlingar kommit igång: På ena sidan TCO:s och SF och på den andra SACO/SR-S och Statens Arbetsgivarverk (SAV)." Citatet är ur februarinumret av *Statstjänstemannen*, organ för den tunga TCO-S-förbundet ST.

● Men kan inte SAV komma runt detta motstånd genom att

säger nej och TCO-S verk svårt att bestämma sig.

## Personalförsörjninge

Huvudmålet för SAV i dande avtalsrörelsen är, Stare formulerar det, at klara statens personalför Här handlar det främst nadsmässiga grupper, o med många vakanser, vidare. På direkt fråga tuella saminingar på h assistenter och frivån — som utsätts för lo kommunernas socialt förhandlingschefen n ning till de stundande lingarna svaret skyld

— Däremot vill j att vi också arbetar f personalförsörjningen vi måste värna om d vilka vi är monopola till exempel lärarna c inom kulturområdet.

## Marknadstrygghe

Som väntar delar inte den fackliga upprördh nansministerns utgiftr limit). Denna gång b men ramarna lär kon i någon form.

— Blir löneökning höga en myndighet

4.26

Robinsons made some attempts to fulfill their social obligations while on duty Henry Catto, the current ambassador to Great Britain, is known mainly for fostering about what a close friend of the president he is and for seldom entertaining. In the words of one political journalist, "These days, it's a rather universal feeling that the embassy is of no intrinsic whatsoever for journalists or diplomats."

Once Robinson's service had ended, he apparently had a difficult time persuading his wife to leave. Martha threw the embassy staff into an uproar by refusing to go to the airport, amid which the flight could be delayed no longer, her husband left without her. She eventually returned to Illinois to join him, but not before serving an apartment in Ottawa, not far from the American embassy.

THE DIPLOMAT'S GIFT OF SPEECH
So, like, it's really important that we, y'know, have lots of missiles in Europe, okay?

Some countries have had more than one awful U.S. ambassador, whether by Washington's design or through plain bad luck.

Switzerland is one. "You've hit the jackpot," says an expert on U.S.-Swiss relations when asked to enumerate about envoys embarrassments. In fact, Switzerland's luck with regard to U.S. ambassadors has been so bad that not long ago, one Swiss newspaper printed photos of several previous U.S. ambassadors under the headline THE AMERICANS TAKE US FOR FOOLS.

Marvin Warren Carver's ambassador from 1977 to 1979, was a savings-and-loan tycoon associated in supporting the New York Yankees, the Tampa Bay Buccaneers and the solid Democrat. He is best known for his poor embassyhood force, the collapse of the Home State Savings Bank, for which he was forced liable to the tune of $4 billion.

Faith Ryan Whittlesey is a right-wing Republican who twice served as ambassador to Switzerland.

fifst in 1980 and again in 1985. On the investigation she had returned to Washington to the White House director of public liaison. Whittlesey was investigated in 1987 for alleged abuses of an embassy entertainment fund and for her hiring practices. One transgression among many was her hiring of a career officer when he re-

**Richard Kneip had an inquisitive mind: "What is this 'Gang of Four' everyone is talking about?" he would ask his staff. "Did you say there are two separate Korean governments? How come?"**

minded her that Switzerland was a neutral country and would not look kindly on her attempts to get Swiss support for the Nicaraguan contras. She also allegedly spent most of an $82,500 embassy fund entertaining and lodging American officials and prominent conservatives even though the money was meant to be used for entertaining businessnationals. Additionally, she was reported to have hired a beneficiary as her return for a $5,000 contribution to the embassy. No action was taken against Whittlesey, but in 1987, as a result of the Whittlesey investigation, the State Department barred all embassies from accepting private donations.

Whittlesey's replacement, Philip Winn, had worked for Reagan or HUD and then stepped over to Winn & Associates, a company he formed with several other former HUD officials. When the HUD scandal broke, he was found to have profited greatly from his past associations. Winn, who was ambassador at the time of the investigation, soon came home, having served for less than a year.

Currently our man in Switzerland is Joseph Gildenhorn, whose only obvious qualification for the post was his willingness to support George Bush and the GOP with $230,000 in campaign contributions. He spends some of the time official langauges of Switzerland (French, German, Italian and was rated unqualified for the

job by the American Academy of Diplomacy, a nonpartisan organization of former ambassadors. The Swiss government may take some solace in the fact that he appears, awoke some of his predecessors, not to be knee-deep in sleaze — so far.

Beautiful Alpine nations seem unusually hard hit, Austria's ambassador-wise. When Helene von Damm rose to prominence as Reagan's personal secretary, the Austrian press displayed a fair amount of nationalal pride over the fact that an Austrian émigré had achieved such success. But when Von Damm returned to her native land as the U.S. ambassador in Vienna, the reaction was quite different. Few members of the establishment each her seriously. Von Damm had been born on a rural Austrian village, emigrating when she was 17. Consequently her finer German there main qualification for the post was the direct German of a provincial teenager, the Austrian equivalent of Valley-speak. And her public behavior was so laughing with her provincial reaction. Her activities were chronicled extensively in Vienna's society and gossip pages, rarely in the same detail in the political news. To the dismay of her embassy staff, she allowed herself to be

4.27

4.28

The initial is yellow, the rest of the breakout is red, on a black triangle. The red and yellow are also used for a sidebar article, visually uniting the parts of this story. *CA Magazine*

**Column structure:**
**position on the page**

4.29

These breakouts run across the tops of five consecutive spreads of a twelve-page story, defining its look and feel. *EMORY COOK* is knocked out of warm red, and the bold phrases are printed green. *Audio*

---

**TOUT CE QUI BRILLE…**

Les emprunts de lingots d'or, comparativement aux contrats de vente à terme, constituent une innovation relativement récente; les pratiques comptables à leur égard ont été grandement influencées par celles que l'on applique aux contrats de vente à terme. Certaines similitudes étaient à prévoir puisque, dans les deux cas, la société minière s'engage à livrer dans l'avenir une quantité déterminée d'or à un prix fixé d'avance.

La méthode de comptabilisation généralement acceptée pour les emprunts de lingots d'or est la suivante : l'emprunteur comptabilise son obligation selon le montant en dollars qu'il obtient de la vente de l'or emprunté. Il n'est pas nécessaire qu'une livraison d'or et une vente aient effectivement lieu : le prêteur peut simplement avancer les dollars équivalant à la valeur marchande de l'or à la date de l'emprunt. Dans tous les cas, la valeur en dollars de l'obligation est établie en fonction de la quantité d'or empruntée et de la valeur marchande au moment de l'emprunt.

Ce principe s'applique même si l'or emprunté est détenu un certain temps par l'entreprise avant d'être vendu, ou s'il fait l'objet d'un contrat de vente à terme. Dans les deux cas, le produit tiré de la vente n'est pas le même que celui qui aurait été réalisé si l'or emprunté avait été vendu immédiatement au comptant. Le gain ou la perte résultant de l'écart entre la valeur marchande à la date de l'emprunt et le prix finalement obtenu constitue un élément distinct qui n'est pas nécessairement pris en compte dans la valeur en dollars attribuée à l'emprunt. L'action d'emprunter de l'or est une opération non monétaire qui doit être comptabilisée à la valeur marchande, à la date de l'emprunt, et les gains ou pertes résultant d'une conversion ultérieure en dollars doivent être traités séparément.

Dans la pratique actuelle, il existe deux méthodes pour présenter l'obligation au bilan. La première consiste à définir celle-ci comme un contrat de vente à prix déterminé et à inscrire un produit comptabilisé d'avance. La seconde consiste à considérer l'obligation comme un emprunt. Quoique les emprunts de lingots d'or présentent des caractéristiques communes avec les contrats de vente à terme d'or (et les contrats de vente en général), ils visent principalement l'obtention de capital et l'emprunteur doit en assumer les frais financiers. Selon les réflexions récentes formulées à l'égard de cette question fondamentale par le groupe de travail sur les problèmes nouveaux du Financial Accounting Standards Board, il convient de considérer ces instruments comme … emprunts (voir *Issue 88-18*).

*Il peut être difficile d'établir un lien entre les quantités d'or produites et le remboursement de l'emprunt*

produit résultant de la vente d'une quantité d'or, égale à la quantité empruntée, au prix par once qui est implicite dans la valeur initiale de l'emprunt.

Il y a des avantages à appliquer une méthode de comptabilisation fondée sur le principe que l'emprunteur de lingots d'or sera remboursé (directement ou indirectement) à partir de la production future : les emprunteurs qui ne réussiraient pas à vendre aux prix courants des quantités d'or au moins égales aux quantités empruntées feraient face à des risques financiers illimités; en outre, il serait peu probable que les prêteurs offrent des conditions acceptables à des entreprises se trouvant dans l'impossibilité de produire les quantités d'or nécessaires au remboursement.

Comme les avances en lingots d'or ne sont accordées qu'aux sociétés qui exploitent des mines d'or, elles ne peuvent être considérées comme une opération conventionnelle; ces avances sont liées de manière inextricable aux réserves minières et aux activités de production de l'emprunteur. Les méthodes de comptabilisation de l'emprunt doivent tenir compte de ce fait. D'autres méthodes qui consisteraient à traiter les gains et les pertes sur emprunts de lingots d'or comme des coûts financiers devant être imputés à l'exercice … fil du temps (ou selon … méthode d'étalement …

4.28

---

**Emory Cook**

**I got into the** *record business because of the* *awful quality* **of American-made discs.**

52    AUDIO/SEPTEMBER 1989

AUDIO/SEPTEMBER 1989    53

4.29

4.30

**INTERVIEW WITH...**

# BILL DAROOGE

*by Patricia Lesser*

4.31

4.32

4.30

Breakouts should make the most salient points visible, giving the browser an opportunity to become a reader. The top of the page is a great place to start. Bold sans serif is set wall to wall (across the width of live area). The lead-in is printed red. *Hippocrates*

4.31

A narrow third column is created at the outside edge of the page, where it is most easily seen. The subject's color photo extends to the edge of live area with the pull quote placed just beneath it, cementing the relationship between the subject and his words. *Nibble*

4.32

A narrow column of white space in the gutter between columns of text guides the eye directly to the breakout, which features a simple illustrative element. Visibility is enhanced by increasing the type weight and the line spacing. A photo and caption are also placed in this central column. *Connecticut's Finest*

**4·33**

This pull quote acts like a caption because it is positioned so close to the photo. The formality of this page is caused by its symmetry: one side mirrors the other. *New Miami*

**4·34**

This breakout shows off the page's unusual column structure. The bold bars emphasize the emptiness of the left edge of the column, which is defined by the vertical hairline rule. Only headlines, subheads, breaker heads, and breakouts extend into the left-hand "mini-column." *The Treasury Pro*

## Open
## line spacing

**4·35**

Opening the line spacing lightens the "color," or grayness, of a breakout. To make added line spacing look purposeful, add at least half the point size of type being used. This example is set in 18-point type, with 12 points of additional line spacing (30 points base line to base line). *Outside*

4·33

4·34

4·35

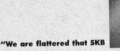

4.36

This pull quote is set in 10-point Futura Extra Black and is 168 points from base line to base line. The photos accompanying the quote help the reader connect the speaker with his thoughts. *Beckman Life*

**Quotation marks**

4.37

Scratchy handwriting is so obviously human-created that quotation marks are not necessary. This is clearly not an ersatz typeset "script" that resembles writing – it's the real thing. *Apprise*

4.36

4.37

## Display initials

**4.38**
The oversize initial acts as a visual target, catching the reader's eye. The breakout is lightened in value by being set with extra letterspacing and a bit of open line space. The initial is printed in blue, the rest of the breakout in red. *New York Woman*

**4.39**
The bold initial cap is centered and sits atop three centered lines of type. The first line is forced to the right by the initial. The underscore with bullets suggests the front view of an airplane, appropriate for an airline company's magazine. *American Way*

**4.40**
A large initial accompanied by a portion of the illustration from the story opener on the previous spread indicates the beginning of this handsome breakout. Color illustration with lavender initial and breakout. *CA Magazine*

Other therapists, both male and female, are less sympathetic and flatly claim their women patients are still single because they either "have trouble with intimacy" or are being "too picky" in their search for a mate. "The women are so drawn to someone who's probably not going to make them happy, for example, macho men—arrogant, self-sufficient men who feel they can choose anyone," says Helen De Rosis, a psychiatrist and associate professor at New York University Medical Center. "The really nice guy who will be supportive they ignore—and that's the guy who will make a good partner in the long run. Then they say there's no one out there."

Those stinging words do ring true for some women. Barbara Fogarty, a striking woman with thick, curly black hair who looks much younger than her forty-nine years, admits, "I pick offbeat, exciting, narcissistic, charming, impossible men who are great in bed but for all those reasons are not very likely prospects for long-term relationships." A divorced business consultant with two college-age children, Barbara says she entered therapy twice a week with a psychiatrist eighteen months ago because "I was getting to the age where I really wanted to figure it out. Maybe I never will marry again, but I'd like to get on with my life."

Her story aside, the "blame the victim" mentality of many therapists (popularized by best-selling self-help books on this topic) seems unduly harsh. It's brutal out there, trying to find someone to love, honor and cherish. Janice Lieberman believes her colleagues refuse to acknowledge the man shortage because it's just too sad. "I think many women may have to come to grips with the fact that they may never marry, or if they do, it'll be to someone who falls short of their ideal," she says matter-of-factly. "In therapy I encourage them to stop leading half lives, to decorate their apartments, to entertain, to go work in a foster home for contact with children, to develop close friendships with other women or married couples. It's true that society isolates them, but they isolate themselves."

Single women don't believe it, of course, but marriage and motherhood are no guarantees for true bliss—as evidenced by all those women wearing wedding bands who are seated in the therapists' waiting room. Many married women were shaken

*M*en often view adversity differently. They blame the fates rather than themselves.

they're also starting to hear from new mothers; raised on feminism, they are now in shock over the drudgery of raising a baby, torn between going back to the office and staying at home, and furious that their previously self-proclaimed liberated husbands aren't being very helpful. "They get tired and angry with the baby, and they hate themselves for it," says Helen De Rosis. "They say, 'Why didn't anyone tell me what it would be like?'" Women who are used to being identified by their powerful and glamorous jobs fear they'll drown in the role of wife and mother. If they aren't bringing in a paycheck, shrinks say, they may start to unconsciously feel that their husbands hold more power in the family relationships. And the men may also feel oppressed by becoming the sole support of the family, given the sky-high costs of living in New York City.

Talking about these multifaceted marital dilemmas in therapy can be comforting, but it's hard to resolve many of these problems when only one member of the couple—typically the wife—is confiding her feelings. "My shrink keeps telling me, 'You can't change his behavior. You can just learn not to let it bother you so much,'" one thirty-six-year-old woman writer complains. "Ultimately, that's not very satisfying." That aside, it's also hard to deal with these issues during a period when society's values keep changing, when one year a woman who stays at home is viewed as a pariah and the next she's a respected protector of the nuclear family.

Naturally, all these concerns—from the heartbreak of remaining single to the intricacies of marriage—evoke childhood memories, images of the kinds of lives today's young women were brought up to expect, of the way they were supposed to act. All patients, of course, talk about their parents in therapy. But given the turmoil of recent years, shrinks say, many women patients feel particularly at odds with their first role model, their mothers. Psychotherapist Lila Rosenblum says career women experience "a lot of conflict over surpassing their mothers." The mothers don't make it easy, often sending mixed messages to their daughters: "Take advantage of the opportunities I never had, dear, but don't you dare be too successful!" But even if their mothers are very supportive, Rosenbl... same young

4.38

### ONCE MORE UNTO THE AUTOBAHN

ler vehicles to be sold in Europe. The result of the test was that they liked the American cars.

"The European journalists drove our cars and Jeep vehicles on Michigan roads, expressways and at our Chelsea, Mich., proving grounds," says Michael N. Hammes, Chrysler's vice president, international operations. "At our proving grounds, they drove a number of our products on a 2.45-mile, high-speed oval to simulate Autobahn speed conditions. The initial driving our high-performance GS Turbo 2 (the European version of the Dodge Daytona Shelby Z) at speeds up to 136 miles per hour." Hammes says the European writers left the Chrysler cars offer "superb comfort at attractive prices."

Chrysler expects to sell 10,000 cars and 10,000 to 15,000 Jeeps in Europe this year, and Hammes says the company is off to a roaring start. "We have 96 dealers in place in West Germany, nearly 40 more retail outlets than our ... of 60," he says. "The

**T**he European marketing effort is just the tip of Chrysler's international iceberg.

plicants who approached us last September at the Frankfurt Auto Show."

All the cars being marketed in Europe carry the Chrysler nameplate. The six offerings are the Chrysler LeBaron coupe and convertible, the Chrysler Voyager minivan, the Chrys-

ler GTS sedan and the Chrysler ES (a version of the Dodge Daytona) and GS Turbo 2.

The European marketing effort is just the tip of Chrysler's international iceberg. Chrysler has a close relationship with Mitsubishi of Japan, in which

supplies the Colt and Conquest vehicles sold through Chrysler-Plymouth and Dodge dealerships.

A joint venture of Chrysler and Mitsubishi, Diamond-Star Motors Corporation will soon produce close to a quarter of a million cars a year in the United States. Chrysler began building a new assembly plant in Illinois in 1986.

Chrysler also has a joint-venture relationship with Maserati of Italy. They have developed and are producing a new top-line sports coupe, the Chrysler TC by Maserati. In April of last year, Chrysler also purchased the Italian specialty carmaker Lamborghini, thus bringing the legendary Countach into the Detroit fold.

Its other international activities include an agreement with First Automobile Works of Changchun, China, under which it provides engine technology and key components for production of up to 300,000 2.2-liter Chrysler engines a year, and a 31 percent interest in Beijing-J...

4.39

4.40

The toughest decisions
are what to eat and
whether to go to the
casino or a bar

4.41

4.42

With the 800
number, consumers
give us immediate
feedback and we
can make immedi-
ate changes.

7

4.43

## Rules

### 4.41

The hefty 18-point rule underscores centered all-cap type in a clearly defined space. This breakout rivets the eye because the contrast with the surrounding text is so sharp. The rule is printed red. *KCET Magazine*

### 4.42

This is a very simple breakout between two horizontal rules. The bold rules accentuate the centering of the copy. Note the generous white space within the breakout, strongly contrasting with the justified gray text. *Business Week*

### 4.43

The hairline rules that separate long vertical columns are interrupted by a pair of 1-point horizontal rules, which sandwich the breakouts in this tabloid. The breakout is purple. *Interchange*

**4.44**

A 10-point rule beneath this breakout anchors it in place. The horizontal rule above the breakout, as well as all vertical rules, are a half point. The color illustration is a detail of the full-bleed artwork on the story opener, making it a breakout as well. *Sales & Marketing Management*

**4.45**

Interline rules are used to define the full column width of this flush-left breakout. *Atheneum*

**4.46**

The bold, expanded typeface is strongly horizontal, a quality that is accentuated by centering between horizontal hairline rules. The breakout type is printed green. *Personal Computing*

4.44

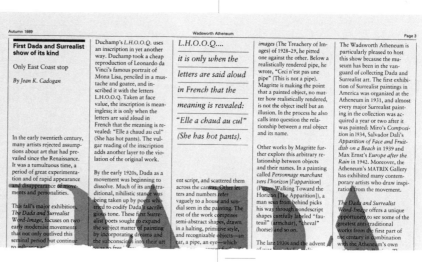

4.45

4.46

4.47

4.48

4.49

4.50

4.47

Vertical hairline rules are used between flush-left columns on this page. The left-hand rule is widened to 4 points for the depth of the breakout. The rules and breakout are printed red. *LDS Hospital Progress*

4.48

An L-shaped rule emphasizes the beginning, top left corner of this pull quote. The initial *I* is printed tan. *Caring*

4.49

An effective juxtaposition of horizontal and vertical rules transforms the photo, quote, and source lines into a single element. Blue type and blue and black duotone photo. *Syracuse University Magazine*

**Box rules**

4.50

This box rule is thickened at top and bottom. The vertical rules are a half point, the horizontal rules are 12 points. The perimeter background is a 10 percent screen tint, which makes this breakout pop right off the page. *Inside Albany*

## 4.51

A drop shadow implies this box rule. This screen tint shadow indicates two edges of a floating card on which the breakout is seemingly printed. *Insight*

## 4.52

This magnificent pull quote is set in black type overprinted on a square color photo of leaves. The photo has been screen-tinted to keep the type legible. Distinguishing this sample are the two printer's flowers, which relate the type to the image. *Caring*

## 4.53

A box connects this dropout pull quote with the color photo. *Cellular Marketing*

## White
## space

## 4.54

An initial cap, larger and bolder type, a stubby rule – all help to make this breakout visible. But what makes it pop is the extra white space surrounding it. The cutout in the text is 9 picas wide, but the centered lines of type are set across a maximum measure of 6 picas, ensuring that white space will separate the typographic elements. *CFO*

4.51

4.52

4.53

4.54

4·55

4·56

4·57

4·55

The "color" of this breakout is nearly the same as that of the text, so it needs the extra white space beneath and beside it. The dropout caption in the photo contrasts well with the breakout. *M*

4·56

This breakout, set in a very peculiar typeface, is given a lot of white space at the outside margin. The dots, printed red, activate the emptiness and suggest humorous flight. *D*

4·57

Breakout or caption? When it is extracted from the text, it is a breakout. When it is new copy, it is a caption. This breakout is pulled from the bottom of the second column of text. *UC Santa Cruz Review*

## Shapes

**4.58**

Relate the breakout to the subject of the article by creating a logical surrounding shape. This story is about a golfer who now lives in Florida. Green type and tee, yellow golf ball. *Gulf Coast*

**4.59**

Create a shape out of the whiteness of the paper itself with a wraparound. This diamond shape evokes a baseball diamond, the subject of the story. *New England Monthly*

**4.60**

This is one of a series of breakouts in one story. Each is designed to look like a memo printed on light blue "stickies," whose edges curl up and cast a gray shadow. *Business Week*

4.58

4.59

4.60

# CAPTIONS

# 5

We like explanations. Even as children, we ask for explanations of the things we see around us. Captions are a printed response to that curiosity. Captions help readers understand what they are seeing and, when the image is complex or puzzling, help them to reach the correct editorial conclusion. Captions serve three functions: they explain the photos; they encourage the reader to want to read the text by summarizing the article they accompany; and they provide another opportunity to give your publication a unique typographic personality.

## Captions
### explain photos

Pictures are always the first things scanned on a page. Reading is work; looking at pictures is fun. Humans simply respond faster to imagery than type. Unfortunately, pictures can be misinterpreted and misunderstood, so captions are added – usually beneath, by tradition – to guide the reader to the intended conclusion.

Captions may explain why the picture is there, they may focus on only a part of the image, or they may put the photo into a different context. Captions should add something to the picture, not merely describe the obvious.

## Captions
### lure readers

Captions can be exploited to entice a reader into a story. Attracted by a picture/caption combination because it breaks the pattern of textual grayness, the reader may then read the headline/deck and breakouts and then the text. Captions are often the entry points for readers because they are so strongly joined with photos – which are great interest-creators – and they are short.

The length of a caption should be neither too long nor too short. Provide enough information to push the reader to the next level of involvement. But a caption contains too much content if paragraphing is necessary. The first few words should be as carefully chosen as a headline's are. Lure readers into completing the caption.

## Captions
### add personality

Every typographic element provides an opportunity to contribute to a publication's distinctive look. And every publication deserves a degree of individuality that sets it apart from its competition, in part because it makes advertisers very happy to be seen in quality surroundings. Captions are among the most exploited elements for distinctive treatment, at the forefront of typographic creativity, along with headlines and breakouts.

---

sic be the
of love,
on. Give me
ss of it that,
iting, the
ite may
n and so
hat strain
! It had a
fall. O,it
o'er my
ke the

**Love sought is good, but giv'n unsought is better.**

sweet sod that beats upon a bank of violets, stealing and giving odor. No

5.01

---

sic be the
of love,
on. Give me
ss of it that,
iting, the
ite may
n and so
hat strain
! It had a
fall. O,it
o'er my
ke the

*Love sought is good, but giv'n unsought is better.*

sweet sod that beats upon a bank of violets, stealing and giving odor. No more 'tis not so

5.02

---

more 'tis no
sweet now a
w's before.
spirit of lov
quick and fi
art thou, tha
withstandin
capacity red
as the sea, r
enters there
what validit
pitch soe'er

sweet now a
w's before.
spirit of lov
quick and fi
art thou, tha
withstandin
capacity red
as the sea, r
enters there
what beats
validity and
soe'er, but

---

## The bard waxes forth

*If music be the food of love, play on.*

Give me excess of it that surfeit, the appetite may sicken and so die. That strain again! It had a idying fall.

O, it came o'er my ear like the sweet sod that breathes upon a bank of violets, stealing and giving odor. No more 'tis not so sweet now as it w's before. O spirit of great love!

How quick and fresh art thou, that notwithstanding thy capacity receiveth as the sea, n'ght enters there. Of what vald'ty and pitch so'er, but falls into abatement and low price, even in a minute.

So full of shapes is fancy that itme excess

L**ove sought**
**is good,**
**but giv'n**
**unsought**
**is better.**

of it that surfeit, the appetite may sicken and so die.

That strain again! It had a idying fall. O, it came o'er my ear like the sweet sod that breathes upon a bank of violets, stealing and giving odor. No more 'tis not sweet now

as it w's before. O spirit of love! How quick and fresh art thou, that notwithstanding thy capacity receiveth as the sea, n'ght enters there.

Of what vald'ty and pitch so'er, but falls into abatement and low price, even in a minute. So full of shapes is fancy that notwithstanding thy capacity receiveth as the sea, night enters there.

What vald'ty and pitch so'er, but falls

5.03

---

*Love sought is good, but giv'n unsought is better.*

5.04

*Love sought is good,*
*but giv'n unsought*
*is better.*

5.05

Love sought is good,
but giv'n unsought is
better. What a deal o'
scorn looks so beauti-
ful in the contempt of
his curl'd lip.

5.06

**LOVE SOUGHT** *is good,*
*but giv'n unsought is better.*
*What a deal o' scorn looks*
*so beautiful in the contempt*
*of his curl'd lip.*

5.07

*Love*
*sought is*
*good, but*
*giv'n*
*unsought*
*is better.*

*looks so*
*beautiful*
*in the*
*contempt*
*of his*
*curl'd lip.*

*What a deal*
*o' scorn*

5.08

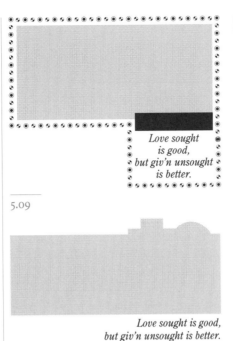

*Love sought*
*is good,*
*but giv'n unsought*
*is better.*

5.09

*Love sought is good,*
*but giv'n unsought is better.*

5.10

**LOVE SOUGHT IS GOOD,**
**BUT GIV'N UNSOUGHT**
**IS BETTER**

**G**ive me excess of it that sur- | ing odor. No more 'tis not so sweet
feit, the appetite may sicken and | now as it was before. O spirit of
so die. That strain again! It had a | great love! How quick art thou. So
dying fall. | full of shapes is it thus fancy.
    O, it came o'er my ear like the
sweet sod that breathes upon a
bank of violets, stealing and giv-    **12**<sup>th</sup> **N A C H T**

5.11

Captions have a built-in contrast because of their attendant pictures. But
more must be done to make them appeal
to the casual reader. Contrast with the
text can be increased by setting captions
bold sans serif (fig. 5.01) or in a smaller,
italicized version of the text face (fig.
5.02).

Given standard text columns and relatively ordinary display typography, captions can become the most prominent
type on the page (fig. 5.03). This path is
not unwise to follow, but it does have one
requirement: your publication must have
a steady supply of good images.

### Relating pictures and captions

Photographs and captions are inherently
joined (fig. 5.04). It is important to design
a typographic system, to write a typographic recipe, that makes this connection
immediately apparent. Some ideas on
caption/picture placement follow.

• A coherent typographic system includes positioning captions in regular
places. Do not move them for arbitrary or
capricious reasons.

• Captions must be physically near the
picture. If they do not actually touch – by
overprinting or dropping out or mortis-
ing – they should not be more than 6
points from the art.

• Captions are ordinarily placed beneath a picture. Forcing readers to look
elsewhere is fine if the caption can be
found easily (by increasing the contrast),
or if the alternate position is necessary because the picture bleeds off the bottom of
the page.

• For a caption to link to a picture, it
must *not* be confused with the text. Leave
at least a line space between the two.

• Connect the picture and caption by
joining them on a central axis (fig. 5.05). If
the caption is set justified, set the last line
centered (fig. 5.06).

• Set the caption to match the width of
the picture only if the caption will not be
too wide to be easily read (fig. 5.07). Do
not weaken the alignment by indenting
the first line of the caption.

• Align a flush edge of the caption with one of the vertical edges of the picture (fig. 5.08).

• Surround the picture and caption with a box (fig. 5.09). One of the elements may break out of the picture for a more dynamic effect (fig. 5.10); this is called a partial silhouette.

Captions can be much more than light smudges beneath pictures. They can be the text or the primary typography, as figure 5.11 illustrates. By far the most frequently used page layout in advertising is called the "Ayer no. 1", after the N. W. Ayer advertising agency in New York, which developed it in the early 1900s. It features a picture on the top two-thirds of the page, a headline immediately beneath the picture, and text and logo at the bottom of the page. This layout has become ubiquitous because it is virtually invisible. It presents information in the most logical order and leaves the design vessel completely unnoticed, throwing all attention to the content itself. What is intriguing about the headline on an Ayer no. 1 layout is that, though it is obviously the primary display typography, it acts as a *caption*, explaining the photo.

Other ways of handling captions:

• Contrast rigid, highly structured pages with less formal caption settings. For example, set captions with one ragged edge with text that is justified (fig. 5.12). Do not hyphenate captions set in a ragged style. Leave space between the caption and text to increase visibility.

• Captions are usually set in a smaller or lighter version of the text type to help make them recede. Sometimes this smaller type is set across the full width of even the widest illustrations with no additional line spacing. Such lengthy lines are very difficult to read if the caption is longer than a single line. This problem is particularly pernicious in desktop-prepared publications with default line spacing, where no one can stop to say, "Too many characters per line! Open the line spacing or shorten the line length." Readers will bear up for two or three lines, but they will rebel and simply not read longer poorly set captions. Forty characters per line is an oft-quoted standard, but captions allow greater flexibility than text, so the maximum characters per line can be increased to sixty.

• Complex, compound captions can sometimes be broken into segments and distributed around a photo (fig. 5.13). Much like the labeling of exploded views, this treatment breaks long copy into bite-size pieces and encourages reading.

• Because captions attract interest, it may be desirable to make a whole story look like a caption or series of captions (fig. 5.14). To do this, you will need a series of photos, fairly short copy, and the willingness to leave some space empty to enhance the picture/caption "easy-read" approach.

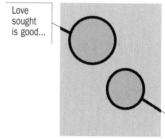

5.12

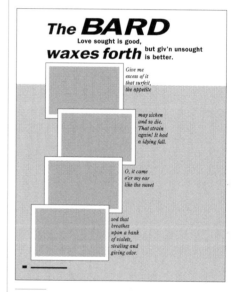

5.13

5.14

Love sought
is good,
but giv'n
unsought
is better.

5.15

Love sought is good,
but giv'n unsought
is better.

If music be the food of love, play on. Give me excess of it that, surfeiting, the appetite may sicken and so die. That | strain again! It had a dying fall. O, it came o'er my ear like the sweet sod that breathes upon a bank of violets, stealing | and giving odor. No more 'tis not so sweet now as it was before. O spirit of love! How quick and fresh art thou, that | notwithstanding thy ca recei-veth sea, nough enters the what validi and pitch but falls in abatement low price, in a minut full of sha fancy that bank of vic stealing ar giving odo Enough, n more! 'Tis so sweet n iot was be

5.16

Love sought is good,
but giv'n unsought
is better.

If music be the food of love, play on. Give me excess of it that, surfeiting, the appetite may sicken and so die. That strain again! It had a | dying fall. O, it came o'er my ear like the sweet sod that breathes upon a bank of violets, stealing and giving odor. No more 'tis not so sweet | now as it was before. O spirit of love! How quick and fresh art thou, that notwithstanding thy capacity receiveth as the sea, nought enters there. | Of what va and pitch e'er, but fa into abater and low pr even in a r So full of s is fancy th on a bank violet, stea and giving Enough, n more! 'Tis sot of love quick and art thou, tl not withou standing tl capacity r sweet now was before spirit of lo How quick

5.17

*L*ove sought is good,
but giv'n unsought is better.

If music be the food of love, play on. Give me excess of it that, surfeiting, the appetite may sicken and so die. That strain again! It had a | dying fall. O, it came o'er my ear like the sweet sod that breathes upon a bank of violets, stealing and giving odor. No more 'tis not so sweet | now as it was before. O spirit of love! How quick and fresh art thou, that notwithstanding thy capacity receiveth as the sea, nought enters there. | Of what va and pitch e'er, but fa into abater and low pr even in a r So full of s is fancy th on a bank violet, stea and giving Enough, n more! 'Tis sot of love quick and art thou, tl not withou standing tl capacity r sweet now was before spirit of lo How quick

5.18

• Superimposing a caption over a picture presents its own set of problems. It neither enhances the realness of the two-dimensional photo nor improves the type's readability, because of the reduced contrast with the background. When superimposing a caption on a photo, place the type in an area of visual plainness. Putting type over a busy background makes it very difficult to read (fig. 5.15).

Regular-weight type is designed to be read on a white background, not a halftone. When placing type in an image area, make the type sufficiently large and bold so that it stands out from the background, whether it is surprinted over or dropped out from the picture. You may also lighten the photo in a rectangle behind the caption.

• The caption can be dropped out of a box, which fully or partially overlaps the photo. This is called a mortise (fig. 5.16).

• A photo can be cropped to make room for its caption (fig. 5.17).

• The caption's initial or first word can overlap the image (fig. 5.18).

The combined impact of well-chosen and well-cropped photos and creatively designed captions can coax the browser into becoming a reader.

5.19

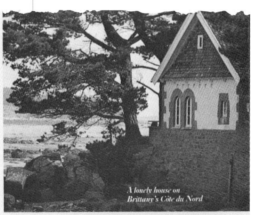

5.20

5.21

## Caption/picture unity

### 5.19

Captions should be located near the photographs. When there is more than one photo, the caption/photo relationship must be very clear. Use rules and alignments to cement that relationship. The captions were set flush left or flush right and aligned with a vertical edge so that each "belongs" with its photo. The caption lines are set fairly narrow – maximum line length is 10 picas – and the white space is kept to the perimeters on this spread. *American Photographer*

### 5.20

A wraparound is an effective means of joining the picture and its caption. This picture, an ordinary portrait, is gussied up to look like a picture of a picture by adding a perimeter and cast shadows. *Institutional Investor*

### 5.21

There can be no stronger bond between caption and photo than actually merging the two. When overprinting or dropping out – especially with process printing – use large, bold letterforms without pronounced thicks and thins. These last tend to fill in with the slightest registration problem, making the type difficult to read. *M*

**5.22**

A potent picture/caption connection can be made by relating the widths of the two elements. These captions match the width of the shoes, creating a distinct column; one caption is set across a wider measure for the larger photo on the right. Note that none of the captions is indented, helping define the picture-wide measure and the column. *Children's Business*

**5.23**

A relationship established by proximity: these relatively enormous words are located immediately adjacent to the silhouetted photo they define. This is also an excellent example of breaking out of the structure imposed by a grid. *The Edge*

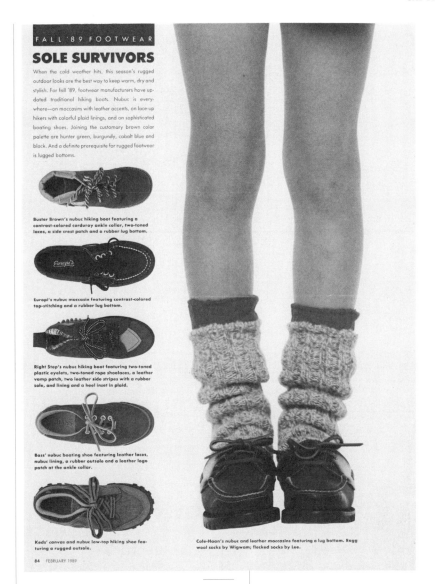

5.22

5.23

5.24

5.25

5.26

5.24
These captions are set flush left, 7 picas in from the left edge of the column, to allow room for the portraits. Interestingly, the 7-pica margin is maintained even when no portrait is available, giving the page strong overall unity. *CIPS News*

**Bold**
**contrast**

5.25
Three typographic contrasts are at work here: boldness, flush-right setting, and column width. The outermost column in this magazine is always 6 picas wide and is used for headlines and breakouts as well as captions. The caption's line spacing remains consistent with that of the text, a nice touch. *Scanorama*

5.26
The boldness of this caption is in extreme contrast with the line-spaced text. This page is set up on a grid of three 13-pica columns. The outer column has been split in half, with the caption running across only half the full measure. This mathematical order makes the page look correct. Color photos and magenta *J. Essence*

5.27

Boldness is only one device used to set this caption apart from its text. The text is set flush left/ragged right; the caption is flush right/ragged left and is not set across the full column width. This added white space melds with the double line space beneath the caption and creates a pond in which the caption sits. *Vistas*

5.28

A bold lead-in, contrasting with the balance of the caption, can demand the reader's attention if provocatively written. *D*

5.29

In this publication, the bold lead-in captions are centered beneath the photo and are never longer than one line. Cumulatively, this creates a significant personality for the magazine. *New York*

5.27

5.28

5.29

## PHILADELPHIA 76ERS

game who's bothered by other teams' fans," he says. "The problems of the road are the travel [the Sixers took a 6:20 flight out of Salt Lake the previous night] and being at the mercy of the hotel restaurant menu and sleeping in strange beds. At home I eat at a certain time and get my sleep. I arrive at the Spectrum at 5:30. Now I'll go back to the hotel, but I don't want to read because I have to spend time concentrating on the

**FEB 22** **3:15 PM**

GMINSKI, WHO DIDN'T GET TIME TO READ IN OAKLAND, MADE THE MOST OF PHILLY'S L.A. LAYOVER

game and I want to stay fresh. So I'll get a bite to eat, watch a little TV and try to get some rest."

Later, while Gminski winds up lunching on cold pasta and other sensible foods at the Airport Hilton salad bar, Barkley treats Hawkins, Dawkins and reserve Lanard Copeland to a postpractice meal at a soul-food restaurant he knows. Short ribs, smothered steak, cream corn, yams, black-eyed peas, corn bread, rice and gravy make up what would never be confused with a training table meal. *General Hospital* plays on a TV set overhead. Talk turns from Jesse Jackson to the players' positive feelings for Lynam and for their recent success. "You know, when you have those feelings when you think you can't lose?" says Barkley. Everyone nods and chews. With the powerful Los Angeles Lakers coming up on Friday and the red-hot Phoenix Suns on Saturday, the Sixers

need to beat the Warriors, who have dropped three straight games.

Barkley believes the primary reason the Sixers have been successful this season is the development of the 6' 3" Hawkins, who as a rookie in 1988–89 relied strictly on his jumper. Since then he has added an array of spin moves and fadeaways, along with a new attitude. "I'm looking to create," says Hawkins. Notwithstanding his winning shot against Portland, he has made only 8 of 24 field goals in the last two games.

"You got to keep shooting," Barkley tells him at lunch. "I will never understand how a great player can lose his confidence." Barkley pays the $68 tab, and the players stumble, stuffed, out into the 2:30 sun to walk a little until they call the Hilton van to come to pick them up.

Two hours before the tip-off, Hawkins is trying to sleep off his short ribs on a wooden bench in front of his locker. Barkley arrives later, and he looks sick. He thinks the creamed corn has caught up to him, although it might be the steak.

Popping Gelusil pills like M&M's before the game and during timeouts, Barkley is not his usual take-charge self from the outset. But no Warrior assumes control either, until Tom Tolbert, a 6' 7" rookie from Arizona, scores eight points in the first 4:14 of the fourth quarter to cut a Philadelphia lead to 86–83. With the score tied 93-all and with 1:34 remaining, Hawkins takes a kick-out pass from Mahorn and converts a three-point

**FEB 23** **2:00 PM**

SMITH LOCATED DOZAL'S BACK-HEALING FINGERS BY LETTING HIS OWN FINGERS DO THE WALKING

**FEB 23** **6:15 PM**

THE SIXER HEAVYWEIGHTS, MAHORN AND BARKLEY, REHEARSED THE FINE ART OF INTIMIDATION

shot for what proves to be his second game-winner of the trip as the 76ers hang on to win 96–95.

FRIDAY, AT LOS ANGELES

While driving a rental car following an afternoon practice, Mahorn backs up traffic on a street near the Forum when he stops the car and jumps into the backseat to pummel Dawkins, who has been slapping the back of Mahorn's head. "On a trip this long," says Mahorn, "you got to get a little crazy."

Meanwhile, Derek Smith, the 76ers' sixth man, is riding to meet a chiropractor, whose name and address are on the torn Yellow Page that Smith holds in his hand. This will be the second time on the trip that Smith has had an adjustment made on his right sacroiliac joint, which slipped out of place during the preseason when Barkley drilled him as Smith tried to dunk. After one elbow, one hip, three knee and two left-eye operations, all since 1985, Smith could update *Gray's Anatomy.* He spends 15 minutes detailing his medical history to Dr. Guillermo Dozal. Dozal's adjustment to his back takes about 10 seconds.

20

---

**5.30**

Each caption in this story begins with a very bold, compact date and time, printed in blue. The line-spaced caption text, set in bold caps, contrasts with the article's text. The two elements combined signal the reader to look at the captions before reading the text and lead the reader through the photos. *Sports Illustrated*

### Italic
### contrast

**5.31**

The use of white space beneath the bold italic caption immediately separates it from the text and binds it to the picture. *Snow Country*

**5.32**

A very simple contrast, italic juxtaposed with the roman text type, combined with a narrower than necessary measure, distinguishes this caption. *Restaurant Business*

---

5.30

Woodcutter, vegetable-grower and ski coach John Caldwell is boiling, because now is when

## THE SAP'S RUNNING

By ANN LYONS

John Caldwell, "the father of the cross-country skiing," is his experience. Even when the sap stops running, he doesn't.

5.31

*Robert M. Dorfman, senior v.p., Health Care and Canadian division.*

5.32

**5.33**

Tucked amid the overlapping portraits, these bold serif italics contrast with the light roman sans serif text. That this caption is printed blue helps make it findable as well. *Directions*

**5.34**

The classic small italic caption (popular with visually sophisticated publications) is set flush left/ragged right, filling a narrow outer column. The size and stress change gives the type a different flavor, but staying within a single type family retains consistency. *In House Graphics*

**5.35**

The typography here is extraordinarily simple; what is interesting is the system of which it is a part. This magazine positions its captions at the top of the live area, with visuals and text beginning at sinkage, which is 13 picas from the top trim. This ensures plenty of white space surrounding a rather subtle caption. Readers quickly become accustomed to looking for the captions at the tops of pages. *Natural History*

5.33

5.34

5.35

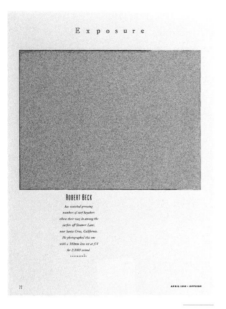

5.36

5.37

5.36

5.36

*EXPOSURE*, a regular department in this magazine, always features just one color photo per page with a brief description of the subject and the technical data of the shot. This handsome typographic understatement allows each photo to stand on its own merits. The typographic contrast is created to differentiate between the photographer's name, always run first on these pages, and the description. *Outside*

## Initial
caps

5.37

An initial cap's function of providing an easily-seen starting point is achieved as this blue initial is indented to the center of the 12-pica-wide caption. The caption is printed warm gray, and the illustration uses the two colors and black effectively in a series of screen tints. *PassWord*

5.38

Centered italics under a full-page photo with a contrasting initial cap. The initial is in the same typeface used for the story's headline, so the connection with the rest of the story is clear. *Pacific Northwest*

**Rules**

5.39

The bold overscore draws the reader's attention. The empty outer column also helps make this caption visible. *Parents*

5.40

The color photos in this story are enclosed by heavy 6-point box rules, which certainly set a tone for the series. The caption, set in all caps to contrast with the generously line-spaced text, has a 4-point overscore that visually connects it to the box rules around the photos. *Cleveland Magazine*

5.38

5.39

became a city in 1961, Beachwood is no ordinary boom town of unchecked growth and hodgepodge zoning ordinances. Rather, like the cutting of a gemstone, the creation of this premier community has been skilled and artful, and its multi-faceted features make Beachwood a standout.

One brilliant facet has been Beachwood's exceptional commercial growth. On a recent afternoon, Mayor Friedman stepped out of his car into a desolate, windswept field.

"See over there," he said, pointing to the horizon. "Isn't that a beautiful sight? On a clear day you can see the Terminal Tower. This is one of the highest spots in Cuyahoga County."

One can also see the future from that vantage point. Friedman was standing on the proposed Chagrin Highlands, a $600-million office complex to be developed by Figgie International, Inc., a diversified Fortune 500 company.

The 630-acre site, slated for completion by 2011, will be the company's new world

ABOVE: SIGNATURE SQUARE OFFICE COMPLEX NEAR I-271. LEFT: FORMERLY A CHURCH, THIS CENTURY BUILDING NOW HOUSES THE MAYOR'S COURT. BELOW: WORLD HEADQUARTERS OF MASTER BUILDERS TECHNOLOGIES.

BEACHWOOD A5

5.40

In the lull before the storm, relax and enjoy Wolf River scenery. If the going gets too tough in the thundering waters ahead, just carry your raft a bit farther downstream and put in again.

66

5.41

5.42

5.41
The hairline rule that frames each page in this story contrasts handsomely with the bolder, 3-point rule above this caption. The thicker rule, printed red, defines the full column width occupied by the caption. *Midwest Living*

5.42
Some mighty heavy 12-point rules are integrated into a system of columns and half columns defined by vertical hairlines. Each story's overscores are printed in a different color: here they are blue-gray; the previous story's are tan. *Electrical Contractor*

**5.43**

The short, heavy rules seem to accentuate the verticality of this page, because the eye jumps from one to the other vertically and because the caption is set in several very short lines. *American Way*

### Boxes

**5.44**

Dropped out of a solid green box, this caption acts as a bridge between the photo and the text by extending beyond the edge of the photo. Notice that the caption is positioned near the picture's subject but does not cover it. *M.*

**5.45**

The bold caption is overprinted on a screen tint, in this case bright green. The green rectangle overlaps the black-and-white photo, bonding the caption and photo into a single element. The green box aligns at the left with the text column, a detail that contributes to a neat, inviting presentation. *Interchange*

5.43

## Your Healthy Child

5.44

5.45

Mit so einem klassischen
Kamelhaarmantel im zeit-
losen Blazerschnitt ist man
immer fein raus. Natürlich
kann man ihn nicht nur zu
Jeans tragen – aber das
kühle Blau harmoniert beson-
ders schön mit dem sanften
Braunton. Mantel: Giddi's,
um 750 Mark; Jeans:
Diesel; Hemd: Mustang;
Rolli: Pringle; Tuch:
Hermès; Schuhe: Deichmann

5.46

**5.46**
The type has been set randomly for the torn-out captions in this fashion article. These torn boxes straddle the edge of the color photos, which end 7 picas from the gutter. *Freundin*

**5.47**
The captions for this corporate photo competition were typed on tracing paper, torn out and photographed on top of hairy paper. The color photos and black-and-white portraits of the winning photographers were superimposed by the printer. This creative and intelligent grouping of three distinct elements is a victory for logical, clear communication. *Partners*

# AMATEUR PHOTOGRAPHERS WIN RECOGNITION AND PRIZES

Darlyne Casey, Trust Em
Benefits, Birmingham, won
Place and $15 for a cand
photograph taken at a f
wedding.

Joyce Fuller, North Office, Cullman, traveled to Hawaii to capture the Best of Show prize in the AmSouth Employee Photo Contest. Joyce won $50 for her photo of Haleakla Crater on the island of Maui.

Martha Sykes, Corporate Marketing, Birmingham, made her trip to Egypt pay off when she won $10 for her Third Place photo in the People Category.

Joy B. Nash, Credit Administration, Mobile, won the $25 First Place prize in the People Category. Joy saw a winning shot when her son and neighbor decided to peek through the backyard fence.

8

5.47

5.48

This box is carved out of its surroundings. Such a treatment requires very even text type to allow the anomaly of the bold sans serif caption to stand out. The caption is printed red. *New England Monthly*

5.49

This box is implied: no borders are actually rendered, but the text and picture are chiseled away to create a visible shape in which the caption is carefully justified. Each of the six captions' last lines in the story is as carefully filled out as these. *Sports Illustrated*

5.48

5.49

his difficulties, he was required by Hooker's bankruptcy lawyers to furnish a non-refundable million-dollar guarantee that he would eventually come up with an offer—a condition he could not meet.

In the middle of the proceedings, Robert Burrick, Conti's attorney, emerged from the back of the crowded courtroom to cross-examine Martin Branman, managing director of Financo, Inc., the New York investment bankers assigned by Hooker to sell Altman's. Burrick focused his cross-examination on the four-week limit that Conti's group had been given to put an offer together.

"Is this a typical amount of time for a deal of this size?" he asked.

"It is not typical, it is a little on the short side," Branman responded.

"About how much on the short side?"

"Well, again, that would range, but I've seen deals get done from start to finish anywhere from one month to four months," Branman said.

"I have no further questions."

"I just have one other question on redirect, Your Honor," said Sheldon Hirshon, a lawyer with Proskauer, Rose, Goetz & Mendelsohn, which was representing Hooker.

...ter. It could...e been take...ame."

He could not understand how a liquidation would be preferable to a sale: Altman's inventory "at cost" was worth $25 million. His $10 million cash offer and the assumption of liabilities would represent a total contribution to Hooker's estate "in the range of $36 million."

Hirshon, however, maintained that a delay would mean a loss of approximately a million dollars a day. He insisted that the court accept a bid that day or liquidate.

"I'm going to ask one last time," Judge Brozman said, "if there is anyone in the courtroom who would wish to make an offer to purchase B. Altman as a going concern now."

A man in the back of the room named Richard Miller rose to his feet to address the court. "Just a couple of comments," he said. "We are a creditor, party in interest, and a member of the Creditors' Committee. We have filed a response that has stated that we are in favor of the sale of B. Altman as a going concern." Miller requested more time for considering the Conti bid and others. He wanted an "opportunity to try and save an institution with more than a thousand jobs in the New York City area alone."

"It is not fair," he continued, "to say that if we don't have a going-out-of-business sale effective tonight, we will lose all this money, we can never save this institution, and that's the end of the deal. That's particularly true, Judge, when

**1989.** Sigoloff decides to liquidate quickly rather than spend any more time looking for a buyer. Beginning the day after Thanksgiving, Altman's going-out-of-business sale is a great success (*center, right*). The shelves are stripped bare in just thirty-seven days—a far cry from the store's hopeful Williamsburg Christmas two years earlier (*left*).

39

5.50

Far left: After gutting the old kitchen, Jim Parks designed a sleek, efficient space that "the whole house revolves around." The black, reflective acrylic surfaces make the kitchen appear to "recede." Center: The dining room—originally a patio—features a skylight, glazed-brick pavers, and a painting by artist Jeffrey Kronsnoble. Below: Separated from the dining area by a pair of louvered doors, the den is Beverly's favorite room. "We can read in it, we can play in it, we can work in it—we can even sleep in it."

SEPTEMBER 1989 TAMPA BAY LIFE 25

5.51

## Cluster captions

*A cluster caption consists of more than one caption joined into a single body of copy. It usually contains directionals (such as top left, bottom right) that indicate which illustration is being described by each caption.*

5.50

The directionals are set in italics and are easily found amid the rigid verticality of Bodoni Bold. This cluster is set in a bolder and larger typeface than the text, indicating that it is to be read before the text. The *1989* is bigger still and printed red, next to a fake duotone photo. *Wigwag*

5.51

This cluster is intended to be read completely. The directionals CENTER and BELOW are set the same as the caption and are not easy to pick out. But this technique gives the cluster a unity that is enhanced by the handsome sandwiching shapes, top and bottom, printed brown and gray. *Tampa Bay Life*

**5.52**

What makes this a cluster caption is the directional headings. The extra space between the individual parts of the cluster caption helps the reader bounce back to the picture when the caption is read. *Pebble Beach*

**5.53**

This imaginative cluster caption echoes the story's deck, which appears on the previous spread. The contrast between square color photos and white space with wiggly type continues throughout this article. This type is as close to illustration as can be achieved without losing legibility. The caption is printed deep red; the kite , navy blue. *USAir*

**MONTAGE**

FAMOUS COUPLES, especially Hollywood stars and their spouses, have been as much a part of the history of Pebble Beach as golf. Whether it's just strolling along the fairways or actually playing them, readily recognizable couples have always managed to upstage the equally famous Pebble Beach landscape—at least while the photographer was present! ▲

**FAR LEFT**
Janet Blair and her husband, Louis T. Bush, early 1940s

**LEFT**
Mr. & Mrs. Randolph Scott, 1949

**BELOW LEFT**
Mr. & Mrs. Conrad N. Hilton, Jr. (Elizabeth Taylor) on their honeymoon, 1956

**BELOW RIGHT**
Mr. & Mrs. Clark Gable, 1956

5.52

...ng five years, too,'' says ... Conover, associate editor of *Kite Lines* magazine.

Real kite mavens own a "wardrobe" of kites suitable for winds of varying velocities. Putting up one kite at a time isn't enough for a kite-lover—25, 50, or even 100 kites flown in a train, on the other hand, are heaven. They are a traffic-stopper, too, as passersby gaze at the seemingly endless chorus line of kites dancing like an airborne version of Radio City Music Hall's Rockettes.

Stunt kites account for the newest

*Left:* The first commercial stunt kites were produced by Peter Powell in 1972. This is an "eight-pack" of Powell kites. *Above:* Flying kites isn't just for kids; more and more adults are getting into the action. *Below:* This 300-foot serpent kite lists for almost $500.

surge in "kitemania." A conventional one-string kite can only go up or down; tradition-breaking stunt models can be steered by a line in each hand, making the kite go either right or left respectively. Dual-line kites, devised in 17th-century England, were refined during World War II and used as moving targets to train soldiers. Flown on 150 to 200 feet of line, stunt kit...

5.53

# 6

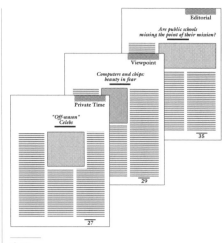

6.01

Department headings are like road signs that help readers find their destinations. They are vital elements in establishing the cohesiveness and strength of your publication's personality. At best, they work hand in glove with your other display typography to organize and highlight your stories and articles. At worst, they are mismatched smudges buried within a publication, confusing rather than easing the reader's search for visual signals.

Departments are topics that appear in every issue. Features, on the other hand, have varying content and a for-this-issue-only specialness. It is unwise to allow departments to outshout features, weakening the features' uniqueness. Departments are toned down by treating their type and imagery in a visually consistent manner (fig. 6.01). The disciplined quieting of department graphics has a profound effect on the perceived cohesiveness and visual personality of a publication.

Relating prominent display type throughout a publication bestows visual unity. Typographically connecting the cover logo, department headings, headlines, subheads, and breakouts is the most visible way of joining the editorial matter. This also separates it from the advertising pages, a differentiation that readers require. The best way to relate all display typography is to use variations of a single typeface (fig. 6.02).

The primary display-type relationship is between the cover logo, or "flag," and the department headings (fig. 6.03). This relationship connects the inside and the outside of your publication, making a more powerful over-all impact on the reader and making your publication more attractive to potential advertisers.

Department headings can be treated in an infinite number of ways. When well designed, they are recognizable bits of typographic fun that often allow the balance of a publication to be considerably less remarkable. Of these limitless possibilities, there are three basic forms: unadorned type (fig. 6.04), type with rules (fig. 6.05), and type with illustrations (fig. 6.06). Choosing which is right for your publication is a matter of finding a complement to your other typographic elements.

Department pages are either clustered in the front and back of a publication or scattered throughout its pages. Separated by advertisements, they must immediately be recognized as editorial material. Departments cannot outshout ads (ad agencies are paid great sums to make highly

*The*
**New Hartford**
*Groseille*

*From the*
**Selectman's**
*Desk*

*Finance*
**Committee**
*Report*

**School board**
**approves budget**
*Compromises on
5.6 percent increase*

6.02

6.03

6.04

6.05

6.06

visible pages), so departments must become visible by being related to one another; they make a *cumulative* impact. Giving departments a like treatment is called **formatting**. Formatting department pages achieves two valuable goals: the pages appear to be a large, unified body, and the preparation of each issue becomes easier with more time available for developing exciting feature graphics, where editorial excitement really belongs.

Formatted department pages must follow a style that is rigidly and consistently applied to enable readers to recognize them. All typographic elements must be handled identically, images must fit into a limited range of sizes, white space must be treated the same from department page to department page. It takes very little to weaken the format "just this once," losing the gain in excitement to messiness.

With restraint and discipline, departments can be the mortar that holds the diverse elements of a publication together. Department headings ought to be attention-getting devices that stop the reader long enough to scan the headline and visuals and then, one hopes, to continue into the text.

### Truck of The Month

*Linens of the Week, Washington, D.C., is featured*

By Joseph R. Schuh

*Joseph R. Schuh is TRSA's manager of textile control and service and distribution.*

Linens of the Week, based in Washington, D.C., was founded in 1953 as a full-service textile rental company. Currently, it operates five plants in three cities: Washington, D.C., Baltimore, Md., and Wilmington, Del.

Last fall, Linens of the Week updated its logo and its corporate image. "We consider each of our trucks to be more than simply a delivery vehicle," says President Alan Bubes. "With 60 trucks covering our marketing area, the potential for marketing exposure is tremendous.

"We wanted to capitalize on that exposure. Our slogan, Your Image Is Our Business,' says what we really deliver — first-class quality linens, career apparel, and ancillary products. We're not just in

the linen business, we're in the image business. We help our customers create a first-class image for themselves."

TRSA's Service and Distribution Committee features this vehicle as an example of what the industry's attention should be in public image.

The committee invites all members to send a photograph of their vehicles as an entry into the Truck of the Month Club. Send an 8-inch by 10-inch color photograph of your vehicle to Joseph R. Schuh at TRSA's headquarters in Hallandale, Fla. Along with a paragraph or two on how you feel your vehicle's graphic design enhances your company's public image. If it is featured as a Truck of the Month, it is automatically entered into TRSA's Truck of the Year Contest. □

*Textile Rental • September 1989*

---

6.07

---

#### LORD OF THE RING

He was a silver medalist in the 1988 Olympic Games in Seoul. The USA Amateur Boxing Federation selected him Boxer of the Year a few months later. He owned the North American Boxing Federation junior flyweight title. And recently **Michael Carbajal** topped off all these accomplishments by capturing the International Boxing Federation title.

The 22-year-old Phoenix native knocked down Muangchai Kittikasem four times before referee Bobby Ferrara stopped the scheduled twelve-round fight at the fourteen-second mark. The feisty fighter has come won all of his fifteen fights and has no doubts about his glorious destiny. "This is what I've wanted since I was six years old. I told everybody that nothing was going to stop me."

#### FIRST AMONG EQUALS

At 19, when most ballet dancers are considering hanging up their pointe shoes, **Beatriz Rodriguez** is still refining her reach and polishing her *out repertory.*

The Puerto Rican ballerina's passion for dance is unswerving. Her interest in dancing began 30 years ago, when she saw a performance of *Sleeping Beauty.*

Her parents agreed to let her take ballet lessons at the Newark Academy of Ballet, but did not take her vocation too seriously. "I don't believe my mother ever thought I would dance to a career," chuckles Rodriguez.

Her mother was wrong. First came the company of the New Jersey School of Ballet, then Richard England's Dance Repertory Company in New York City, the Joffrey II Dancers and finally the Joffrey Ballet.

Although the policy of the company is not to single out any dancer as principal [all-star, no-star], Rodriguez clearly enjoys a special status. She often represents the company at fund-raising functions, she's always the first to go across the floor in company class, and her dressing rooms are better. She's first among her equals, whether dancing the Chosen One in *Le Sacré du Printemps, Juliet in Romeo and Juliet,* or Columbine from Spain in *The Nutcracker.*

Sometimes she worries about having to let dancing go, and sometimes she dreams about marriage and children. But, like being Hispanic, dancing is an integral part of her nature.

"I have often tried to explain who I dance. It's this very Hispanic feeling, very comfortable to me. It's a feeling like speaking Spanish."

#### ARTISTIC DIPLOMACY

"When you believe in something, you go all the way."

Since 1985, Puerto Rican artist **Frank Diaz Escalet** has been doing just that, in the face of red tape and indifference. He's not quite there yet, but almost. On November 1, his one-man show [135 pieces spanning decades of artistic endeavor and including a variety of media] will open at the prestigious Nasprisk Museum of Prague. Diaz Escalet, 52, hopes that his self-taught brand of primitive Impressionism,

depicting slices of everyday life ["real life"] will appeal to Eastern Europeans the common ground shared by different peoples in the world.

Achieving this longstanding dream was not easy. Diaz Escalet's wife and manager, Marlseh, fired off almost 1,000 letters to local officials, government agencies, and other institutions in an effort to interest interest her husband's goodwill art tour. So far, the couple has raised only a portion of the money it will takes to set up his exhibit in Czechoslovakia, and they are still actively searching for funds. Diaz Escalet's work has hung in the Smithsonian and the National Gallery in Washington, D.C., and is meant by such personalities as explorer Jacques Cousteau.

After Prague it will be a long time before the pieces return to Diaz Escalet's home in Kennebunk, Maine. The plan is for the art tour to make a stop in the Soviet Union.

*Funeral in Florence (Acrylic, 1989)*

#### FROM MANES TO METAL

**Reynaldo "Sonny" Rivera**'s love for art started in grade school in his village of Mesquite, New Mexico.

His first medium can best be described as somewhat unconventional. After all, beavers are not often associated with brushes, canvas, or chisels. For twenty years, Sonny Rivera sculpted hair. Until he decided it was time for a change. In 1978, he sold his shop and went to art school, first in Chicago, and then in Mexico and Italy.

Today, Rivera's work can be found in museums and private collections in Arizona, New Mexico, Florida, and abroad. In a style reminiscent of Frederic Remington, his bronze horses, his favorite theme, burst with strength and dynamism. His latest commission, however, involves a more corpulent animal. Three life-size bronze buffaloes by Rivera have recently been installed at the entrance of the North American Exhibit at the Rio Grande Zoo in Albuquerque, New Mexico, which is scheduled to open in October.

#### DEDITOS DE ORO

What do Burt Reynolds, Dolly Parton, and the Eagles have in common? They all own dolls by designer **Manuel Carvar**, 37, the textile wizard from Cuidronan, Mexico.

Carvar, who was already sewing pants and shirts at the age of eight, emigrated to the United States at the age of 21. He wound out making "regular clothes," but found with that line of work, he soon moved to tailor clothing. Here he was in the right vicinity, and even fulfilled a childhood fantasy by putting together toys for his and Chrysler Moore, a.k.a. The Lone Ranger. an experience he describes as his "most beautiful moment" — a real professional moment.

Carvar opened his own shop, Manuel's, in 1976, avoiding the ritzy of Delphi Yonkers, Conway Twitty, and Linda Ronstadt, who go wild over his one-of-a-kind wearable art.

In addition to his shop in North Hollywood, Carvar this year opened a shop in Nashville, Tennessee, and plans to open other stores in Atlanta, Texas, and New York. The whole subtlety is the cafe, not only clothes, but also jewelry and luggage.

As Carvar told *Elle* magazine, "his offbeat vocal success its way through his creations."

"In America we have such a tremendous reprint, a heritage that we never show. My interest is in bringing it back, to nurture the acculturation of the American tradition."

—By Lia Giron

---

6.08

---

---

6.09

---

6.07

This department heading consists only of type. Notice that it aligns flush left with the byline and bio and that the headline aligns flush left with the text. Retaining consistency in the sinkage at the top of the page and in the emptiness of the leftmost column throughout the department pages in this publication is very important. *Textile Rental*

6.08

The Helvetica Ultra Compressed of this department head has been given cast shadows on a desktop computer. The letters are printed in warm orange with 60 percent gray shadows. The white space at the head of the page has been purposefully left open, enabling this compelling department head to receive the reader's full attention. *Hispanic*

6.09

Crayon calligraphy appropriately suggests the quick scrawl of a busy mother who grabs the only tool at hand – since all pens and pencils have presumably been long since lost by her little crumbgrabbers – in this heading. It is repeated in a reduced size on subsequent pages. *Family Circle*

6.10

The contrasting typefaces, one bold sans serif and the other custom-drawn calligraphy, echo the cover logo, which also appears at the top of each page. Department headings in this publication are always printed in two colors, deep red and a 40 percent black screen tint, and are consistently styled to fortify the publication's design personality. *Virginia Leader*

6.11

Verticality and redness make these headings stand out in a visually active, typographically dynamic publication. The headings always appear in the upper left corner of a left-hand page. Display type throughout this publication is set in variations of Futura, printed in either black or warm red (100 percent magenta and 100 percent yellow). Mixing the typeface variations creates continuity throughout the issue. *Elle Deutsch*

6.12

Contrasts are made obvious in this heading. Bodoni Bold all-cap roman type is printed in a color that changes for each issue. The Bodoni Bold lowercase italic is printed in solid black. A strong relationship with the cover's logo has been created. *Sara Lee InterChange*

6.10

6.11

6.12

6.13

6.14

6.15

6.13

There are several typographic contrasts at work in this heading: typefaces (Aachen Bold and Century Old Style italic, both of which are used throughout for display and text type), color (*THE GOODWILL GAMES* is printed in a different color on each page, *COMIN' ATCHA* is always in black), horizontal and curved base lines, and tight and open letterspacing. *View*

6.14

These department heads are unified by the use of the same typeface, though capitalization and size change from page to page. In addition, an emphasized word is always printed in warm red, while the rest of the head is printed black. Occasionally the brackets are printed with a 40 percent black screen tint. They contribute an overall sense of fun and frivolity to this publication. *Glamour*

6.15

The combination of two fonts creates this distinctive heading. Sharp letterform contrast is necessary to make each word readable when fonts are blended like this. Note the apostrophe in *WHAT*'s is clearly downsized to make it less prominent. Attention to such details exemplifies the difference between typesetting and typography. *Domain*

## Type
## and rules

### 6.16

This screen tint gradation was easily done on a desktop computer. The style, suggesting a developing photographic print, is well suited to a photography publication. Sufficient change from tint to tint was achieved by using 30 and 60 percent screens and solid black. *Photomethods*

### 6.17

Department headings can be made more visible by being run in from the side of the page. In this publication the color of the calligraphic type varies from page to page, but the underscore remains black throughout. The publication's logo is repeated on every department opener, and the word GRAPHICS in the logo is written in the same way as in the department headings, unifying inside with outside. The logo is dropped out of solid black, is surrounded by a half-point box rule, and always bleeds at the head margin. *Step-by-Step Graphics*

### 6.18

The simple, bold, warm red overscore insists that the reader notice this department heading. *National Geographic Traveler*

6.16

6.17

6.18

6.19

6.20

6.21

6.19
A page-wide overscore accentuates the space not occupied by image or type below. The open letterspacing adds to the rich feeling of spaciousness. *Santa Barbara Magazine*

6.20
Rules for department headings need not be simple straight lines. These wiggly rules are always set across 6 picas, though the headings vary in width. *Washington Flyer*

6.21
This is a simple, elegant treatment. The 18-point-thick bold underscore is run in deep purple (100 percent magenta and 70 percent cyan). The purple rectangle brings the reader's eye to the top of the page, where the fine cap/small-cap setting identifies the department. *Sports Afield*

**6.22**

These marvelous department headings use a peculiar typeface that give this publication a distinctive look. The underscore of dots helps make the headings unique. These departments always start on a left-hand page and begin with a text-free left column. Note the "off-center centering" of this page's layout. *Trump's*

**6.23**

Depth can be achieved by using screen tints, even in one-color printing. This example has a 20-point 40 percent black rule bleeding off the head margin. The rule aligns flush left with *BREAKS*, and the heads are given generous white space all around. The hairline rule that encloses the copy adds further distinction to this treatment. *Waste Age*

**6.24**

Variations of squashed and squeezed Univers illustrate how exaggeration can overcome typographic differences. Though the type is always printed black, the 4-point overscores change colors within each issue, adding to their visibility. *Life Association News*

6.22

6.23

6.24

6.25

6.26

6.27

## 6.25

In an interplay of vertical and horizontal, this overscore partially overlaps condensed letterforms. The overscores are printed in various flat screen-tint colors with black type. These headings appear on continued pages at about half size. *Tampa Bay Life*

## 6.26

These headings are placed flush right and dropped out of a 13-pica-wide color bar. The bar, which changes colors with each new heading, is integrated with a hairline box rule that surrounds the live area of the page. The headline's underscore is printed in the same color as the department heading. *Down East*

## 6.27

The upper, outer corners of pages are key signal areas for the reader, so these departments are relatively easy to find amid the ads. The colored overscore extends over the outer two columns. Illustrations are sometimes popped into the dedicated white space and occasionally cover the letterforms. *Online Today*

6.28

A department heading must be findable. The bar is printed in warm red and is suspended from the head trim. The complementary type is printed black, and the heading is given plenty of white space. *Modern Maturity*

6.29

This bold vertical rule contrasts with the hairline horizontal rule, which is set to the width of the longest line in the heading. Note the envelope artwork repeated next to each writer's name, a great way to add charm while reinforcing the idea of the *Letters* page. *AmSouth Partners*

6.30

A unique department heading treatment that opens horizontally and continues vertically on subsequent pages. The opener is set in 24-point type, reduced to 12 points on the following pages. This example shows the department head as a tab that signals the page's contents quickly. *Tappi Journal*

## STAYING WELL

### Don't shrug off chest pains

Scenario 1: You're having an argument when suddenly your chest tightens like a vise. You feel dizzy, can't catch your breath, and a dull pain radiates down your left arm.

Scenario 2: You're watching TV and eating pizza when you feel mild discomfort in your chest for several minutes. You shrug it off and take an antacid tablet.

Which one could be a heart attack? Would you believe: either one.

Any chest pain that persists for more than a few minutes—or comes and goes over a period of hours or

KAREN STEEN

"We have [all] heard about men and women rushed through the doors of emergency wards clutching their breastbones only to discover that what they are suffering from is too much

as you age. (b) Denture wearers rarely require regular dental care. (c) A little bleeding after brushing and flossing is normal. (d) People with early stages of periodontal (gum) disease have no symptoms and suffer no discomfort. (e) Older persons are at greater risk for cavities than are 14-year-olds.

A. a, b and c are myths; d and e are facts.

Q. Of the approximately two dozen brands of dental-implant systems, how many have been accepted by the American Dental Association? (a) none; (b) 1; (c) 11; (d) 19; (e) all of them.

A. b; three others have been "provisionally" accepted.

Q. After you have brushed and flossed, plaque reforms within: (a) 1

6.28

## LETTERS FROM SATISFIED CUSTOMERS

6.29

Vibration Analysis

### Finding press section vibration sources using synchronous averaging

David A. Beck

*Four case studies show how synchronous averaging can be used to isolate the causes of vibration in the press section.*

When a vibration analyst is asked to find the cause of vibration on a paper machine, he or she is faced with a formidable task. A paper machine contains many rotating parts and many highly loaded structures, any of which can cause vibration. It is up to the analyst to determine which part of the machine is the root cause of the vibration. In earlier years this would have been a very difficult process. Now, with the advent of computers and digital signal analysis, the analyst's job has been greatly simplified. In particular, one form of analysis called synchronous averaging allows one to directly determine the source of vibration and to study the characteristics of the source so that ways to reduce vibration can be found.

#### How synchronous averaging works

For synchronous averaging, an analyst uses a setup similar to the one shown in **Fig. 1**.

In this typical setup, vibration sensors are attached to the vibrating elements. In this case, the sensors are attached to upper and lower moving housings of the press

roll from the raw vibration signal.

Another way of showing how synchronous averaging works is displayed in **Fig. 3**.

In this multiple-spectra plot, the two Fast Fourier Transform spectrums shown were derived from the two curves in Fig. 2. It is obvious that the raw signal's spectrum is very complicated and contains many frequencies. However, after synchronous averaging, only a single major peak is left, which is unequivocally due to the press part with which we synchronized. In this case, we synchronized with the top press roll, so this single peak is the vibration caused by the top press roll. The entire synchronous averaging technique thus comes down to placing the vibration sensors on the machine and then moving the trigger around the machine, effectively isolating each element in the machine in turn until the problem is found.

The heart of the time synchronous averaging technique is being able to get a good stable trigger once per felt, or roll, revolution. While the paper machine is operating, obtaining a reliable trigger can be a major problem. Typically it is not practical for the

6.30

6.31

6.32

**6.31**
This heading is neatly aligned with the three columns beneath it. The sharply reduced *TO*, the pair of solid ballots, and the beautiful all-cap Palatino typeface combine to make a simple, elegant heading. *Annapolitan*

**6.32**
A 12-point overscore printed with a 70 percent black screen tint is neatly integrated with a series of vertical and horizontal rules. The width of the gray rule is adjusted to match the width of the heading. *ABA Journal*

**6.33**
Rules can organize the page. These hairline rules overlap a very visible area of tone that hangs from the head trim. The typeface Friz Quadrata is used throughout this publication for display type, including the cover logo. *Educational Leadership*

## Trends

## Science

DOUGLAS M. LAPP

**Resources for Hands-On Science**

Children, especially young children, learn science best when they have a concrete body of experience on which to base abstract concepts. Hands-on experiences are also the best way to spark the enthusiasm of young learners. For these reasons, the National Science Resources Center (NSRC), a joint initiative of the National Academy of Sciences and the Smithsonian Institution, has begun a number of programs to bring hands-on science to elementary schools.

*Spreading the word.* First, NSRC serves as a clearinghouse for the dissemination of information about science teaching materials, including the innovative materials developed by the seminal curriculum projects of the '60s and '70s. Our Science Teaching Resource Collection is a storehouse of information about past and present programs, an "institutional memory" for the field of science curriculum development. Through this collection and computerized database, educators can access ideas and approaches that have been tested over time.

Using this collection we have pub-

hands-on science manageable for teachers.

These modular units are designed for teachers who do not have extensive backgrounds in science. They make use of inexpensive and commonly available materials, and each explores a topic that can be successfully investigated by elementary students. Examples of units are *The Life Cycle of Butterflies* (grade 2), *Electric Circuits* (grade 4), and *Experimenting with Plants* (grade 6). After the original development in classrooms, each unit is field-tested in additional classrooms across the country. The first three units will become available to schools in spring 1991.[2]

*Providing support.* NSRC's third area of effort is outreach to schools. During the past two summers, NSRC has held Elementary Science Leadership Institutes at the Smithsonian Institution for teams of teachers and administrators, who have come from 32 school districts and 25 states across the nation. During an institute, participants attend workshops on high-quality curriculum materials, participate in discussions on curriculum and other inservice educa-

and distribute the science kits used in hands-on programs.

Currently our nation's schools are not imparting an enthusiasm for science that capitalizes on youngsters' innate curiosity and their need to make sense of what they observe. To correct this, Luther Williams, of the National Science Foundation's Directorate for Education and Human Resources, urged "a general rebuilding, starting [with] better basic instruction in grade schools," as well as teaching that engages "students actively in the scientific process."[4] Through its programs, NSRC is sending this message by fostering support for science instruction that is in tune with both the potential of young people and our society's needs.□

[1]Copies of *Science for Children: Resources for Teachers* are available for $9.95 (or less, for quantity orders) from the National Academy Press, 2101 Constitution Ave., Washington, DC 20418. For more information or to order, call (202) 334-3313.

[2]For more information, write to the Carolina Biological Supply Company, c/o Richard Franks, 2700 York Rd., Burlington, NC 27215, or call (919) 584-0381, ext. 225.

[3]To obtain additional information about

6.33

**6.34**

Part of a handsome, more involved box ruling system, this department head has an overscore that matches its width. The head's open letterspacing contributes a great deal to the look. *CASE Currents*

**6.35**

An elaborate scheme of rules and shapes has been added to simple typography for a unique heading solution. The overscore, matching the heading's width, is printed in warm red (solid magenta and solid yellow), and the triangle is printed in blue. All else is black. *Inside Sports*

**6.36**

This department heading makes full use of color. SPORT is overprinted black on yellow, MAIL is knocked out of deep blue, and a warm red rule extends across the head of the page. The two vertical hairline rules, indicating the three-column format, are printed in magenta (registering yellow would be too difficult on such a fine rule). *Sport*

---

LETTERS

# The Numbers May Be Misleading

*A president challenges how we perceive two-year college attrition*

Arthur Levine's "Defying Demographics" [June] notes that two-year institutions have a "disproportionate number of minority and poor students." The author goes on to conclude that this situation "clusters the student groups with the lowest retention rates in the institutions with the highest attrition rates."

I offer this challenge. Place two-year college students with the lowest retention rates in an elite college and observe the result. My guess is the students will experience even higher attrition rates. In all likelihood, the elite college simply would not have the ........ services required to ...... ...

office should run the show. After all, the public relations staff knows the campus better than any outside counsel, and having a centralized effort will cause less confusion when dealing with the media.

Second, the campus president should have realistic expectations about media coverage. Like it or not, most reporters were there to cover the summit—not to do stories about Rice. And finally, don't forget campus sources. Make sure your PR plan includes your own expert faculty.

Pretty basic stuff. But the basics make or break an event. In this case, we were pleased with the amount of coverage Rice received from the summ-...... .....ing the in-

him he didn't carry the topic far enough. It's one thing to produce a style manual and quite another to gain its acceptance across campus. But we did just that this spring at Cabrini College.

We'd spent months working on an institutional style manual and, for its unveiling, held workshops to educate staff and faculty on their role in the larger contexts of PR: creating and changing perceptions.

First we cultivated senior staff by charging deans and vice presidents to spearhead a college-wide movement to incorporate our editorial recommendations in their work. Most did. Those who didn't, as one aca-....... .... discovered with a jolt, found

6.34

---

# THE FAN

## By KEVIN DOBSON

## Baseball Trains You For Life

My GREAT PASSION is baseball. I just love the sport, mainly because it's been a training ground for me, a springboard to confidence and determination. Once I un-

nurtured and cared for; you'll burn them out if you take the game too seriously.

As for my own son Patrick, I've already had great times with him at the ballpark. He was with me last year at Dodger Stadium, when at a Hollywood Stars game I hit this long fly ball. It kept going, going, going, and 55,000 people in the stands are all saying to themselves, "Here's an actor hitting a home run." Well, the ....... ... looked ..

6.35

---

# SPORT
## MAIL

**NOLAN RYAN**

I praise Randy Galloway's article on Nolan Ryan ("Beers With Nolan Ryan," April). Not everybody who plays baseball is in it just for the money. A contract to Nolan Ryan is as good as his word. Your article stands as a tribute to a man who will one day be in Cooperstown.

Bryan Kroeger
Wausau, Wisconsin

Ryan is a perfect example of what hard work and dedication can do for you. Everyone thought he was washed up, but Ryan proved them wrong . . . just as Joe Montana did.

Jason Hawiszczak
.. Hanover, New Jersey

basketball god.

Navin Kamath
Nesconset, New York

George Castle says Ernie Banks preceded Michael Jordan as Chicago's best-loved athlete. How could he forget Walter Payton and what he did for Chicago sports, not to mention the Bears?

Jason Gelber
Los Angeles, California

Jordan is the caliber of athlete who could easily make the transition from one sport to another. With his I-love-to-win attitude and dedication, I'm sure he can succeed at any sport he wants to play. So the NBA and PGA may produce a new kind of elite athlete—one who gives us explosive power

6.36

6.37

6.38

6.39

**6.37**

The use of hairline and 12-point rules in addition to mixed serif and sans serif typefaces and deep sinkage make this heading unique. It is greatly simplified and reduced on continued pages, but the connection is still evident. *CA Magazine*

**6.38**

Using color or texture creates a recognizable department heading. The type in these headings is always centered and overprinted in black on one of several pastel screen tints. Notice the contrast of the condensed, vertical letterforms with the broad, horizontal color bar. *Food & Wine*

**6.39**

This heading is dropped out of solid black, but it is tipped sideways and bleeds off the upper outer corner of the page, suggesting a tab in a looseleaf binder. This system makes finding departments very easy. The vertical headings in this publication are very similar to the cover logo. *Golden Years*

**6.40**
The type in this heading has been vertically aligned so the "pinstripes" do not obscure the words. Representing a department heading literally is an intriguing idea, but it is very difficult to create a unified series, which is also important to the cohesiveness of a publication. *Executive Edge*

**6.41**
Department headings can be unified with other typographic elements, as in this case, with a headline. *DH Headlines*

**6.42**
Tabloid publications have large 17- by 11-inch pages. Organizing these big pages is more difficult than organizing a standard-size page. This tabloid has developed a system where department headings are almost always at the top of the page, making it easy for the busy reader to scan for subjects of interest. These heads are dropped out of red bars that extend over, and define, their portions of the page. *AIA Memo*

6.40

6.41

6.42

## AMÉRICAS
# ¡Ojo!

### POR HENRY GOETHALS

#### A la pesca de riqueza

**Con unas** pocas notables excepciones, los países latinoamericanos deberían tomarse unas vacaciones y "salir a pescar". Podrían ser las vacaciones más fructíferas de su historia.

La región está finalmente comenzando a mirar hacia el mar en busca de sus recursos marítimos. Pero hasta la fecha pocos países han aprovechado el botín que yace frente a sus playas.

Las excepciones consti-

#### Ni palo ni astilla

**En el sur** de Chile se encuentran algunos de los bosques más antiguos del mundo, que cubren las abruptas montañas costeras y las innumerables islas del archipiélago chileno. Al igual que los antiguos bosques de la costa del Pacífico de América del Norte, los bosques chilenos de las regiones de Valdivia, Norte de la Patagonia y Magallanes se ven amenazados por las actividades madereras multina-
cionales.

6.43

---

*Attitude,*
*Competence,*
*Teamwork*

### Servicing a custom program

Recently, representatives from Industrial's San Diego and San Francisco divisions and Home Office met with the program administrators and association insurance committee representatives on two Custom Programs. The two programs are Northern California Bowling Proprietors' Association (NCBPA) and Bowling Proprietors' Association of Southern California (BPASC). They met to agree on underwriting criteria for bowling center security personnel. The meeting was precipitated by a major loss in Southern California involving a security guard who fatally shot a bowling center patron. Realizing

that the security personnel risk is as great in Northern California as it is in Southern California, Sr. Director Gregg McDermont, H.O. Custom Programs, called a meeting for members from the NCBPA and the BPASC to work out an underwriting agreement that would benefit both programs.

"If this had been an individual risk," he notes, "the loss might have encouraged us to either drop the account or exclude this risky coverage. The nature of a Custom Program, however, is to recognize all needs of a particular business and do our best to figure out how to address them." ∎

One of the benefits Industrial provides for its employees is a library—at every Industrial office. Not just a library of insurance-related periodicals and books, but a library filled with magazines and books on every subject imaginable, from best-sellers to classics.

The libraries make a very positive first impression on visitors, as the following letter, written by an attorney to the Orange division, attests:

Gentlepeople:

I happened to be in your office last week to have a brief conference with one of your workers' compensation claims representatives, and chanced to notice your employee library collection. The fact that almost all of the recent best-sellers in fiction and non-fiction categories were there, and,

will be willing to copy. And, at least for a few moments on a hot summer afternoon, I envied your employees' access to a fine selection of popular books. . . . Industrial is taking into account [employees'] personal enjoyment of literature and recognizing their intellectual interests outside of their workday world of claimant,

Custom Progr

6.44

---

6.45

---

### 6.43

Combining very different typefaces produces an interesting department heading. AM RICAS, its underscore, and the headline *POR HENRY GOETHALS*, are all black. *¡OJO!* is printed red. *Américas*

### 6.44

A very heavy overscore defines the space that this heading's freeform initial and traditionally set type fill. Initials like this can be found in clip-art resources. The initial, overscore, rules, and initial o are printed in teal green; all else is black. *Intercom*

### 6.45

This heading is loaded with contrast: reverse type, digitally condensed type, all-cap and all-lowercase type, roman and italic type, and dots and shapes. This is a very unusual, and very recognizable, creation. SHORT is printed warm gray. The square bleeds off the top outside corner, making the department easily seen by page-flipping readers. Continued pages have the same artwork, but it is reduced 50 percent. *Syracuse University Magazine*

## Type and illustrations

### 6.46

A department heading can be combined with an illustration. The star is the consistent illustrative element repeated in each of these department headings. Interesting here are the compound names all including *STREET* (the name of the publication) and the typographic alterations used. *The Street*

### 6.47

This heading is created by dropping the type from a four-color reproduction of a torn colored paper corner. This effect is also convincingly achieved in two-color printing by combining screen tints (for example, 80 percent red and 20 percent black) if you start with a good torn edge. *CV Magazine*

### 6.48

Pictograms created from clip art have been added to flush-left headings and a page-wide hairline rule. The pictogram images have been unified by placing them in similar 5- by 4-pica black shapes. Note that bleeding an image to the perimeter of the black field makes it appear more dynamic. *American City & County*

6.46

6.47

6.48

6.49

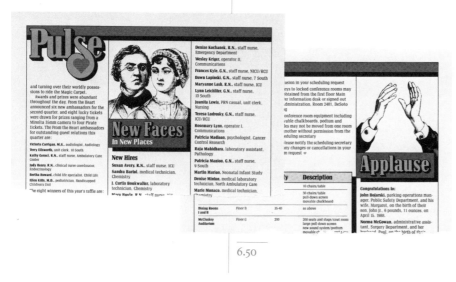

6.50

6.49
This pictogram is printed in 100 percent yellow, 10 percent magenta, and black to communicate its traffic-sign reference most convincingly. It is highly visible, located centered at the head of the page. *Caribbean Travel and Life*

6.50
These line-art illustrations are steel engravings taken from clip art, printed black on white. The headings make outstanding use of two-color printing, combining several shades of green and black screen tints. The various tint combinations give the headings great depth and considerable visual attraction. The job of creating these headings is made much simpler by having all elements fit within the visible external grid structure. *Children's Hospital of Pittsburgh Pulse*

6.51
LETTERS is a department heading that receives a good share of special handling, perhaps because it suggests its own solution. This cancellation mark was created on the desktop and surprinted on the black type in 20 percent magenta. *BN News*

## LETTERS

**WHY NO LOGO?**

I am a carman apprentice at the Havelock shops (Lincoln, Neb.), who was recently recalled to work after a seven-year furlough. During those seven years, I worked as a master machinist (journeyman) in an aerospace manufacturing firm where only the highest quality and pride in our workmanship were allowed. We were required to stamp our name (and reputation) on every order of parts we built, and NASA could trace every single part all the way back to individual machinists if they needed to. This gave me the feeling of "signing my name" on every part, and I was proud of the hardware I produced.

Now that I'm back to my first love (railroading), I see that many of the carmen and *managers as a whole have*

*nized by the distinctive Cascade green paint. The BN initials and numbers on the side and ends of freight equipment fulfill the requirements of the Association of American Railroads' rules, while the logo application only added cost to the repainting of our cars.*

*"Burlington Northern has nearly 5,000 cars scheduled to be painted in 1988 and 1989, including many of our predecessor cars, so all savings toward this program are very important. These savings, nearly half a million dollars annually, represent the funding for additional employees and material at Havelock to produce a higher quality car for our customers and support BN's commitment to Service By Design.*

*"Havelock Shops have a personalized symbol, which presently is not being applied to newly painted*

We often wondered if anyone cared because officials that set the rules *never* work on Christmas Day.

Little children don't understand why. Do we?

By early January, again the phone rang saying "you are cut-off" with no concern about our welfare. Our kids used to say, "Daddy, did they lose your name again?"

Years later it's still the same story. Kids and grandkids are coming home but "Grandpa" is not there. Grandchildren don't understand any better than their parents did.

For us and most BN families, our traditions will have to be formed — after retirement.

*Emma Turner*
*Moorcroft, WY*

**THANKS BUT**

*is intended to serve as a symbol of pride to its recipient and as a positive example to fellow co-workers. The pin is a symbolic reward, not a monetary award, that expresses the company's appreciation for a job performed properly, which means free of any on-duty lost time injury and disciplinary action. This recognition is provided in an effort to improve relations as well as to give positive reinforcement. We appreciate Mr. Lysaker's concern and would welcome additional input regarding the award program."*

**COAL DUST FLYIN'**

*From the coal mines in Wyoming*
*'cross the heartland to the shore,*

6.51

**6.52**

Another *LETTERS* heading that is inspired by a postmark. Here an original postmark was scanned into the computer and printed with "jaggies," to suggest the unevenness of a real cancellation stamp. *LETTERS* is printed in red for emphasis. The clipart pen, printed red, has also been scanned into a computer and printed with jaggies. *Current*

**6.53**

The computer-created symbols for each of these departments are unified in identical starburst shapes, always located in the top outer corner of the page. With such enticing symbols, it is best to leave the type comparatively simple. *Adeptations*

**6.54**

Another series of dissimilar symbols is joined by a shared shape. These symbols, almost always mortised into the middle of the text, become visible because their darkness contrasts with the grayness of the surrounding text in this newsprint publication. *VeloNews*

6.52

6.53

6.54

6.55

6.56

6.57

6.58

6.55
Letters carefully fit together (making excellent use of the Avant Garde characters) act as a backdrop to another road-sign illustration. Printed only in black, this heading attains great visibility because of its darkness and because of the added diagonal rules. *Kansas Telephone Times*

6.56
The handsome inline typeface is complemented by similarly handled illustrations, which are all based on an inverted triangle. Printed in one color, they always appear in the upper left corner of left-hand pages, making them expected elements and very findable. *View*

6.57
Each of these charming pieces of custom-made artwork introduces a brief article. Notice that the bylines are letterspaced to the full column width and that the typeset department headings are placed wherever space allows at the top of the illustrations. *New England Monthly*

6.58
These full-color department headings go well beyond mere labels, becoming focal points on the page. The illustrations and flat screen tints broaden the spectrum of what department headings can be. These headings also have subheads that further explain what the page contains. *TravelLife*

**6.59**

This unique heading demonstrates an outstanding integration of imagery and letterforms. It is quite large and extends fully across the head of the page. It was created in three steps: the type was set, the first and last letters were altered, and the photos, converted to line art with a mezzotint screen, were added. *Jacksonville Today*

**6.60**

This publication commissions new department headings for each issue. Each series emphasizes type or imagery to varying degrees and features illustration, painting, photography, and design as media. Generally printed in full color, these department headings play a major role in defining each issue's unique personality. Initial caps are also created, to be used on the same page as the department head, thereby connecting head with text and reinforcing that issue's special look. Shown here is a representative sampling from eight issues. *Wigwag*

## TRIVIAL PURSUITS

Locations where most accidents occurred in Jacksonville in 1987 (through November):

| | |
|---|---|
| Mathews Bridge, center span | 49 |
| I-95 and Phillips Highway | 48 |
| Atlantic Boulevard and St. Johns Bluff Road | 44 |
| Beach Boulevard and St. Johns Bluff Road | 42 |
| I-295 and Blanding Boulevard | 42 |
| Blanding Boulevard and 103rd Street | 38 |
| I-295 and San Jose Boulevard | 37 |
| I-95 and 20th Street Expressway | 36 |

6.59

Can the Viralizer really cure the common c...
**James Gorman** reports.

An upstart in the pet cemetery business sp...
some time with **Tracey Seltzer.**

**Susan Moritz** takes a gardener's look at what florists do to flowers.

**Patricia Storace** says that Randy Travis k...
what women want.

In *Black Rain*, **Luc Sante** finds out what happened after the bomb fell.

**Witold Rybczynski** visits the birthplace of postmodernism.

**Alexander Kaplan** stays up all night.

Identification is no problem: the eye is drawn to them at once. The difficulty comes when I've actually picked some and brought them home. A salad of dandelion greens brings me close to gagging. And the same is true with other foraged greens and with the commercial ones closest to them—cress, for example, or corn salad or chicory. It would be one thing if I simply disliked greens, but I don't. It's just that in eating them I walk a tightrope between pleasure and actual physical revulsion. It's like the edginess I feel eating blood sausage or tripe gumbo—there's something in all of this that cuts a little too close to the bone.

A salad of buttery lettuces made piquant by a few bitter greens is one thing; a whole plate of fresh-picked weeds is another, no matter how charming their names. Here, then, is the problem of the traveling Tuscan salad bowl posed me: its confidence of appetite.

"Field salad" is a hot item in certain culinary circles these days, but there has always existed in Maine—as in Tuscany—a deep-rooted native hunger for the local greens. I'm not the only one around here on the lookout for them, first of spring. Between times a local

**John Thorne** considers the dandelion's essential otherness.

y favorite cookbook right now is Pino Luongo's *A Tuscan in the Kitchen* (Clarkson N. Potter, 1988). The food is good, simple, and full of character, as if it were made out of the stuff of someone's actual larder...

*frittata di pasta*, another flask that holds a simple *condimento per insalata*—salad dressing—and an empty salad bowl. The salad itself, "tiny field rugola, aromatic herbs, and wild spinach," would be quickly gathered from the fields around the house.

It all sounded very good, but what stuck in mind after I turned the page...

6.60

# 7

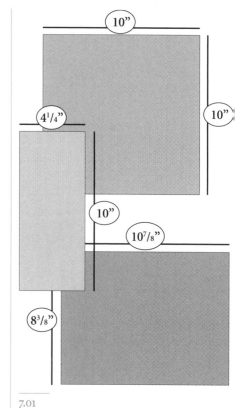

7.01

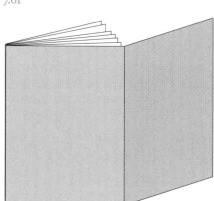

7.02

Long ago, when printed material was very rare, alluring, informative covers were unnecessary. The very existence of a document was reason enough to take time to read and absorb it.

Today, of course, printed communication is so plentiful that readers must control how much of it will gain their attention. It is therefore vital to be able to indicate immediately the contents, or at least the kind of information, contained in a publication. The science and art of announcing information, its style and immediacy, are what cover design is all about.

Covers create expectation in the reader. They lure the reader into browsing through the issue. Their function is the same as that of the teaser that television networks broadcast to lure viewers to watch the evening news. They supply a sample of what is to come that engenders a sense of needing to know *now*.

If a cover is uninteresting or cluttered, readers will not rush to get inside. Conversely, if readers notice one or two items on the cover that appear worthwhile, they will open the publication. If a sidewalk store window display does not show products passersby want, in a way they will notice, customers will not come inside where the goods are to make a purchase. So it is with covers: if the best stuff out front does not catch the reader's attention or arouse the reader's sense of immediacy or appeal to the reader's self-interest, the reader will not make it inside where the goods are.

The cover is the single most important page of a publication. It establishes identity from issue to issue (while simultaneously signaling a new issue) and claims territory distinct from the competition. A cover must reflect its own identity and personality. It must communicate a sense of worth and urgency. It must fascinate, tease, and involve. And it must relate visually to the pages within.

Four elements, all equally important, must be kept in balance when designing a cover:

• *Format:* Shape and size, use of a frame, texture, weight, thickness – all these establish recognition and continuity. A standardized cover format creates history, value, confidence, trust, and loyalty.

• *Logo:* The publication's title, it defines who you are. The symbol must be personalized and applied consistently everywhere. The issue date should be incorporated into the logo.

• *Illustration or visual:* Imagery both intrigues and signals a new issue.

• *Cover lines:* These blurbs provide other reasons to pick up the issue. Well-

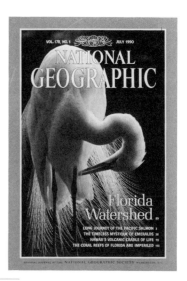

7.03

written cover lines catch more readers than imagery, but imagery attracts readers in the first place.

### Format

• *Shape and size:* Advertising sizes dictate inside page size which in turn dictates the size and shape of the cover. But some publications have moved away from tradition and produced square or tall or wide formats (fig. 7.01).

A gatefold cover can be a powerful attractant if used correctly (fig. 7.02). Be sure the gatefold's story unfolds as the cover is opened. Intrigue readers by showing half the image, with the visual "punchline" on the second, inside, panel.

• *Framing:* A frame around the page can become a recognizable and memorable design device. *Time's* red border is so recognizable it can be purchased printed on mirrors. Similarly, *National Geographic* is known for its yellow border, which is used on nearly all marketing pieces and correspondence as well as on the cover of the magazine (fig. 7.03).

To avoid a me-too look, consider an eccentric, off-center border (figs. 7.04 and 7.05) or a partial border (figs. 7.06 and 7.07). Be sure to leave sufficient border to disguise crooked trimming; ¼ inch is usually the minimum.

• *Texture, weight, thickness:* The heft of a publication is usually indicative of its success. It signals the amount of advertising the publication can attract – many magazines gain weight in the two months before Christmas and go on a crash diet in January for lack of advertising pages. It indicates whether the publication is healthy. *Sports Illustrated's* swimsuit issue is one of their fattest because advertisers know that particular issue will attract many readers.

Many publications' covers are printed with an ultra violet (UV) coating to make them shiny and more tactile. UV coating is a protective, ultra-shiny coating that hardens under UV light. It imparts a sense of quality and substance to a publication, to which readers seem to respond.

Some magazine covers are enclosed by a second, uncoated sheet that is some-times cut narrower than the cover (fig. 7.08). On it are printed cover lines or special messages (for example, "This is your last issue!").

Some publications are printed on unusually textured stock or use colored paper or paper with visible additions (little hairs, for example). All these add to the immediate recognizability of the publication.

### Logo

The logo says who you are. The symbol must be personalized and applied consistently on all printed materials. It should be closely related to the department headings and, perhaps, to the headline typography. These typographic connections unify the editorial matter, creating a cohesive visual product.

The issue date and other secondary information should be integrated with the logo to reduce visual clutter.

To enable readers to find a publication on a crowded newsstand, the logo must be the dominant element (fig. 7.09). It should also be dominant if good visual material is not always available.

If a publication is not sold at a newsstand, the logo need not be run at the top of the cover. Indeed, the logo does not even need to be horizontal (fig. 7.10). Marvelous personality and easy-to-execute flexibility can be created by developing a system in which the logo can be placed in any of half a dozen positions, depending on the shape, quality, and internal composition of the visual elements.

### Illustrations

The purpose of a cover illustration (a term that includes both drawings and photos) is to pull the reader inside. Drawings allow a wider range of graphic techniques than photos and lend themselves to showing concepts, ideas, and humor. Photos, on the other hand, are more believable because they are more realistic. Beauty for its own sake – using either artform – may be admirable, but it will not necessarily increase reader interest.

Whether to use a large or a small picture depends on the quality of the imagery. A cover-sized enlargement requires in-focus, well-lit, well-developed, dimensional imagery that is interesting. If you cannot count on professional photography or if you know the photographs will be taken on an inexpensive, do-everything camera, design a format in which imagery occupies only about half the cover (fig. 7.11).

Bleeding an image makes it more dynamic by implying continuation. Bleeding on all four sides of the page makes an image look much larger – so large, in fact, that it appears uncontainable on the page. But full-bleed photos require an area of relative blandness in color and texture to provide space for cover lines. If no such background field exists, the cover lines should be placed in an area of screen tint color somewhere around the perimeter of the page.

Although reader interest is highest when a cover contains a single focal point, it is sometimes worthwhile to have two pictures on a cover. If the two photos are directly related, they can be joined in a "split-screen" treatment, to make a single visual impression (fig. 7.12). If the two pictures are not related, one should be considerably larger, telling the reader that it is more important. A full-bleed image with a smaller, secondary image mortised within is visually dynamic but requires careful cropping of the bigger photo so its subject is not hidden (fig. 7.13). A partially silhouetted primary image with the sec-

ondary image placed beneath the logo provides a flexible system (fig. 7.14).

Readers respond particularly well to pictures of other people. Because portraits look a lot alike, covers with them should be distinguished by printing an area in a distinctive color, including a secondary, nonperson image, or changing the color of the logo.

Many feature stories concern trends or ideas, which must be conveyed by the cover. A concept cover is an idea presented in visual terms. The problem is to find a visual symbol that is not a cliché yet is understandable. A concept cover must be more than merely a visual pun; it must address and illuminate the meaning of the lead article.

All-type covers are recognized as being special because they are so rare. They should be reserved for special issues because of their focus on substance. They are inexpensive and easy to produce but become hard to distinguish from one another if used often (color changes alone are not well remembered). All-type covers sometimes include tiny pictures, which allow the type to be dominant.

## Cover lines

Imagine a magazine cover that has just one image and one headline. No matter how important the subject being shown, some readers will fail to respond. Instead of gambling on one idea to bring in the crowds and losing some, give the reader a selection of great reasons to pick up the issue and open it. Cover lines persuade readers to pick up a publication by providing several "appeals." Newspapers do the same thing with their headlines.

Words are critical to readership. Loyal readers, those who already find value in a publication and make time upon its arrival to read it cover to cover, will read

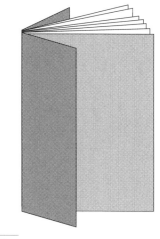

7.08

7.09

7.10

7.11

7.12

7.13

7.14

7.15

anyway. It is the casual and the harried reader for whom cover lines are a necessity.

Cover lines should present the most important contents, usually only feature stories. Lesser listings dilute the importance of all the cover lines and can overwhelm the reader.

The primary cover line describes the main visual, so it must at once be similar to other typography on the cover and act as a caption to the picture (fig. 7.15).

If cover lines are to be superimposed on imagery (a full-bleed photo, for example), sans serif type is much easier to read and has greater weight when reversing out of a four-color screen image. Sufficient contrast between type and background must exist, or cover lines will be illegible. The more sophisticated and upscale the publication, the more restrained the typography should be.

Repeat the wording of the cover lines exactly on the contents page and on the opening page of each story. It's a reward readers expect for having found the right page.

7.16

7.17

7.18

**Format:**

**shape and size**

7.16

This tabloid cover is 9¹ by 13 inches. The large page is exploited by running the nameplate (or logo) up the side. The logo is set in contrasting typefaces, with the word TALK printed in a second color. *TimesTalk*

**Format:**

**framing**

7.17

A half-point box rule printed in warm red frames the live area of this cover. A frame is activated by breaking an element out of it, in this case, a brochure cover, placed on an angle. Note the use of light and heavy rules to define areas, and that the banner fits a simple four-column structure. *Focus On Healthcare*

7.18

White space at the head, foot, and right side of this cover create an eccentric, or off-center, border. The placement of the horizontal rules, ancillary copy, and the logo at the head of the page are all carefully considered to allow the whiteness to remain. Dedicated white space (such as the right-hand column) is best used to emphasize something important within it. Corporate logos qualify, especially if a bison in a field of white. *Teller*

**7.19**
The imagery on this publication's cover
fits a distinctive format. The bottom of
the photo always bleeds, and the subject
of the photo is silhouetted within rigidly
maintained borders. The logo is printed
in two colors that are selected from those
in the photo. Cover lines, set flush left, are
placed flush left anywhere on two vertical
axes that align with the logo and the date-
line, providing both flexibility and consistency. *Textile Rental*

**Format:**
**texture, weight, and thickness**

**7.20**
The coated cover of this publication is enclosed by a second, uncoated sheet that is
cut with a curvy edge. Cover lines are
printed on this flap; when it is opened, the
cover art remains uncompromised.
*Wigwag*

7.19

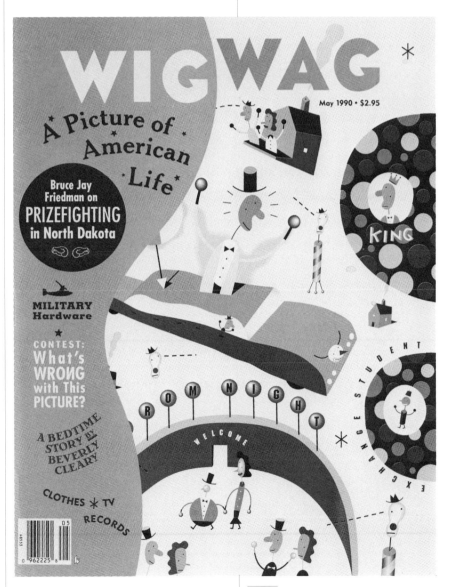

7.20

7.21

7.22

7.23

## Logo

### 7.21

The logo is the dominant element on this cover. It is printed in a different premixed ink color for each issue. Note that the ascender and descender overlap the half-point rules to unify the nameplate and that the base line of the date aligns with the bottom of the descender. Indeed, everything aligns with something on this well-organized cover. *Update*

### 7.22

This desktop-created flag makes good use of drop shadows by integrating them with rectangular panels and second color. The shadows are printed 20 percent red, the 12-point rule is printed solid red, and all else is black. *CIPS News*

### 7.23

All the elements on this flag are carefully aligned, making it very handsome. THE has been downsized to match the width of the U, the rule above ST PAUL aligns with the serifs on PULSE, and the vertical edge of the P in PAUL aligns vertically with the box rule around the text. *The Pulse*

7.24

The logo and descriptive copy have been unified by stacking words under the stylized apostrophe. The full-bleed, full-color cover has TRUMP'S printed metallic gold.
*Trump's*

7.25

This logo shows obvious evidence of digital manipulation. It is a playful experiment with the normal logo (shown inset). The modified logo is printed black on a yellow circle with remnants of red and blue around the edges of the letterforms.
*Dialogue*

7.26

A highly structured logo can give an otherwise freeform cover the organization and recognizable consistency it requires from issue to issue. The MAI in DOMAIN has been kerned to achieve optical evenness. The open letterspacing of THE LIFESTYLE MAGAZINE OF TEXAS MONTHLY perfectly aligns the width of the phrase with that of the logo, creating an effective relationship between two elements that should appear to belong together.
*Domain*

7.24

7.25

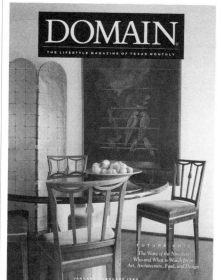

7.26

Vol. 3 No. 2 Spring 1990

## Protecting fish habitat

*A healthy economy requires a healthy environment.*

Our Common Future
The Report from the United Nations World
Commission on Environment and Development, 1987

The environment can be simply defined as the place where we live. It follows that words, economic growth and development must take place within the natural laws that govern our environment. Jobs and environmental protection not only can happen together, they must, if we wish to keep our planet and ourselves alive.

"Taking the idea of sustainability and putting it into action is difficult," says Dennis Deans,

careful and we have to be conscientious.

"Those strategies must include ensuring that industrial developments are environmentally sustainable."

And it's here that Fisheries and Oceans is already at work, implementing the concept of sustainability through their fish habitat management policy.

The fish habitat policy applies to all development projects and

7.27

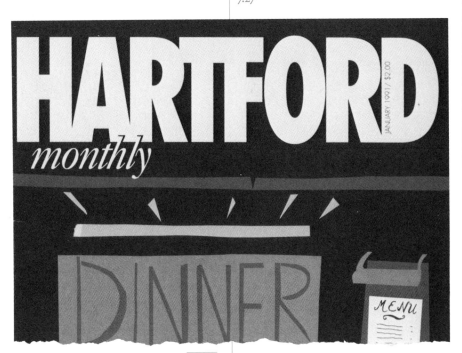

7.28

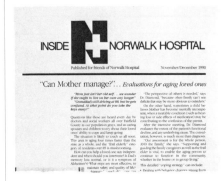

7.29

**7.27**
This elaborate flag shows how effectively overlapping unifies separate elements. PACIFIC is given secondary importance by reducing its size and placing it in an oval on top of TIDINGS, which can absorb the coverage with no loss of legibility because it is so big. The wavy logo relates to the whole by interrupting the perimeter box rules and the background screen tint. The original is printed in black, aqua, and light orange. *Pacific Tidings*

**7.28**
Flags are made more attractive when a clear hierarchy is established. MONTHLY is not as important or as descriptive as HARTFORD, and this hierarchy is clearly communicated through typographic contrast. *Hartford Monthly*

**7.29**
This example shows the integration of a logo with the name of the publication, which has been sized to match the height of the horizontal stroke of the cross. The publication's title is a playful pun on the logo, which itself illustrates "insideness." *Inside Norwalk Hospital*

**7.30**

The logo of any publication deserves customized typography. This minimalist approach is quite effective, imaginative, and appropriate for the word being illustrated. *Newsline*

**7.31**

This logo is designed to emphasize the word ADEPT, which is an acronym for the organization's name. The triangular panel always bleeds off the head trim and overlaps the artwork. *Adeptations*

**7.32**

Positioning the logo vertically is very dynamic. A logo need not be run horizontally across the top of the cover if the publication will not be sold at newsstands. Note the carefully mitered kerning on ENTERPRISE with its chopped-off serifs, as well as the placement of the volume, number, and date. The logo and all rules are printed dark blue; all else is black. *Enterprise*

7.30

7.31

7.32

7.33

7.33
This downward-pointing logo rests in open space, which contrasts with the exoskeletal format on the rest of the cover of this tabloid publication. DEP, the period, and the horizontal rules are printed light blue; all else is black. *DEPtoday.*

7.34
A publication's logo configuration must be applied to the department heads for consistency. Graphic embellishment has been used to unify this logo (on the outside) with the department heads (on the inside), creating a potent visual personality for this tabloid. *PaperAge*

7.34

7.35
The type in this logo is printed red, set flush left and enveloped by a field of black. The department heads echo the flag by being similarly placed in consistently sized fields. *Nation's Business*

7.36
The flag for this monthly is placed in any location that is convenient to the imagery. It can appear as either a "solid" or a "transparent." Colors are selected from those in the imagery. Note how the ampersand hangs beneath the base line, implying "underneathness." *Brake & Front End*

7.35

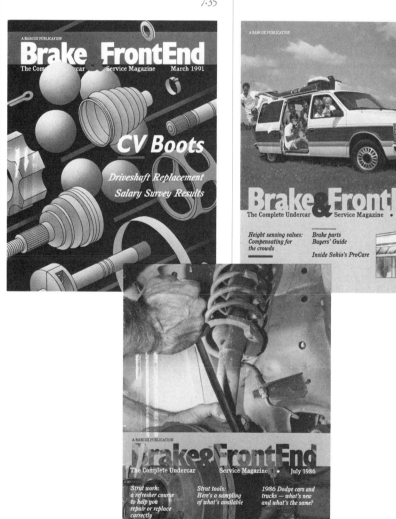

7.36

7.37

7.38

7.39

## Illustrations

### 7.37

This publication always runs a full-color, full-bleed photo on the cover. Full-bleed photography is especially desirable when the subject is photogenic, though it need not be the world's most beautiful islands. Note that, even with this exquisite imagery, cover lines are still used to draw the reader inside. The logo's colors change every issue. *Islands*

### 7.38

A nearly life-size, full-bleed face always appears on the cover of this publication because *vis à vis* is French for "face to face." The theme is continued throughout the issue with a regular series of interviews, each starting with a head shot. The life-size portraits on these covers are startling and editorially expressive. *Vis à Vis*

### 7.39

What do you do if high-quality cover art cannot be guaranteed every month? Design a format that makes the primary visual small but still eye-catching, even if the artwork is a publicity shot or taken by an editor rather than a professional photographer. This publication's cover format calls for the photo, usually of a piece of automotive hardware, to be silhouetted on the top edge and bled on the bottom and both sides. A smaller portrait accompanies a pull quote and the cover lines. The top background and the logo colors change for each issue. *Automotive Rebuilder*

7.40

Concept covers illustrate a complex point by combining two or more symbols to provide a fresh slant on an idea. An audio tape, representing the process of interviewing, is painted red, white, and blue to resemble the Texas state flag, which represents the interviewees. The result is integrated with the three-word headline in a simple format, showing off the concept with unadorned directness. *Texas Monthly*

7.41

Sometimes an idea is so powerful that the best way to express it is with type. This publication, which is very aware of typography, relies on all-type covers with some regularity. But each is given a unique design to look quite different from the others. *New Perspectives Quarterly*

**Cover lines**

7.42

Cover lines should be typographically consistent to look "of a piece" and to reduce clutter on the cover. Here they are run across the head of the page. Only feature stories are listed, to attract readers with the most substantial "appeals." *Medical Economics*

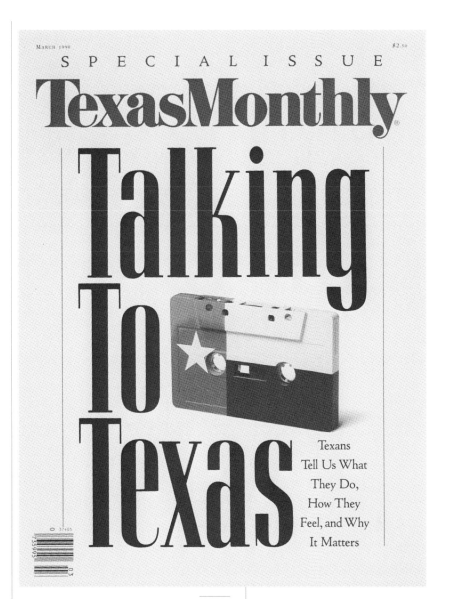

7.40

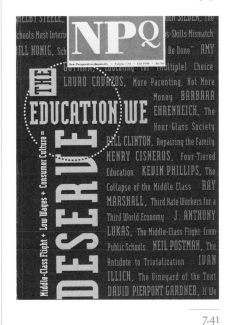

7.41

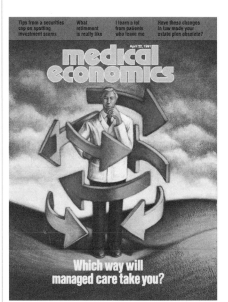

7.42

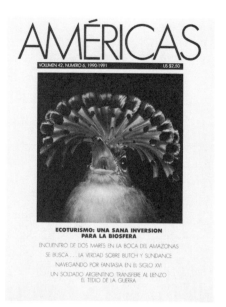

7.43 | 7.44

7.45

**7.43**
These cover lines are set as continuous copy at the bottom of the page, with red bullets separating the items. This oversize magazine is 9 by 11$^m$ inches, with the images printed in four duotone combinations (black plus another color). *i-D*

**7.44**
The title of the cover story (on ecotourism, or seeing the wilds – such as this royal flycatcher – firsthand) is set bold, to stand out from the other cover lines and to act as a caption, placed beneath and describing the photo. Covers can have only one cover line or as many as six; more than that overwhelms readers. *Américas*

**7.45**
The cover story's line should always be set larger, in contrasting type, so it will be seen first. The cover lines can be set flush left or centered, as shown here, depending on the requirements of the photo. Note the additional cover line in the upper right corner. *Travel Holiday*

**7.46**

An ingenious system of alternating flush-left and flush-right copy with images blends verbal and visual incentives to open this publication. The tight minus line spacing in the primary cover line darkens the color of the copy and makes it stand out. *InterCity Magazine*

**7.47**

These cover lines are connected to the edge of the page by a horizontal rule, which is printed in the same color as the logo. A complete contents listing is shown on the back. Note the distinctive logo typography and the use of textured pattern. This cover is printed in pastel colors, with a full-color photo wrapping around the spine. *Pebble Beach*

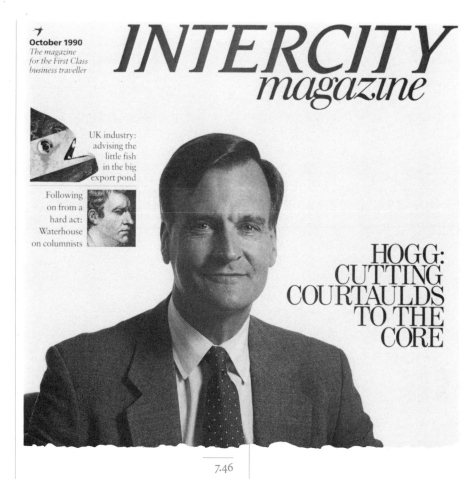

7.46

7.47

Taking on the '90s

7.48

7.49

7.50

**7.48**
A single cover line is knocked out of a screen-tinted area of a full-bleed photo. The date, placed vertically in a bar of yellow along the spine, is a nice detail. *Interest*

**7.49**
The addition of page numbers turns cover lines into a contents listing. The horizontal rules, added to define the column width, and the headlines are printed purple. *Eye on LSSI*

**7.50**
This simple contents listing is designed not to fill all the space available. It does, however, contribute to the handsomeness of the cover and give brief descriptions to pique a reader's interest. Newsletters of fewer than eight pages probably do not need a contents listing, as readers find it easier simply to leaf through the issue. With four-page newsletters, readers do not think of page 3 but of an inside back cover. *Network Newsletter*

**7.51**

The contents listing, flag and date, volume and number are printed black in the center of this cover, which is preprinted in full color. A certain sameness is evident issue after issue because the artwork does not change. However, this publication is issued only three times a year, so sufficient time passes between issues to make the new copy's arrival noticeable. *The ALAN Review*

**7.52**

The cover can actually be the contents page, as this publication illustrates. The space is divided to make each story findable, and artwork is used to attract readers to select stories. This publication has a great deal of editorial material, so it continues its contents onto a gatefold. To save space, it uses a less flamboyant layout on the second page. *Folio:*

7.51

7.52

# CONTENTS

# 8

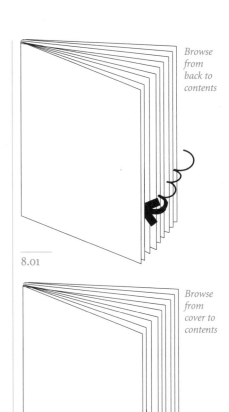

*Browse from back to contents*

8.01

There are two ways to read a publication, front to back and back to front. When readers work back to front because, say, they enjoy checking regular sections before the feature stories, they are satisfied to discover stories as they progress toward the front of the publication (fig. 8.01). Readers who work from front to back, on the other hand, are more apt to pause at the contents page for an overview of what the issue contains before leafing through it (fig. 8.02). They prefer to discover the issue in the order the editors have presented it.

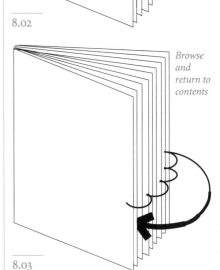

*Browse from cover to contents*

8.02

Because the contents page is often read after a preliminary scan of the issue (fig. 8.03), it provides the reader with a second chance to discover an article. The contents page should therefore present the article titles, summaries, and images as appealingly and intriguingly as possible.

*Browse and return to contents*

8.03

The contents page – or a briefer contents list in newsletters – is essentially redundant. All its information is contained elsewhere, in greater detail and with more hooks to catch the reader. So why would a reader – or a designer – spend any time on the contents page? A good contents page must, at the very least, be a clear, simple guide to the issue. But it can be more than that, hooking the reader with its own abbreviated persuasive appeals to turn to a story opener right now.

The material on the contents page must be organized in such a way that it builds excitement and anticipation in the reader. It should communicate the issue's worth, value, and fullness as well as its articles' locations. Ideally, it should whet the reader's appetite for the issue.

Fullness is not the same as busyness. Fullness suggests depth and quantity, whereas busyness is a symptom of not having chosen a clear hierarchy of information. A busy layout has too many elements jumping out at the reader, resulting in none of it being noticed. It repels readers. White space is as important on this page as on any other. Design some emptiness into your contents page.

The first step in creating a good contents page is for the editors to decide what they want the page to accomplish. What should it show off? Which elements will be emphasized? How wide is the range of subjects covered? Will there be brief descriptions of the articles, or will headlines stand alone? Will there be visuals? Are the authors' names more important than the titles of their articles? Is color available? Is more than one page desirable or possible?

The contents page must be easy to use. Clear typographic organization is the

8.04

8.05

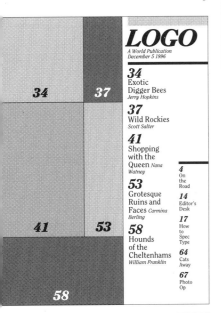

8.06

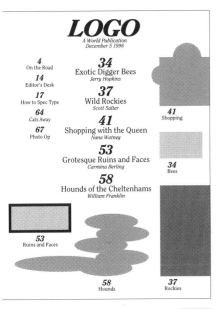

8.07

most important aspect in attracting readers. Article titles should jump out and page numbers should be placed near the headlines to avoid confusing gaps of space. Leaders, or rows of dots used to guide the eye across expanses of emptiness (fig. 8.04), are less effective than folios located immediately before or after story listings (fig. 8.05).

Contents pages can be type dominant or image dominant. If images are used, recycle color separations by showing same-size details of images as teasers. Photos may be neatly organized vertically up the side or horizontally across the page's top or bottom (fig. 8.06), or placed in a seemingly random pattern to contrast with structured type (fig. 8.07).

Emphasizing some elements, and necessarily deemphasizing others, creates contrast, which attracts readers. If all elements are treated equally, the page is gray all over and is more likely to be skipped. Clearly organized elements make skimming the page easy. Contents typography must exhibit obvious hierarchy. Titles must be worded exactly as they appear on story openers. A change in the headline wording from the contents to the opener causes confusion.

The contents may be on the cover. The difference between cover lines and a bona fide contents listing is that the contents gives page numbers. Cover contents listings are nearly always supported by a complete contents listing inside the publication, because an issue usually contains more elements than space can accommodate on the cover.

The contents should appear on the same page or, in a newsletter, in the same place, in every issue to make it findable. Some readers will turn immediately to page 5 for the contents if they are conditioned to do so. Four-page newsletters do not need a contents listing because the document is so short that readers find scanning the actual pages easier. A possible exception to this rule is four-page

tabloids, which, because the page size is 11 by 17 inches, contain more stories per page and may indeed benefit from a listing on the first page.

As the examples in this chapter affirm, information on a contents page can be organized in many ways. Whatever system you adopt, it must provide an immediate inherent visual indication announcing what this page is: a well-designed contents page does not need to be labeled "Contents."

8.08

8.09

8.10

## All type

**8.08**

Newsletters have contents sections, usually somewhere on the first page, rather than full contents pages. This all-type treatment, located at the bottom of the tabloid's first page, features large page numbers and reiterated headlines. All-type contents must contrast sharply with the text and headline type to be visible on the page. *PC News*

**8.09**

This newsletter's contents section is located just beneath the flag on the first page. Notice that the contents elements align with the three-column grid, giving it a unified, handsome appearance. The second color (purple here) changes with each quarterly issue. The two horizontal rules, the date, the page numbers beneath the contents listings, the captions at bottom right, and the duotone photos are all printed in the second color. *Executive Update*

**8.10**

This is a sixteen-page full-color newsletter printed on very good paper with a typographically flavorful contents section on the front page. The copy is broken into three styles: page numbers are white on the light tan background; titles are bold, condensed sans serif in black; and descriptions are light sans serif in black. *Step-by-Step Electronic Design*

.11

The hierarchy of information is quite clear in this example, with titles on the left above the dotted line, bylines on the right beneath the dotted line, and big folios centered. Such organization provides simple logical differentiation among kinds of information. *Adeptations*

.12

This contents spread lists features on one page and columns and departments on the other. The feature titles are repeated on the cover with page numbers, making it very easy to turn immediately to a topic of special interest in this learned and purposely dry professional publication. A different screen tint is surprinted on the cover and behind the center area of the contents spread of each issue; here, it is yellow. *Journal of Cash Management*

8.11

8.12

8.13

8.14

**8.13**

Big, bold headings (such as DAS NEUE JAHR ERFOLG UND MEHR, MODE, BEAUTY UND GESUNDHEIT) are printed solid warm red, helping to create a distinct hierarchy of information. The simple flush-left and flush-right settings create a clean page, a notable achievement given the many elements that must be included. The hand image is lifted from a story within, but having no caption, it is used here purely as decoration. The very glamorous portrait is a reproduction of the cover photo with a detailed caption listing the makeup the model is wearing. *Elle (Deutsch)*

**8.14**

A 9-pica/22-pica/9-pica column structure gives this page a vertical stress. The condensed Univers folios contribute to the vertical feel. The features are given emphasis with brief summaries, whereas departments are merely listed by title. The lone image, which upsets the strict symmetry of the typography, is positioned on the outside, visible edge of this verso (left-hand page). Its caption, the 22, connects it to its article, "The Bloom Boom." *Gift Reporter*

**8.15**

The folios have been given 1-point overscores in this simple system. It is easy to find departments and features; the latter are set double width and placed on the more important, outer part of the page. A single photo emphasizes the lead story. *View*

**8.16**

Similar to figure 8.15, these folios hang in the column margin along with the department headings. The white space gives this page a light, airy feeling. *Phoenix Home & Garden*

**8.17**

This contents page makes terrific use of typographic contrasts in size, line spacing, and column width to involve the reader. This spread includes, on the left page, the contents, whose titles and folios are printed in a reddish brown, and on the right page, the editor's note (the initial is also printed in reddish brown), purpose statement, and masthead, or staff listing. Notice how much white space remains despite the complexity of information; the openness makes the spread appealing. *America*

8.15

8.16

8.17

NEW YORK ALIVE (ISSN 0734-7189) is published bimonthly for the Business Council of New York State, Inc., 152 Washington Ave., Albany, NY 12210. Subscriptions: $14 one year; $27 two years. Single copy price $2.50. Second-Class Postage paid at Albany, N.Y., and at additional mailing office. Postmaster: Send address changes to NEW YORK ALIVE, Box 6389, Syracuse, NY 13217.

8.18

The American School Board Journal (ISSN 0003-0953) is published monthly in 1991 Dues St., Alexandria, VA 22314 by the National School Boards Association, an educational association incorporated not-for-profit. Copyright © 1991 by the National School Boards Association. All rights reserved. The American School Board Journal is registered in U.S. Patent and Trademark Office. Second class postage paid at Alexandria, Va., and at additional mailing offices. Subscription rates: United States and possessions, $48 a year; Canada, $58 a year; foreign mailing $60 a year; single copies $5. Single copies $4. Change of address? Send change of address information and a label from a previous issue to The American School Board Journal, 1680 Duke St., Alexandria, Va. 22314. Allow four to six weeks for address change to be processed. Subscription renewal information must reach School Board's Washington area office before expiration date to ensure uninterrupted delivery. POSTMASTER: Send address changes to The American School Board Journal, 1680 Duke St., Alexandria, Va. 22314.

16 *Centennial celebration*

20 *Lee Iacocca*

26 *Rainbow curriculum*

JANUARY 1991                                                                                                1

8.19

FLASHBACK

*Så går det løs i mørkt-diskotaket. Så de 15 førlæller vi, hvordan 2500 kg querdelede kaffer-grejl skaber et forrygende slamfeste af lyt og lyd.*

▲ *Med et 16-km højt glitter fotoaber componere på Metereologisk Institut, hvortien consecutive oplister og over Danmark. Læs reportagen side 18.*

◄ *Rundt flot lyd, der kan betales? Ta de 59 prøvetester vi HI FI & elektronik's nye fraeselt subwoofer - med nemgtor bygge-beskrivelse.*

*Hører glade, vår overikken spiller! Denne fejlen med ime er udgel tel stand samligt som en CD-spiller med radiven. Læs testen side 36.*

3

8.20

.21

[ ]his Brazilian magazine contains so many
[s]tories that a spread is deemed the best
[w]ay to show off the wealth of material.
[C]onsequently, a vertical column of pho-
[t]os runs up the outer edge of each page.
[T]he clear structure of this spread, fol-
[l]owed with great discipline, allows the
[d]ramatic silhouetted chaise longue to
[o]verlap the vertical red rule and bump
[i]nto the text. *Casa Claudia*

**[T]ype and imagery:
[h]orizontal**

[8].22

[W]hite space has been retained on this
[p]age as a vertical separator between items
[a]nd as a means for showing off the logo.
[T]he three most important images,
[c]ropped as squares, have been clustered at
[t]he top of the page. *Varian Magazine*

8.21

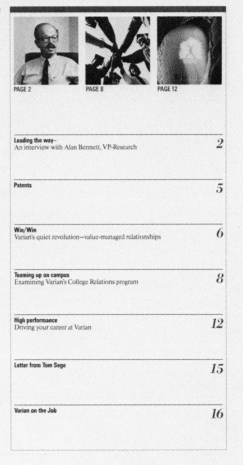

8.22

# The Bottom Line

HOME WELCOMES CARTERET

For Employees of The Home Group, Inc.                    September 1988 Vol. 2 No. 7

## Carteret Bancorp Joins The Home Group

On August 8, the acquisition of Carteret Bancorp was completed. With this addition Home Group doubled its assets and became the 20th largest financial services company in the United States.

"The Carteret acquisition completes The Home Group's restructuring into a major diversified financial services organization providing a substantial position in East Coast markets and enabling us to offer a full range of financial services," said Marshall Manley, President and Chief Executive Officer of Home Group. "We welcome Carteret employees as the newest members of The Home Group," said Manley. "We're confident that under the continued leadership of its current senior management, Carteret will make a significant contribution to the success of our Company."

Carteret is one of the largest savings institutions on the East Coast. It employs 2,084 people and has 124 retail banking or loan production offices in New Jersey, Florida, Maryland, Virginia, New York, North Carolina, and Washington, D.C. Headquartered in Morristown, New Jersey, the bank has $6 billion in assets and is the second largest thrift in the Garden State. The merger, approved by the Federal Home Loan Bank Board, resulted in Carteret becoming a wholly-owned, separately-managed subsidiary of Home Group.

The Home Group will have more than

The Home Group, Inc.
September 1988

* 20th largest financial services company in U.S.
* $13 billion in assets
* $3.5 billion in revenues
* 10,000 employees throughout U.S. and Canada

Home Group President and CEO Marshall Manley (right) welcomes Carteret Chairman and CEO Robert O'Brien to Home Group headquarters in New York before the start of a special presentation to top management held earlier this year.
More about Carteret on page 2.

$3.5 billion in revenues, $13 billion in assets and 10,000 employees. Carteret provides retail and mortgage banking services. It is also active in consumer and corporate lending. Through the other Home Group subsidiaries (Home Insurance, USI Re, Commonwealth Insurance, Imperial Premium Finance, Gruntal, Home Capital Services and Sterling Forest), the Carteret Savings Bank "Our businesses complement each other. We can tap broader markets and offer a complete range of competitively priced products to meet the needs of today's consumers."

O'Brien called the deal a good one for everyone concerned. "Our merger is indicative of a trend in the financial services industry," he added, stressing his belief in financial industry consolidation.

He said the savings and loan charter is the most valuable franchise in the industry. "But at the same time," he said, "you need the capital to maximize the value of that charter. And the average thrift is finding it hard to get that capital."

pany offers property-casualty insurance, reinsurance, mutual fund management, investment programs, corporate finance, asset management and stock brokerage services.

"The combination of Carteret and Home Group will result in a strong financial services company," said Robert B. O'Brien, Jr., chairman and CEO of Carteret.

*Michael Corey*

## Home Group Celebrates Three Years of Achievement

On September 3, 1988, Home Group celebrated its third anniversary as a public company. In this relatively brief period of time, the Company has changed dramatically. When it was established in 1985 it was considered primarily of insurance operations. Now it has expanded to investment services and banking. We thought it would be useful on this anniversary to recount the major events that resulted in its restructuring from insurance to a truly diversified financial services company. This period also marks a turnaround in the Company's profitability.

In 1985, the first year after The Home Group's spin-off from its former parent, City Investing Company, The Home came far in its objective of making the Company a major force in its industry. A review of every operation and the expenses for each

area of the business resulted in the redirection of resources and energies. The new organization provided a foundation for future growth and profitability.

The Home Group's performance in 1986 was one of solid achievement. After three consecutive years of losses, the Company posted a pre-tax operating profit and made significant progress in reestablishing itself within the U.S. property-casualty industry.

A number of factors combined to make 1987 a milestone year. Operating income rose to $119 million from $15.1 million reported for 1986; revenues and assets continued to increase; Home Group was approved for listing on the New York Stock Exchange; and the first regular quarterly dividend was declared. Also, Gruntal Financial Corp was acquired and an agree-

ment was reached to acquire Carteret Bancorp.

The following are highlights of the first three years of The Home Group.

### 1985
* Annual revenues totaled $2.0 billion; assets $5.0 billion.
* To revitalize The Home Group and restore its balance sheet, the life insurance subsidiaries were sold for $130 million and Home Insurance issued preferred stock to add $271 million to the Company's surplus.
* The Home Insurance Company's reserves were strengthened by approximately $250 million.
* Book value per share, which measures the net worth of a company, was $19.03 at year-end.

### 1986
* Acquired Imperial Premium Finance to substantially enlarge The Home's premium finance business and complement the basic insurance operation.
* At year-end, the Company reported operating income of $15 million and net income of $79 million (including $66 million of nonrecurring credits). Annual revenues grew to $2.2 billion and assets were $5.7 billion.
* Combined ratio for insurance operations dropped to 116.0 from 135.7 reported in 1985.
* Company repurchased approximately 2.5 million shares of its common stock.
* Book value per share at year-end was $22.19.

*Continued on page 3*

### I N S I D E

**4** Geo. T. Scharffenberger

**5** Training

**6** Kids' Money Camp

**7** Historic Airlift

8.23

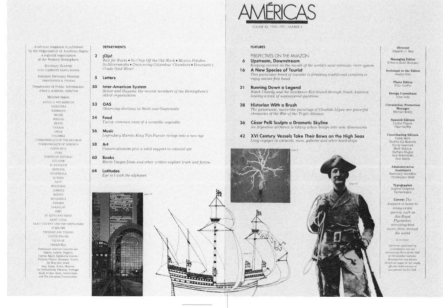

# AMÉRICAS
VOLUME 43, 1990-1991, NUMBER 6

Américas magazine is published by the Organization of American States, a regional organization of the Western Hemisphere.

**Secretary General**
IVÁN CLEMENTE JOSÉ A. SOARES

**Assistant Secretary General**
CHRISTOPHER R. THOMAS

**Department of Public Information:**
JORGE A. BARBOSA, DIRECTOR

**Member states:**
ANTIGUA AND BARBUDA
ARGENTINA
BARBADOS
BELIZE
BOLIVIA
BRAZIL
CANADA
CHILE
COLOMBIA
COMMONWEALTH OF THE BAHAMAS
COMMONWEALTH OF DOMINICA
COSTA RICA
CUBA
DOMINICAN REPUBLIC
ECUADOR
EL SALVADOR
GRENADA
GUATEMALA
GUYANA
HAITI
HONDURAS
JAMAICA
MEXICO
NICARAGUA
PANAMA
PARAGUAY
PERU
ST. KITTS AND NEVIS
SAINT LUCIA
SAINT VINCENT AND THE GRENADINES
SURINAME
TRINIDAD AND TOBAGO
UNITED STATES
URUGUAY
VENEZUELA

Permanent observer countries are Algeria, Austria, Belgium, Cyprus, Egypt, Equatorial Guinea, Finland, France, Germany, Greece, the Holy See, Israel, Italy, Japan, Korea, Morocco, the Netherlands, Pakistan, Portugal, Saudi Arabia, Spain, Switzerland, and The European Community.

**DEPARTMENTS**

**2 ¡Ojo!**
Bait for Bucks • No Chip Off the Old Block • Mexico Polishes Its Silversmiths • Uncovering Columbus' Chambers • Venezuela's Crude Gold Mine?

**5 Letters**

**50 Inter-American System**
Belize and Guyana: the newest members of the Hemisphere's oldest organization.

**53 OAS**
Observing elections in Haiti and Guatemala

**54 Food**
Yucca: common roots of a versatile vegetable

**56 Music**
Legendary Mambo King Tito Puente swings into a new age

**58 Art**
Conservationists give a solid support to colonial art

**60 Books**
Mario Vargas Llosa and other writers explore truth and fiction

**64 Latitudes**
Eye to I with the alphabet

**FEATURES**

**PERSPECTIVES ON THE AMAZON**

**6 Upstream, Downstream**
Keeping current on the mouth of the world's most intricate river system

**16 A New Species of Tourist**
This particular breed of traveler is forsaking traditional comforts to enjoy nature first hand

**21 Running Down a Legend**
Butch Cassidy and the Sundance Kid blazed through South America leaving a trail of unanswered questions

**28 Historian With a Brush**
The panoramic, movie-like paintings of Cándido López are powerful chronicles of the War of the Triple Alliance

**36 César Pelli Sculpts a Dramatic Skyline**
An Argentine architect is taking urban design into new dimensions

**42 XVI Century Vessels Take Their Bows on the High Seas**
Long voyages in caravels, naos, galleons and other hard ships

**Director**
Edgardo C. Reis

**Managing Editor**
Rebecca Read Medrano

**Assistant to the Editor**
Gladys Soto

**Photo Editor**
Felix Gaetho

**Design Consultant**
John Jody

**Circulation, Promotion Manager**
Michael Reilly

**Spanish Edition**
Carlos Viguría
Pilar Gaetho

**Contributing Editors**
Caleb Bach
Rosita Gili Marteño
Betty Guertink
Mark Holston
Bárbara Mujica
Jack Robertello
Gert Smith

**Administrative Assistants**
Rosemary González
Christopher Shell

**Typographer**
Rupert Graphics Technologies

**Cover:** The Amazon is home to many exotic species, such as this Royal Flycatcher, stretching bird facets from around the world.

Opinions expressed by contributors are not necessarily those of the OAS or its member nations. Reproduction and reuse stories on maps do not imply official endorsement or acceptance by the OAS.

8.24

---

**8.23**

This tabloid runs its contents at the bottom of the first page (a pun on its name?). It is an image- and folio-dominant system, requiring that the same image appear on the designated page. A brief title or description, knocked out of light blue, is provided for each item. Note the rhythm of the section: each image is cropped to the same size, the folios are all set the same size, and the one-line titles are edited to fit the bars. *The Bottom Line*

**8.24**

Beginning 10 picas from the head trim, the consistent sinkage used in this magazine, these contents listings simply extend until they are complete. The remaining space is used for visuals from the issue. The tiny folio placed next to each image allows readers to connect an image to its headline. This contents system is easy to produce for each issue because of the built-in flexibility of the white space at the bottom of the spread. *Américas*

**8.25**

Five features are clearly emphasized in this involving contents spread. Brief headlines accompany each photo in a distinctive typeface, each printed in one of four colors. The rest of the contents listings are easily read in the screen-tinted box beneath. All page numbers are printed in warm red. *Travel & Leisure*

**Type and imagery: blended**

**8.26**

This music publication is chock-full of articles and recording reviews (it comes with a full-length compact disc so readers can listen to a segment of each of the reviewed recordings). Consequently, the contents page is a very busy place. It looks as active and vibrant as possible, yet elements are still quite findable because the captions relate directly to the headlines, and because excellent contrast has been created between primary and secondary type elements. *Classic CD*

**8.27**

The second of two left-hand pages (each designated by the vertical CONTENTS title printed in warm red), this department-biased format has pronounced vertical columns enhanced by hairline rules. The square halftones' heights are cropped to fill each column evenly. *Men's Fitness*

8.25

8.26

8.27

8.28

8.29

8.30

8.28
8.28
These columns are built up from the bottom of the spread, ending where they will. No attempt is made to fill the space, leaving a magnificence of whiteness at the top of the spread. The department headings are printed in different colors. *Entertainment Weekly*

8.29
Integrating pictures with the contents type provides great flexibility when laying out the page. These five pictures move the eye around. The headlines and copy beneath function as captions. *Aetnaizer*

8.30
Feature stories are placed in the left-hand column, leaving the outer margin for less important stories and departments. An excellent typographic contrast has been created: features are set centered and all else is set flush left. Page numbers and headlines are screen tinted to 80 percent black. The reader can scan and find topics of interest very easily. *Continental Profiles*

**8.31**

This spread is clearly intended to be fully read. The descriptions of each article are long, but they are written to intrigue. Note the indents of the department's headlines and bylines. These deliberate white spaces make the folios pop right out. *Personnel Journal*

**8.32**

This contents scheme is typical of the magnificent art direction in this publication. The copy and folios (which are printed in warm red) are set in a 17-pica-wide column. Stories are separated by half-point rules. Extended half-point rules connect images with specific descriptions, a great way to make design relationships visible. *Look at Finland*

8.31

Cover photo: Snow board enthusiasts Photo by Kuvasuomi

Editor-in-Chief: Bengt Pihlström Managing Editor: Ann-Mari Pihlström Photo Editor: Aila Kolehmainen Art Director: Martti Mykkänen English Translation: The English Centre, Diana Tullberg Administrative Board: Ralf Friberg, (Chairman). Risto Hemming, Matti Linnoila, Ann-Mari Pihlström, Bengt Pihlström, Boris Taimitarha. Look at Finland is published four times a year. Opinions expressed in feature stories and articles do not necessarily reflect those of the publishers or editors. Publishers: Finnish Tourist Board and Ministry for Foreign Affairs. — Please apply to the editors for permission to use material appearing in this issue. Editorial address: P.O.Box 625, 00101 Helsinki, Finland. Tel 90-40 30 11, Telefax 40301333. Subscriptions: Finland FIM 50. Europe and overseas (air mail) USD 15. Single copies: Finland FIM 10 without purchase tax. Subscriptions can be sent to the Editorial address. Payments can be sent to our post giro account No. 1140-0 with the Postipankki bank, Helsinki. Orders can only be made for one calendar year at a time. Printed in Finland by Sanomaprint Vantaa 1990. ISSN 0024-6379

8.32

8.33

8.34

## Mortises

**8.33**
A mortise is a panel that is fully surrounded by an image or a color. This quarterly has a unique way of indicating the season: run a full-bleed, full-color photo across the spread. The mortised contents (on the right) are balanced by a panel on the left containing the editorial and masthead. *Connecticut's Finest*

**8.34**
This is the first page of a special section in the publication. Its mortised contents listing echoes the design of the section's listing on the main contents page. It is printed in red, white, and blue on a full-color photo. *U.S. News & World Report*

8.35

A full-spread illustration has been used a second time as background for the mortised contents listing, which is a recto, and the first of two contents pages. The departments are listed on the next page using a very different, but related, system. The two pages are related by typefaces, hairline rules, and the size of the folios. *Hippocrates*

**On the cover**

8.36

Perhaps the most famous contents-on-the-cover treatment belongs to *National Geographic*, which has been using it since 1896. The difference between cover lines and contents is that cover lines do not include page numbers. While this publication does have a more complete contents page, even it does not list departments. It merely describes the five feature articles in two or three sentences each and shows a representative color photo. *National Geographic*

8.35

8.36

# 9

A byline gives the author's name. A bio (short for biography) is a brief profile of the author, giving pertinent details that express his or her competence to take the reader's time.

The presentation of bylines and bios indicates the importance of the author. Readers are served by being told up front – somewhere on the first page of an article – who is doing the talking. If the author is not on the staff of the publication, a bio is extremely helpful in describing why the writer is qualified to discuss the topic at hand.

A byline format should be developed and used throughout a publication to make finding the names easy and to make visible those infrequent times when the author is extraordinary and truly deserves to have the byline trumpeted by breaking the normal format.

There are eight locations for bylines. They may be: placed near the headline or department heading (fig. 9.01), integrated with the headline (fig. 9.02), placed near the deck or subhead (fig. 9.03), integrated with the deck (fig. 9.04), placed near the text (fig. 9.05), integrated with the text (fig. 9.06), placed in a separate column (fig. 9.07), or integrated with an image (fig. 9.08).

Bios are often run at the end of an article because it is easy to tack them on there. No preplanning is needed to fit them. But a bio at the end cannot induce a browser to read unless, of course, the article is only one page, making the bio immediately visible. With multiple-page articles, readers have long since made their decision to read by the time they find the bio. It is far more helpful to place the bio on the opening page.

Bottoms of pages are far less valuable than tops: readers always start at the upper, outer corners when flipping through an issue, scanning individual pages from upper left to lower right. It is therefore a good idea to put a bio at the bottom of the opening page of an article. It is easily found yet will not interfere with headlines or primary visuals.

To avoid cluttering the opening page, distinguish the bio from the text but relate it to the surrounding type. Make it recognizable by contrasting its type size or style with that of the text, with which it is most easily confused. Set the bio in the same typeface as the text but in italics, or in a smaller size, or flush left if your text is justified. It needs its own typographic "flavor."

Sometimes bios are separated from the stories by being grouped on a single page near the front of the publication. This makes them appear even more important

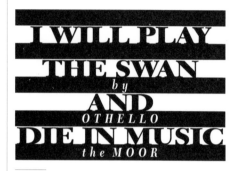

9.01

9.02

9.03

9.04

ou? Over hill, over dale, through bush, through brier, 'er park, o'er pale, through flood, through fire, I do wander everywhere. Swifter than the moon's sphere, and I serve the fairy queen o dew her

orbs upon the green. The cowslips tall her pensioners be, in their gold coats spots you see. Those rubies, fairy favours, in those go to seek some dew-drops here, and hang a pearl in any

## Starveling A. Tailor

9.05

you? Over hill, over dale, through bush, through brier, o'er park, o'er pale, through flood, through fire, I can wander anywhere. Swifter than the moon's sphere, and I serve the fairy queen, o dew her orbs upon the green. The cowslips tall her

— *by* —
**STARVELING A. TAILOR**

pensioners be, in the gold coats spots you can see. Those be rubies, few fairy favours, in those freckles live their saviours. I go seek some dew drops here and hang a pearl in every cowslip's ear. Over hill, over dale, through bush, through

9.06

he moon's sphere, and I serve the fairy queen, to dew

*B by* Robin *Goodfellow*

9.07

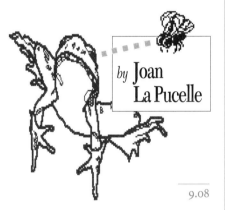

*by* Joan La Pucelle

9.08

of dull Octavia. ll they hoist me up show me to the uting varletry of dnsuring Rome? her a ditch in Egypt gentle grave unto Rather on Nilus' d lay me stark na- and let the water ; blow on me. His egs bestride the ean, his rear'd arm ted the world, his oice was propertied s all the atuned heres, and that to

9.09

a ditch in Egypt be tle grave unto me! her on Nilus' mud ne stark naked and he water flies blow me. His legs be- le the ocean, his 'd arm crested the ld, his voice was bertied as all the ed spheres, and to nds. But when he int to quail and ke the orb, he was ttling thunder. For bounty there was winter in't, an au-

9.10

— — — — — —
*CLEOPATRA is a thoughtful and passionate author who has a gift for languages. This article, written in collaboration with Plutarch, originally appeared in the Macedonian Herald Sunday Magazine.*

9.11

friends. But when he meant to quail and shake the orb, he was as rattling thunder. For his bounty there was no winter in't, an autumn that grew the more by reaping. His delights were dolphin-like. They show
*Continued on* 8

— — — — — —
***Cleopatra** is a thoughtful and passionate author who has a gift for languages. This article, written in collaboration with Plutarch, originally appeared in the Macedonian Herald Sunday Magazine.*

9.09

tumn that grew the more by reaping. His delights were dol-phin-like. They show'd his back above the element they liv'd in. In his livery walk'd crowns and crownets, realms and is-lands were as plates dropp'd from his pocket. ●

— — — — — —
***Cleopatra** IS A THOUGHTFUL AND PASSIONATE AUTHOR WHO HAS A GIFT FOR LANGUAGES. THIS ARTICLE, WRITTEN IN COLLAB-ORATION WITH PLUTARCH, ORIG-INALLY APPEARED IN THE MACEDONIAN HERALD SUNDAY MAGAZINE.*

flies blow on me. His legs bestride the ocean, his rear'd arm crested the world, his voice was propertied as all the tuned spheres, and that to friends. But when he meant to quail and shake the orb, he was as rattling thunder. For his bounty there was no winter in't, an autumn that grew the more by reaping. His delights were dolphin-like. They show'd his back above the element they liv'd in. In his livery walk'd crowns and crownets, realms and islands were as plates dropp'd from his pocket, smashed upon the forestage in

and can serve as an alternate contents page: the reader may peruse the contributors' page to learn who sounds interesting and, by extension, what should be read first.

A bio is enhanced by including a photo or drawing of the author. It is always more interesting to see images that tell something about the subject. Another bland mugshot (head-and-shoulder formal portrait) does not tell much. Select authors' photos by their descriptive quality – their content – rather than their ordinariness. Ask authors to supply their own photos: you never know what you will get. The pictures may be quite descriptive because they will show the authors as they view themselves.

The byline, bio, and photo must not add clutter to the page. Make them align or agree with other elements on the page. Photos and bios should be united by placing a box rule around them or by wrapping one around the other or by some other means that makes the two elements appear as one.

Bios can be placed at the end of the text on the first page of a story (fig. 9.09), at the conclusion of the story on the jump ("continued on") page (fig. 9.10), or in a separate column on the opening page (fig. 9.11). A horizontal rule is often placed above a bio to define its beginning. These are very easy to add. Software programs install overscores automatically if you first define a typestyle as "Bio" and include an overscore as part of its makeup.

# The Dairy Case

THE WOMAN ON THE PHONE HAD a voice that could melt the wax off a Gouda. U.S. Customs, she informed, had intercepted a load of imported Cheshire that looked suspiciously like cheddar sneaking into the country under a fancy alias. Probably trying to dodge import duties. Could Mike give them a positive ID?

Michael Tunick, cheese detective, didn't think twice before he took the job.

Tunick gets the kind of case that won't yield to the probing of your average shamus, who doesn't know jack cheese about dairy products. Regular police procedures don't work either. You know what they say: You can grill cheese all night, and it will won't talk.

That's where Tunick comes in. Mild mannered yet au Milquetoast, he knows how to pressure a tough customer. He does it with a texture-profile analyzer—a machine that measures stress tolerance by mimicking the chewing process—instead of with threats. None of that "Hi, curdbull, keep it up and you'll be buggin' macaroni" stuff. And the only heat Tunick packs is the differential-scanning calorimeter he uses to measure the melting properties for various suspects, often it's the only way to unmask an adulterated mozzarella, or maybe a "butter" that's known to its close personal friends as Oleo.

Tunick's a chemist. His turf, the U.S. Department of Agriculture's Eastern Regional Research Center, is the venerable 55-year-old lab where instant mashed potatoes and concentrated fruit juice were invented. The center is a mile or so outside Philadelphia, where Tunick grew up. As a boy he showed no early signs of a calling. A healthy appetite for cheese steaks, sure, but he didn't sit around reading Havarti fava mysteries. In 1973, when most other college kids were doing pot cheese, Tunick started at the center as a trainee; he was hired full-time in 1977.

Tunick introduces his boss, chemist Virginia Holsinger, one of the researchers who came up with a milk for the lactose-intolerant. She heads the Milk Components Utilization Research Unit's 20-person team. "We do the kind of longer-term, higher-risk research that universities can't afford to do," she says. Recently the unit took a shot at keeping good cheeses from going bad, and it paid off. "Wire-brassed cheddar earmarked for special federal projects like the school-lunch program was ripening faster than the government could use it," she explains.

"Three years of experimentation and two more of shelf-life studies proved that it is possible to freeze a large volume of cheddar, then thaw and process it without any significant damage.

"The detective work—we've done milk and butter, not just cheese—is just a sideline."

But don't the gumshoe and the research scientist walk the same mean streets? What is it but sleuthing when you're trying to find a better way to treat tannery wastes, as Tunick did when he worked for the center's Hides, Leather, and Wool Research Unit in 1977. ["We came up with a way for

DISCOVER • JUNE • 1992 **33**

*Were it not for the dedication of an unsung cheese whiz, the nefarious plot of the mozzarella mob might never have been uncovered.*

9.12

---

# REPORTER

## BY JOE NICK PATOSKI

### MUCKRAKER OF THE BIG BEND

When Jack D. McNamara moved his family back to his hometown of Alpine in 1983, all the retired Marine Corps lieutenant colonel wanted to do was build an adobe house and relax. But once he realized how news is disseminated in the sparsely populated Big Bend, his plans changed. "Out here, you don't walk to the newsstand, pick up the daily newspaper, and read about local events," he says. "The dailies we get out here are from San Angelo and Odessa. Nobody is here in the trenches for the day-to-day battles." Worse, he noticed, the weeklies in Brewster, Presidio, and Jeff Davis counties shied away from controversy.

McNamara became convinced that he should do something about it after joining a group opposed to the construction of a new federal detention center. Attending a Brewster County

1988, with Jack writing most of the copy and Bonnie and Kathleen doing the typing, layout, and production. They chose the name *Nimby News* after Jack saw the acronym for Not In My Back Yard in the pages of *Atlantic Monthly* and figured, "That sounds a lot like us."

The job of media watchdog comes naturally to the 52-year-old McNamara, who served as the press officer for the Marine Corps in Washington, D.C., during the Watergate era and later

was a persuasive argument that it would provide jobs," he says. "But we were worried because a community like Alpine has a lot of retirees and tourists, and we felt a prison would be a negative force. We were active because it *was* in our back yard. After that, we made a decision to go forward on criminal justice issues because there were a lot of strange things going on in what we call the Borderland."

Since then the paper's pages have been

9.13

---

## With department headings and headlines

9.12

The byline on this department page is joined to the department heading by a 6-point red rule. The rule's redness visually connects it to the vertical red bar bleeding from the head trim that sets off the headline's initial τ. *Discover*

9.13

A "force-justified" byline is the same width as the department heading. Force-justifying will make the ends align, but in extreme examples so much letterspacing is inserted that legibility is compromised. The title of the article here is deemphasized by being set in 16-point type and being placed at the top of the first column of text. *Texas Monthly*

**9.14**

Sandwiched together with the department heading between a pair of half-point rules, this byline at once becomes lighter (less visible) and is embellished by letter-spacing. *Pulse!*

**9.15**

The byline is dropped out of an 18-point rule that extends across the top of the page. The bio is placed beneath the department heading (printed blue) and a 2-point rule. *Men's Health*

**9.16**

The byline and brief bio (really just an affiliation) is treated the same way on the opener of every article in this trade journal. Notice how important the two solid ballots become on this simply designed page. They alone give the page its personality. *Journal of the Institute of Nuclear Materials Management*

### RCA Reissues Complete Toscanini; Polskie Nagrania Label Releases 13-CD Set

#### CLASSICAL
BY ALLAN KOZINN

During the first seven years of the CD era, collectors of historical recordings have been intensely disappointed with many of the CD transfers of Arturo Toscanini's recordings. And Toscanini partisans, who are legion and vocal, have complained vehemently that RCA's handling of this important legacy has been scandalously sloppy for decades — ever since the '60s, when the company reissued a sizeable chunk of the Toscanini catalog in electronically rechannelled stereo LP pressings.

Now BMG Classics, RCA's parent company, had decided to redress these grievances by embarking on an ambitious and organized reissue series. The plan is to do the job right, once and for all, in a project that will run through 1992, the 125th anniversary of Toscanini's birth. All told, there will be 82 mid-price RCA Victor Gold Seal compact discs (or 81 cassettes) of material, taking in every

on the stage of Carnegie Hall in April that the CDs would eventually be issued separately (as well as in an 82-disc edition) by 1992. The introductory offerings are basic: Beethoven's Nine Symphonies, recorded with the NBC Symphony between 1949 and 1952, plus the Leonore Overture No. 3, from 1939 (RCA Victor Gold Seal 60324-2-RG, 5 CDs); Brahms's Four Symphonies, recorded with NBC in 1951 and 1952, and filled out with the Double Concerto (with Mischa Mischakoff and Frank Miller) and various shorter orchestral and choral works (RCA Victor Gold Seal 60325-2-RG, 4 CDs); and a Verdi box.

Without getting into a detailed discussion of Toscanini's approaches to Beethoven and Brahms — these are certainly known quantities by now — the uninitiated should know that these are taut, streamlined readings in which clarity, power and forward movement are highly prized. It is not quite accurate ... all Tosc-

(BMG Video 60332-6-RG on laser disc; 60332-3-RG on VHS) and a 1949 Verdi "Aida" with Herva Nelli, Eva Gustavson, Richard Tucker, Giuseppe Valdengo and the Robert Shaw ... Video 60331-6-RG on

solid 1962 Rowicki recordings included in the Polish series.

The Polish recordings are, however, concise and generously packed. Of the six discs in the Lutoslawski series I would recomm ... I did ...

*9.14*

## Phil Dunphy on
# MEN'S Fitness

Phil Dunphy, "the man who trained Bruce Springsteen," is a physical therapist, exercise physiologist and the man in charge of HEAR (Health through Exercise and Rehabilitation) and The Gym, two fabulous fitness facilities in New Jersey.

# FAT LOSS
### Part 2: Fighting it off

Want to burn more fat? Use more of your body.

You burn more fat with an exercise that works your arms *and* legs than one that just works your legs. You burn more fat when you exercise standing up because you're also carrying your body weight.

Those simple rules form the basis of this "fat-burning rating" of machines you might find at the nearest health club, gym or Y. Here they are, from the best fat burners to the least effective:

of the machine with it set at a high level are wasting their time.

**Treadmill:** You're standing, which is good. Swing your arms and raise the incline level for a little extra work.

**Rowing machine:** Better than a bike because you're using your arms and your legs, but very few people can pace themselves slow enough so that they can last for 30 to 45 minutes. It's also the machine where people tend to have the worst form. Keep your back straight; don't lean

there's two escalators side-by-side.(or a set of stairs). *Walk* up and down them (you should *never* just ride an escalator—it's like having free time on a StairMaster—use it!) for half an hour, and then walk from one end of the mall to the other again to cool down.

It's a great workout and bad weather won't hold you back. Same thing with an airport. I was talking with our esteemed editor McGrath about this column and found out that we both do the same thing to kill time between planes: walk from one end of an airport to the other.

If you're in Chicago or Atlanta you'll get an Olympic-level workout. And no matter which airport you're in, power-walking to kill time not only burns fat, it also loosens you up enough that you won't feel stiff after you get off the plane.

Stuck in a hotel in a strange town? Climb up and down the stairwell for an hour. *Always* take the stairs every chance you get. It builds up your endurance *and* it gets your body used to exercise.

Increase your everyday activity. Walk

*9.15*

## Physical Protection Philosophy and Techniques in Czechoslovakia

Jan Lukavsky
Czechoslovak Atomic Energy Commission/CsAEC
Czechoslovakia

The physical protection in Czechoslovakia/CSSR is understood as one of the basic conditions for the safe utilization of nuclear energy. From this point of view, the physical protection measures are part of the nuclear safety requirements. The Nuclear Safety Law is the basic legal document for the physical protection area. In CSSR a very tight connection between the physical protection system and the State System of Accountancy for and Control of Nuclear Material/SSAC is also established. Combining regulatory activities in the field of nuclear safety, accountancy for and control of nuclear materials and physical protection into one complex system enables the minimization of unauthorized removal of nuclear material. This minimizes the possibility of sabotage and also implements effective protection against both inside and external threats. The physical protection is a very important complementary measure to the other ones which assure low risks from the technical and human failures.

The IAEA's document INFCIRC/225 (Rev. 1), "The Physical Protection of Nuclear Material", is applied as a basis for the physical protection measures and requirements concerning nuclear material storage and utilization. The categorization of the nuclear material based on INFCIRC/225 (Rev. 1), as well as the other requirements relevant to individual categories, is valid in CSSR. In 1981 CSSR signed and in 1982 ratified the Convention of the Physical Protection of Nuclear Material. Without waiting for the validation of this document, the convention's requirements become obligatory immediately, and they are applied to both the domestic and the international transportation.

Both documents mentioned above focus on nuclear material, and they do not consider the risks which can arise from the malevolent act against the nuclear facility. However, considering the measures for the physical protection of the nuclear facility, not only must the characteristic of the nuclear material itself be taken into account, but also, the characteristic of the nuclear facility must be considered.

In CSSR each enterprise is obliged to ask the CsAEC for a license before receipt of the nuclear material and it is obliged to seek an extra license for siting, construction and operation. The application for the license has to be supported by the safety reports confirming that all nuclear safety, accountancy, and physical protection requirements are fulfilled. The content of the safety report chapters concerning the physical protection is as follows:

• Evaluation of the geographical location;
• Evaluation of the facility design;
• Description of the physical protection system;

• Evaluation of the relation between the facility operational conditions and the effectiveness of the physical protection system;
• Evaluation of the physical protection system reliability;
• Description of the quality assurance programs for the component fabrication and for the system construction; and
• Description and evaluation of the response activities plans.

The license issued by CsAEC can be controlled using additional conditions. In order to control how the information given in the safety report reflects reality and how the license conditions are fulfilled, the CsAEC has a right to carry out inspections. If anomalies are found, the CsAEC's inspector is authorized to ask the operator to introduce complementary measures, to check the system performance, and in serious cases, to ask the facility to shut down. Of course, this is valid for the anomalies in the field of the physical protection, as well as in the field of nuclear safety. The evaluation of the facility geographical location, the facility design, and the risks resulting from the malevolent acts against the facility represent the basis for the physical protection system design. For each facility, determining which event represents the greatest potential harm to the public, for example the radiation release from the reactor fuel due to core meltdown, is necessary. The physical protection system then is built with the aim to minimize the possibility of such an event. The sensitivity of each facility component to the malevolent acts is determined by the following factors:

• Significance for plant safety;
• Radioactive material inventory;
• Complexity of the intruder's access; and
• Design resistance against the sabotage.

Based on this approach, the optimization of the physical protection measures is carried out with respect to the individual facility components. This means that more complex physical protection requirements are applied to more sensitive parts of the facility, and simple requirements are applied to less sensitive parts. The categorization of the nuclear facility components is based on this principle. The nuclear facility components are categorized, as well as the nuclear material in the INFCIRC/225 (Rev. 1), into three categories. The INFCIRC/225 (Rev. 1) requirements can be used as guidelines for the physical protection of the nuclear facilities such as nuclear power plants, research reactors, laboratories etc.

The conditions for the safe operation of the nuclear facility are created during its construction. From this point of view, the quality

*9.16*

# George's Corner

## Tribute to a Great Life
*by George Pennebaker, Pharm.D.*

A few weeks ago I was shocked to read in the paper that Bob Noyce had died. Knowing that most readers of this magazine

in the accomplishments of others. Bob possessed all of those qualities. We met when I got into a car that was to take the two of us from a hotel

thing to contribute to the conversation or activity. He also was sincerely interested in what other people were thinking and doing. He listened with

9.17

---

## Minicourse

One night when Alexander the Great was just about ready to give up on his siege of the stubborn city of Tyre, he dreamed of a dancing satyr. Aristander, the dream interpreter traveling with the army, told Alexander his dream foretold the conquest of Tyre. Aristander figured out the dream by splitting the word "Satyros" into the two words "sa Turos"—Greek for "thine is Tyre." Alexander, fortified by the interpretation, attacked and conquered the city.

The ancients took dreams as divine prophecies. To learn the future, one only had to interpret a dream's elements correctly. As Freud wrote, "Throughout the whole of the Hellenistic-Roman period the interpretation of dreams was practiced and highly esteemed." But somewhere along the way this became disreputable, as undertaking for the superstitious. Dream interpretation hit an all-time low, wrote Freud, when people used dreams to figure out "the numbers fated to be drawn in the game of lotto."

At the beginning of this century Freud tried to revive the old idea, but with a new twist. He said the dream hides not a divine message but a wish from the dreamer's unconscious. A dream is formed when the unconscious wish seeks release in the dreamer's conscious mind. In order to slip past a censor that guards the conscious mind and thus protects the dreamer's sleep, this wish disguises itself. Alexander's dream (though it did turn out to be prophetic) was not a tricky way for the gods to tell Alexander he would conquer Tyre, but an elliptical expression of Alexander's wish to conquer Tyre. Thus Alexander's successful siege was not the fulfillment of divine prophecy, but simply a wish come true.

Despite the changes, Freud's view has a lot in common with the ancient belief. Both assume that a dancing satyr is never just a dancing satyr. Both assume that to figure out a dream's latent meaning, one must interpret. And both are frowned upon by scientists who believe that dreams are purely somatic, nonpsychical events. Knowing full well the scientific view, Freud wrote, "Let us embrace the prejudice of the ancients and of the people and let us follow in the footsteps of the dreamers of antiquity."

Nothing much has changed. Scientists still abhor

### Scientists are again debating the reasons for our dreams

By Sarah Boxer

# Inside our sleeping minds

dream interpretation. In the last 30 years, however, the revolt against Freud's theory has gathered new momentum. Armed with fresh neurobiological evidence, a coterie of scientists is on the rampage against the Father of Psychoanalysis. With a vengefulness that seems positively Oedipal, they are out to prove that dreams are not elliptical messages from the unconscious—that they have no latent meaning at all.

The big, dirty secret about Freud, say these scientists, is that he never really understood the biology of dreaming. In an 1895 paper titled *The Project for a Scientific Psychology*, Freud tried and failed to link his psychological theories with neurobiological ones. And yet, his critics say, he had the gall to create a dream theory. With Freud as their whipping boy, these scientists promise to build a new dream psychology on the study foundation of the neurophysiology of dreaming, a science that has come into its own in the last three decades.

*Sarah Boxer is a freelance writer living in New York City. She has contributed articles to Discover, Sports Illustrated, Metropolis, The Village Voice and The New York Times Book Review.*

MM   October–November 1989

9.18

---

# THE CODEPENDENCY CONSPIRACY

IN A LARGE CONFERENCE room at the Center for Recovering Families in the heart of upscale Houston, a group of well-dressed people shut their eyes and tried to remember that period in their lives long ago, before they were stricken with the most devastating emotional disease of our age.

"I want you to remember the house you lived in as a little kid," the speaker said in a soothing voice, "and I want you to see your mom and dad, brothers and sisters." Among the 32 people in the room, most of them professionals, were a successful Florida dentist, a New Mexico doctor, a chemistry professor from the Northeast, a California corporate executive, and a furniture Houston realtor. They had each spent $700 for the four-day program to discover that they had been stricken by a vague but deadly psychological

illness, one that was turning them into self-destructive addicts and would eventually lead to their ruin.

Indeed, the people in the room were about to be hit by the latest buzzword of the American self-help movement, the word that practically overnight has come to stand for most of humanity's ills, the word that many have heard but few understand—the dreaded "codependency."

"I want you to see a small child coming out the front door," said the speaker. Houstonian John Bradshaw, a stocky, bearded, 56-year-old ex-seminarian, whose books and lectures on family relationships have become survival manuals for hundreds of thousands of readers. "That child is you. Walk over to him. Tell him that you know better than anyone else what he has been through—his suffering, his abandonment, his shame."

**Codependency gurus insist we don't know how sick we are. In our family struggles we have lost our true selves . . . .**

## BY SKIP HOLLANDSWORTH

118 / FEBRUARY 1990

**Do you crave love and approval? Do you overeat, watch too much TV, or think about sex all the time? You may be suffering from codependency. Or then again, you may just be human.**

From somewhere in the audience came a sob. One woman was shaking her head, her face a crumble of grief. The members of the group were being asked to reach that time in childhood when they were pure, natural, and innocent—perhaps the only time, according to Bradshaw, when their lives worked, when they were not victims of codependency.

"This," Bradshaw said, his voice nearly a whisper, "is your *inner child*. Tell him that all the people he will ever know, you are the only one he will never lose."

I sat at the back of the room, slightly skeptical and more than a little confused. For the past couple of years, I had been hearing more and more people talk about being codependent. They would blame their failed relationships on codependency and would even tell codependent jokes ("What happens when a codependent dies? Someone else's life flashes before his eyes"). I had come to the New Life Family Workshop because I was perplexed. Although I knew that codependency was a term

**. . . To find our codependencies, we must strip ourselves bare and journey into the dark recesses of our lives.**

originally used by counselors to describe the dynamics in an alcoholic family and although I knew some therapists had expanded the meaning to include anyone who depended on anything outside himself for his feelings of self-worth, I did not understand how the concept had captivated the imagination of such a large segment of society.

Yet codependency has helped usher in an astonishing new self-help age in America that focuses on addictive behavior. What were once considered only bad habits are now potential "diseases." People eagerly acknowledge that their codependency has been the cause of their "addictions" not only to chemical substances like alcohol but even to such impulses as the constant desire to fall in love, to overeat, or to watch too much television.

The codependency movement has created a proliferation of twelve-step groups, modeled on the principles of Alcoholics Anonymous but dealing with topics ranging from excessive

TEXAS MONTHLY 121

9.19

---

9.17

In this publication, the byline is always placed beneath the headline, in this case *TRIBUTE TO A GREAT LIFE*. The department heading is dropped from a screen tint, which changes color on each page. What makes the top area of this page work so well is the unity achieved by aligning the bottom of the photo with the hairline rule beneath the byline. This format is flexible: two-line headlines merely steal some of the screen tint behind the department heading. *ComputerTalk*

9.18

Altering only a single font's size, a three-level hierarchy is created on this opener (a full-bleed photo is on the facing page). All three segments of display type have been set flush right. The headline and deck are aligned on that right edge, and the byline is base-aligned with the first word of the headline. These relationships make a simple display type treatment very handsome and inviting. Notice that the author's bio is conveniently located on the first page of the story, making it easy to review her credentials to determine whether the article is worthwhile. *Modern Maturity*

9.19

This unusually large byline extends across the full width of the live area of the page. It shares both the width of the headline and the same Helvetica Bold all-cap typeface. Both are printed in a light warm gray screen tint. Notice how the white space is used to make the huge display type unavoidable and the images more visible. *Texas Monthly*

**9.20**

The use of an appropriately distressed typeface in the headline makes the byline, set in all caps dropped out of a 20-point rule, a satisfying treatment. The bios are placed at the bottom of the first column of the story. *Américas*

**9.21**

Binding a piece of type with a line is very easy with a computer – perhaps too easy, as the treatment is used arbitrarily and inappropriately all the time. This example uses curved base lines intelligently to convey being underwater, a very suitable application. *Sports Illustrated*

EL 7 DE NOVIEMBRE de 1908, dos policías bolivianos mataron a tiros a dos bandidos norteamericanos en San Vicente, un pueblo minero situado en una árida y ventosa hondonada a 4.300 metros de altura en la Cordillera de los Andes. Aunque desde entonces han transcurrido ocho décadas, los historiadores que se dedican a investigar las aventuras de los bandoleros aún discuten si los hombres que murieron ese día eran Butch Cassidy y el Sundance Kid. Algunos investigadores incluso han sostenido que el tiroteo nunca ocurrió.

Gracias a Hollywood, Butch Cassidy y el Sundance Kid (cuyos verdaderos nombres eran Robert Leroy Parker y Harry Alonzo Longabaugh) se convirtieron en los más famosos integrantes del Wild Bunch (la Pandilla Salvaje), una indefinida confederación de bando-

*Daniel Buck es miembro de la junta asesora de la* National Association for Outlaw and Lawman History. *Anne Meadows es una escritora que reside en Washington, D.C. Ambos colaboran con* South American Explorer.

leros que a fines del siglo XIX y principios de este siglo se dedicaban a asaltar bancos y trenes en la región situada al oeste de las Montañas Rocosas.

A fines de siglo, las pandillas de bandoleros se hallaban en retirada en el oeste de los Estados Unidos. El telégrafo y el teléfono permitieron a las cuadrillas de alguaciles expulsar a los bandidos de los caminos, la fotografía ayudó a identificar sus escondites, y los Pinkerton y otros detectives profesionales, contratados por los ferrocarriles y los bancos, persiguieron a los bandoleros después de las redadas de los alguaciles.

La mayoría de los miembros del Wild Bunch habían muerto, o estaban presos o prófugos para marzo de 1901, cuando el Sundance Kid y su compañera Etta, con el nombre de Harry A. Place y señora, se embarcaron en Nueva York en el vapor *Hermínius* con rumbo a la Argentina. Cassidy se les unió en 1902, y los tres vivieron pacíficamente durante varios años en el valle de Cholila, en el norte de la Patagonia.

En esa época, el norte de la Patagonia era una región fronteriza escasamente

# EN BUSCA DE UNA LEYENDA

POR ANNE MEADOWS Y DANIEL BUCK

Butch Cassidy y el Sundance Kid huyeron a América del Sur hace noventa años. Una partida internacional de historiadores los ha estado persiguiendo desde entonces

AMÉRICAS **21**

9.20

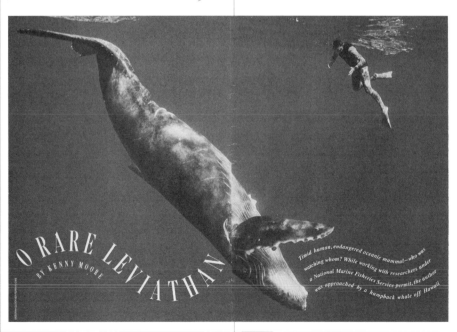

O RARE LEVIATHAN
BY KENNY MOORE

Timid human, endangered oceanic mammal—who was watching whom? While working with researchers under a National Marine Fisheries Service permit, the author was approached by a humpback whale off Hawaii

9.21

# MODERNIDADE ANTES E DEPOIS DA REFORMA

Ainda atual, apesar dos seus 63 anos, esta construção passou por uma reforma que criou novos espaços, mas não alterou a proposta inicial do projeto: o compromisso com a modernidade.

REPORTAGEM: MARIA AMÉLIA O. SANTOS
FOTOS: JUCA MORAES

R io de Janeiro, 1927. Ergue-se aos pés do Pão de Açúcar uma construção com as marcas do mais puro estilo moderno: linhas retas, panos de vidro e grades em tubos de metal. Rio de Janeiro, 1990. Uma reforma amplia a casa, redimensiona sua distribuição interna e, sem alterar seus traços, acrescenta alguns elementos do atual Freestyle — tendência nascida nos Estados Unidos propondo formas originais em arquitetura e mobiliário. Eis a trajetória desta casa em três pavimentos, cujos 350 m² de área construí-

**1.** Amplas aberturas em vidro traduzem o espírito moderno da obra, onde grades de tubos metálicos substituem os muros.

**2.** A garagem cedeu lugar à entrada para a nova copa e ganhou teto rebaixado, cujo recorte contorna a coluna estrutural.

**3.** Ladeada por tijolos de vidro, a porta principal tem piso tubular e fica sob a marquise, que ganhou rebaixo e luz embutida.

AR 90

A&C 85

9.22

decks

## 9.22

The byline and photo credit of this are set in 7/8 bold caps and usually follow the deck, as shown here. There is a clear structure of information, from most important (the headline) to progressively less important, until the reader is led to the text. The captions are brief and easily identified by number. *Arquitetura & Construcao*

## 9.23

The byline is incorporated flush right on the last line of the deck in this publication. A reporter associate is always credited at the bottom of the text's first column. Note also the caption's bold lead-in, in a contrasting typeface. The variety of typographic flavors makes this page interesting. *Fortune Magazine*

CORPORATE PERFORMANCE

## THE FIX IS IN AT HOME DEPOT

Fixing up the old homestead, that is. This champion supplier of the do-it-yourself-prone shows it's possible to provide top-of-the-line service at bargain-basement prices.

■ by Bill Saporito

9.23

**9.24**

The treatment here is similar to that of the previous example but uses a more unusual divider between deck and byline. The white space on this page has been consciously manipulated to make each element distinct and invitingly brief yet remain cohesive as a part of the whole page. *Chicago*

**9.25**

This byline is part of the third level of display type. Its boldness makes it more visible than the deck, trumpeting the author's importance. *American Heritage*

**9.26**

The ultimate marriage of byline and deck is to incorporate the author's name into the descriptive copy. The formal typographic relationships on this page are enriched by the warm red *TASTE*. The bios and pictures of major contributors, including the author of this article, are on the editor's page at the front of this magazine. *Mirabella*

9.24

9.25

9.26

GRAB BAG

# Monuments to Romance

BY HARRY DEVLIN

The development of my personal interest in architecture—specifically 19th-century houses—can be traced back to my college years. The journeys between my home in Elizabeth, New Jersey, and Syracuse University were frequent and the routes I took were varied. Those were late Depression years and the roads through Pennsylvania and New York were memorable for their noble houses in sad decay.

On leaving Elizabeth for the journey north, the first structure to fire my youthful imagination was a hotel, the Cochran House of Newton, New Jersey, which has since been destroyed. It was a masterpiece of carpenter's lace and latheman's art. On Route 11, in Great Bend, I saw my first Greek Revivals. A little further on, at the approach to Binghamton, there rose a great deserted Victorian that might have been home to the Magnificent Ambersons.

Another, in Flemington, New Jersey, was Roselawn (my painting of which is shown above). Roselawn grew from the viewer's

*Adapted from Portraits of American Architecture. Copyright 1989 by Harry Devlin. Published by David R. Godine, Horticultural Hall, 300 Massachusetts Avenue, Boston, Mass. 02115.*

left to right. The original house under the tall, leaning chimney was a farmhouse built in the earliest years of the 19th century. Sometime in the 1870s the Italianate porch was added and in the 1880s the Stick style elements were attached. The Second Empire tower was possibly part of another house moved to the site. In time a *porte cochere*, extended porches, and a 20th-century addition were added at the right. In the center of the building a cube with a slight Mansard roof was built on the porch. Legend insists that it was a fresh-air infirmary for the ailing wife of the owner.

Since this portrait was painted, the exterior of Roselawn has been handsomely restored, and the reds, blues, and creams make the splendid old house at the end of the town a source of community pride. In 1987 developers razed half of the structure to accommodate an out-of-scale office building entirely alien to the community. Residents of Flemington were outraged.

Roselawn is among more than 60 structures featured in *Portraits of American Architecture*, a volume of text and 72 paintings capping my 40-plus years as an artist and enthusiast of Victorian architecture.

There is a yearning to know more about an old house—to see beyond the bricks, wood, and mortar into a dwelling that may have sheltered generations of a family or, perhaps, nurtured the tangled plot of a Gothic tale. In writing and painting *Portraits of American Architecture* I wish to encourage that very romanticism by celebrating the Victorian era in America, an epoch that produced vital, exuberant, and miraculous architectural expressions—miraculous because the extraordinary circumstances and climate of the period will never occur again.

**HARRY DEVLIN'S** artistic career spans nearly all of the 50-plus years since his graduation from SU in 1939. Having served during World War II as an artist in Navy intelligence, he became a successful and frequent illustrator for such national magazines as *Life*, *Collier's*, and *Saturday Evening Post*.

Devlin has illustrated 16 children's books written by his wife, Wende, and from that experience he decided in 1965 to produce an informal primer for children on domestic architecture, titled *To Grandfather's House We Go*. It became the first of a series. His latest book, *Portraits of American Architecture*, is excerpted in this article.

48 • SYRACUSE UNIVERSITY MAGAZINE

9.27

---

## "If People Pull Down Nature..."

Last spring a friend and I went for a walk through the neighborhoods surrounding Swarthmore, Pennsylvania.

*by Richard Louv*

50 • SEPTEMBER/OCTOBER 1990

9.28

---

ARCHAEOLOGY in the CLASSROOM

Last year, more than 250,000 children across the United States and Canada were able to watch, and even maneuver, a robot exploring two American naval vessels from the War of

*Pictures telecast by the remotely controlled robot Jason included ... this image of an 18-pound carronade on the starboard side of the schooner Hamilton. The ship sank during the War of 1812 and is now at the bottom of Lake Ontario.*

# HIGH-TECH

by ANNA MARGUERITE McCANN

66 ARCHAEOLOGY

9.29

---

## With text

**9.27**
This byline is placed between two hairline rules and replaces the first two lines of text in the middle column. The bio is interestingly handled: a portrait bumps out of a 20 percent warm gray screen tint, which defines the bio's space. *Syracuse University Magazine*

**9.28**
Wrapping the text around the byline makes the author's name at once visible and honored, like a framed work of art. The ornamental leaves are printed in colors selected from the main illustration. *Sierra*

**9.29**
This boxed byline is partially embedded in the text and partially hangs into the wide outer margin, which it shares with a detail photo and an unavoidably tempting caption. *ARCHAEOLOGY IN THE CLASSROOM* is knocked out of a bar that represents a file folder's tab. The bio is at the bottom of the facing page, where readers can find it quickly. *Archaeology*

## In a separate
## column

### 9.30

A narrow 7-pica column on the outside margin is designed into the format of this publication to hold decks, hanging initials, and bylines and bios. The remaining dedicated white space lightens and brightens each page, making it look less weighty and more attractive. *American Printer*

### 9.31

A bold lead-in to the text umbrellas a very small, very tightly cropped portrait. Except for the department heading *ADS* (printed in purple), the byline and headline combination is the largest type on the page. Notice how wonderfully that outside column of whiteness has been used. It shows off each of the most important elements on the page: the department heading, the byline/headline, and primary visual. *Blitz*

9.30

9.31

● UPFRONT ● **POLARIZED RELATIONSHIPS** ● **RELAXATION TIPS** ●

# PERSON TO PERSON WITH DR. POPE

My husband and I can't stop fighting. I say he starts it. He says I do. In the beginning, we seemed so "together." Now we are opposite about everything. I want to talk it through. He walks away and continually avoids discussion. When we do talk, I seem to cry a lot and he becomes even more rational and intellectual. I think we need more time together. He thinks we need space. How can I convince him I'm right?

Suzanne Pope, Ph.D., is clinical director of the Colorado Institute for Marriage and the Family in Boulder, Colo.

Couples tend to fight around the very things that attracted them to each other in the first place. If your husband was attracted to you for your warmth and sensitivity, he now finds you too emotional and too dependent. If you were attracted to his apparent power and clear idea of who he was, you now complain that he's selfish and doesn't care enough about his marriage.

In the beginning of a relationship, people are usually attracted to some characteristic in their partners that they feel they lack in themselves. It's as if the union creates a necessary balance, as well as the possibility that some of the desirable characteristic might rub off.

Some examples of the characteristics that complement each other in relationships are: thinking/feeling, responsible/carefree, aggressive/passive, and optimistic/realistic.

However, over time, each person begins to view their partner as becoming *too extreme* in the very characteristic that once was attractive. The "optimist" becomes the *eternal optimist* who can never address a problem, so nothing ever gets discussed or solved. The "realist" becomes a *wet blanket*, who always sees what's wrong with a new idea and has a list of complaints or problems for anyone who'll listen. Interestingly, the couple still *balance* each other, but to do so they have had to play extreme versions of their former roles.

This polarization occurs when a series of misunderstandings or misreadings of each other are not checked out or discussed. The optimist simply sees

his partner up, so he becomes more optimistic, and vice versa.

Sometimes external stressors, such as financial or career problems, can contribute to these positions becoming even more extreme and rigidly held. Each person is convinced that they are right in holding this perspective. After all, you might think, isn't it necessary given your partner's position?

Breaking the cycle requires moving out of the *extreme position.* A good start is to consider that perhaps you have inadvertently helped to create your partner's position by being so extreme in your own.

All it takes is one person to begin acting or talking like their spouse—in essence, assuming your partner's position—to create a significant change.

Try taking a less extreme version of your position—or, better yet, reverse roles altogether. Ironically, you may find that the role your husband has been playing is one that you identify with, also. You just haven't been able to experience it because your spouse has taken the position first.

For one month, don't try to talk everything through. And when you do talk—hopefully initiated by him—draw on the more rational and intellectual side of yourself— the parts you haven't been relying on so much lately. Put your emotional side back on the shelf for a while. Let him begin to feel emotions, if there are any to be expressed, without being inundated by your well-developed emotional tidal wave. Develop your own outside interests and need for space. It might be a relief to take the burden of solving the "relationship problem" off your shoulders for a while.

If you worry about the relationship a little less and become more preoccupied with taking care of yourself, your husband has room to worry about your marriage a little more. The two of you have a chance to assume the original balance that attracted you to

9.32

---

# Star
## Properties

*Hollywood's decorators are sorcerers' apprentices. The sorcerers are the movie stars, directors, studio bosses, and agents who hire them to realize*

their fantasy blueprints. These clients, after all, can afford both budgets thanks to their own track records creating dreams for other people. Decorators to the stars turn the stuff of such dreams—often expressed in a client's chance phrase or a phrase ripped from a magazine—into just the right creation screening room or long red swimming pool or hillside of cactus and pepper trees. More akin in spirit to movie set designers than to Park Avenue schoolmarch/housewife crowd, Hollywood's most successful decorators are a checkered and eclectic group.

The best-known member of the group is **Waldo Fernandez**, a team player who is a co-owner of Trumps, a fashionable power restaurant, as well as the driving force behind Waldo's Designs, where he sells his sodeum "California look" furniture. Forty-three-year-old Fernandez is a recognizable figure, tooling around

town in his black Bentley Turbo R, sporting an Armani suit or, more often, jeans and T-shirt, strolling through his silvery black mustache, and greeting friends in a warm lilting accent that unearths his Cuban roots. In recent years Fernandez has grown away from the "Waldo look" once unlike the Michael Taylor look) that made his interiors so recognizable from his first job for director John Schlesinger in the early seventies, on through the houses of luminaries like Elizabeth Taylor. "I could do it with my eyes closed," Fernandez now says of the overstate white-on-white or beige-on-beige sofas and oversized tables awash in natural light that made him famous.

Having started out as a Twentieth Century Fox set designer for *Doctor Dolittle*, *Planet of the Apes*, and *Hello, Dolly!*, Fernandez is experimenting these days with a few cinematic interiors. He is at work on a hairdressing

**By Brad Gooch**  Produced by Charles Gandee
**Photographs by Tim Street-Porter**

### Contributors Notes

**Dorothea Walker,** who has been an HG contributing editor for forty-five years, searches for the imaginative and original in San Francisco-area interior design. One of her greatest finds was decorator Michael Taylor, the subject of her article in this month's issue. "I first met Michael who he was in his early twenties. Whenever he'd come to my house, he'd always tell me what he thought was wrong with it. Despite his frankness, it was clear he had an extraordinary talent."

**Tim Street-Porter** left his native London for California twelve years ago and has since focused his camera on his surroundings. "The whole of L.A. is like one large outdoor studio that has excellent light, climate, and architecture." Street-Porter helped bring the California issue to life by capturing Expert creative director Stone Tompkins at work and play and by presenting some of L.A.'s hottest decorators at home. He is working on two photography books, a compilation of L.A. residences and a history of fireplaces.

**Dania Martinez Davey** sees her role as HG's new art director as a chance to sharpen her eye for the telling detail. "When laying out a story, I first approach the images as a journalist trying to tell an engaging story. Then I go back and act as a designer, aiming to pictures that highlight a single detail or motif that will catch the reader's attention because it's wild or intriguing." In her fifteen years for the California issue she across an earlier spin-seasonal West Coast style—"designs that leave little distance between indoors and out."

9.33

---

**9.32**

The bio appears beneath a protracted quote, which is really a question to which the author addresses her response. The bio is set flush right across a maximum measure of 7 picas and is accompanied by a playful rule system for emphasis. *Your Personal BEST*

**9.33**

This byline appears at the bottom of the opening page's text, a fairly common approach. But the bio appears on a separate page (not just in a separate column), up front under the department heading *CONTRIBUTORS NOTES*. The idea is to lure readers into articles by making the contributors worthy of their own pages. Readers survey the contributors and then cross-reference them, via the contents listings, with their articles. *HG*

With
magery

9.34
Department authors are each shown in a
black-and-white photo mortised in a
color swatch that fades at the bottom. The
fading panel ends just before the text begins with a noteworthy initial. The byline
is placed just beneath the photo.
*MacGuide Magazine*

9.35
This byline overlaps the image in three
discrete bars. The bio is sandwiched between two 1-point rules, printed red, beneath the first column of text. *Xploration*

9.36
This byline is literally made into an illustration by becoming a hockey puck (the
story is about two New Yorkers who play
in the National Hockey League). The type
was bound to a circle and reversed out of
black. *Sports Illustrated*

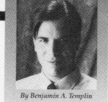

EDITOR'S LETTER

# Talking 'Bout A Revolution

By Benjamin A. Templin

A lot has been written about the revolution the Mac caused in publishing. Desktop publishing not only spawned a cottage industry of newsletter and brochure typesetters, it also changed the way traditional publishers put together their books, magazines and corporate reports. That the Mac made it so easy for "anyone" to publish good-looking documents caused the "professional" operators a little anxiety. And they have good cause to be nervous. Just like the first, there's a second revolution on the horizon — in color desktop pub-

Good things come in threes, and the third revolution you'll be seeing is in *MacGuide* itself. In our January issue, you saw our new look and feel. Now, with the debut of the monthly, you get a taste of *MacGuide* on a more regular basis. In addition to our color DTP coverage, you'll enjoy articles relating to doctors, lawyers, engineers, salespeople and business executives. Then check out our new reviews section, "GuideLights," for miscellaneous products. Other new additions include Jahan Salehi's "Open Line" column which will focus on communications issues, ranging from on-line services to hard-wiring a Mac to other, less friendly computers.

You'll find divergent opinions on Apple's treatment of *System* software. Steven Bobker sees potential for Apple's treatment of the OS in "The Last Byte," while Larry Husten rallies against Apple's policy in his new "Power Utilities" column.

In any revolution, some traditions and policies must inevitably change. As Macintosh products become more sophisticated, so has the way we judge those products. To see how we've fine-tuned the *MacGuide* review process, read

9.34

9.35

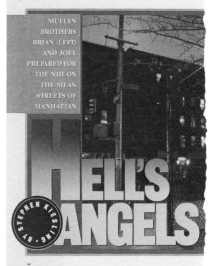

9.36

# 10

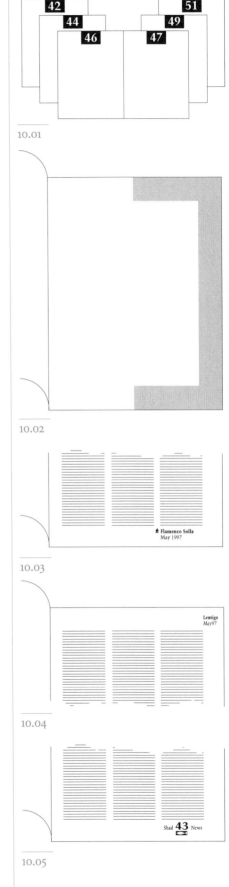

10.01

10.02

10.03

10.04

10.05

**Folios are page numbers.** They are odd on right-hand pages and even on left-hand pages (fig. 10.01). Right-hand pages are called *rectos*, which is Latin for "right," while left-hand pages are called *versos*, which is Latin for "reverse."

Folios must be easily visible to readers who have visited the contents page and are flipping rapidly through a publication to find a particular article. At minimum, folios must be positioned consistently. The outside margin and the outer half of the head or foot margin are obvious locations because they are the most visible parts of the page (fig. 10.02). It is not necessary to put a folio in the lower outside corner, where it traditionally seems to have been stuck and is now placed by default.

A foot line, so named because it typically appears at the bottom of the page, contains the name of the publication and the publication date (fig. 10.03). The foot line is also called a running foot or a footer. When it is placed at the head of the page, it is called a running head or header (fig. 10.04). The foot line is useful for readers who tear stories out for future reference or for passing on to others because the content is particularly well written and valuable. With a foot line, the source of the story is automatically recorded.

Folios and foot lines should be combined into a single perceived element on the page, to reduce the bits and pieces that make a page look sloppy. Their combination is a design opportunity that can dra-matically enhance the overall appearance of a publication with very little effort. As in any multi-element relationship, the issue of comparative emphasis must be addressed. Emphasizing the folio over the foot line in this relationship will make it more findable (fig. 10.05).

The folio/foot line unit can be centered at the foot or at the head of the page (fig. 10.06). It can be aligned with the edge of a text column, looking eccentrically off-center (fig. 10.07). It can be in the upper outer corner or the lower outer corner (fig. 10.08). It can be in the outside margin, where the page-turning thumb goes (fig. 10.09). Or it can be elsewhere in the outside margin.

The folio/foot line can be embellished with rules or with bullets (fig. 10.10). It can be placed in a shape (fig. 10.11). It can be connected to the edge of the page (fig. 10.12). Or it can be integrated with imagery (fig. 10.13), particularly useful in feature stories when the art conveys some significant aspect of the story.

It is not necessary to have a folio/foot line on every page, particularly, for example, if every story opens on a recto. A

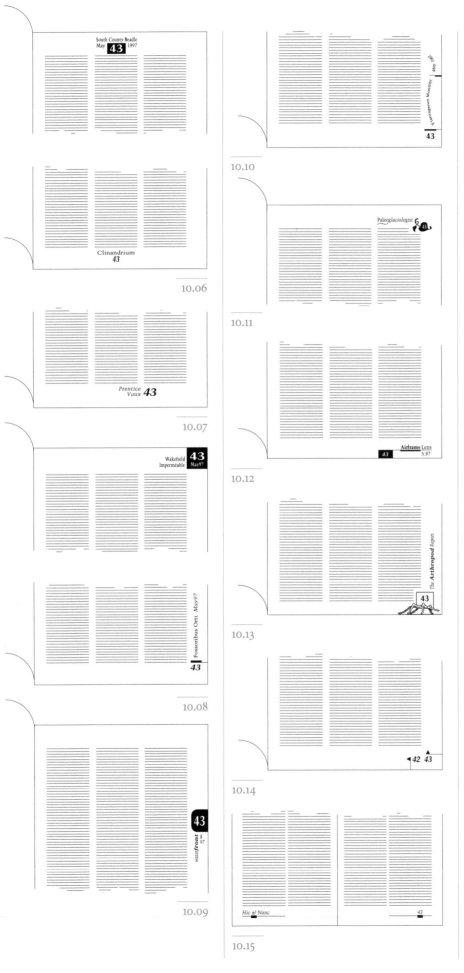

10.06

10.07

10.08

10.09

10.10

10.11

10.12

10.13

10.14

10.15

variation of the recto-only folio is including both folios on only one page (fig. 10.14). It is also possible to place the folios, for example, only on rectos, and foot lines only on versos (fig. 10.15). Or put folios on every page, and split the foot line so the publication title appears only on versos and the publication date only on rectos.

Creating unexpected folios and foot lines enhances your publication's personality. Use the following examples as ideas, developing and altering them to achieve unity with your other display typography.

juice. The RDA is 60 mg.

**Microwave alert:**

Containers and packages used in microwave cooking may be releasing potentially harmful synthetic chemicals into food—even when they're labeled "microwave safe," reports the Center for Science in the Public Interest. *Problem:* The FDA doesn't regulate microwave cling wraps, dishes and containers. In addition, a 1988 study found that *every* microwave "heat-susceptor" (thin pieces of metalized plastic included in packages to brown food products) tested released harmful substances into food.

Heat the oil in a large no-stick frying pan over medium-high heat. Add the links and sizzle until burnished on all sides, about 8 minutes. *Serves 4.*

*Note: Serve warm with whole-grain toast. Or make quick breakfast sandwiches by filling pita halves with shredded lettuce and turkey links.*

buttermilk and ¼ cup all-fruit apricot preserves in a blender.

◆ Combine the juice and pulp of 2 oranges with ¼ cup maple syrup in a blender and process until smooth.

◆ Blend chopped fresh fruit, such as peeled kiwi, with lime juice.

◆ Heat 1 cup frozen raspberries with 1 teaspoon honey in a small saucepan. Bring to a boil and cook for a few minutes to reduce slightly. *Serves 4.*

BODY BULLETIN ▼ NOVEMBER 1990
**2**

10.16

...RLD

*LEFT: BOB WAGNER. STYLED BY EVA PUSTA.*

...at Paris, disregarding the dozens of shiny ... parked in front.

Right at the corner, a visit to Cartier is a "must." Between imposing gold columns, exquisite windows show off the firm's latest line of jewelry, Indes Galantes, which is based on designs done in the early 1900s by Cartier for Indian royalty, using pearls, carved gems, gold, and platinum. Indeed, there is enough sparkle to illuminate a maharaja's palace. The pièce de résistance of the collection is a dramatic necklace with carved green agates that sells for 91,000 francs, about $18,000. More reasonably priced are small brooches in the form of ladybugs, bees, tigers, and elephants: to let your entourage know that you are a friend of nature.

Louis Vuitton, down the street, offers a dazzling choice of classic luggage. Are you tired of those now ubiquitous initials? (They became Vuitton's trademark back in 1896 and have been around for nearly a century.) If so, the leather purses and carry-

...Royce and Bentley ... that are always...

PAN AM CLIPPER
FEBRUARY 1991 **27**

10.17

The multi-task capabilities of future workstations will result partly from advances in "connectivity." This is the ability to link computers with facilities such as faxes and printers on each office floor into local area networks (LANs), and then, using fibre optics, to connect LANs into communications networks extending across the country.

"Using industry-standard LANs, we will dramatically increase the applications which can be performed at the branch level. It will be easier, for example, to

extended to most Royal Bank locations during the 1990s, says Mr. Heckman.

These networks will in turn be backed up by satellite communications, which will also be used for transmission to remote areas and for offering improved service in mobile branches.

**Long-distance meetings**
One of the most useful services to be offered via new telecommunications networks will be videoconferencing. Such facilities, which enable employees in

quiries, transactions and sales of all banking products and services.

The Service Reference File will expand to include important additional client data and will continue to be the cornerstone of many new business and systems initiatives. This computerized file will provide a complete picture of each client by linking personal, financial and service information. It will be an important factor in the successful 1990s implementation of our sales and service program.

*Please turn to page 25*

interest · March 1990 · page 16

10.18

Vol 4, No. 9                                        September 1990

$2.25

**LOSE WEIGHT** *naturally*

N E W S L E T T E R

**Fit and Fabulo...**

T hank you. Jane, Cher, Sylvester and Raquel. You have shown us that reaching 40 doesn't have to mean it's time to throw in the towel in the Battle of the Bulge. But what most of us in our 40s would like to know is, can we achieve long-term slenderness without a constant struggle? Or must we fight creeping middle-age spread with the vengeance of a Rambo?

...causes. For the other 30 percent, heredity is the problem. That's good news, parents, because it means there's a lot you and your child can do to get that excess weight off.

*Taking Action*
Before you do anything, though, it's critical to get your pediatrician's advice. While you may think your child is overweight compared to her friends or siblings, children vary. A doctor can provide an objective assessment and determine how serious the problem is—or if there really is a problem at all.

If the child is overweight, restricting calories until the child loses weight is, at best, impractical, and at worst, potentially dangerous. What overweight children need is a flexible, low-fat eating plan to follow, in which portion size and between-meal snacking are kept to moderate levels.

...a walk in a zoo, make a resolution to do family fitness activities together every week.

*In with the New*
On the food front, the first thing you need to do is look inward. In your refrigerator. In your cabinets. In your oven. Are you really buying and preparing low-fat, high-fiber foods? Are the cabinets clear of fatty chips and cookies and has your freezer been declared an ice-cream-free zone?

At home, move the focus away from food. When the family gathers to play games or talk, do it away from the dining room and the kitchen. Make a new rule: No eating anywhere in the house except at the dining table. Everyone has to abide by this rule, including the grown-ups.

Support your child's school program that teaches good nutrition in the classroom. Get the PTA and school authorities to ban junk

...weight loss be on the agenda. And that should be initiated only after weight gain has stopped and after the entire family is eating healthy foods. Then you can explore with a physician a safe way for a child to lose 5 to 10 percent maximum of weight at the rate of a pound or two a week, over 5 or 6 weeks.

Weight loss should then stop, and children should stay at that level for several months before losing any more, if indeed they still need to lose. Weight-loss diets for children must be constructed carefully by pediatricians or pediatric nutritionists and should always include a 10 percent increase in physical activity.

*Dr. Blackburn is an associate professor of surgery at Harvard Medical School and chief of the Nutrition/Metabolism Laboratory at New England Deaconess Hospital, Boston.* ●

LOSE WEIGHT **5** *naturally*                September 1990

10.19

---

## At the foot of the page

**10.16**
The foot line contains the name of the publication, the publication date, and ordinarily also includes the folio. This example's folio and the triangle just above it are printed red. *Body Bulletin*

**10.17**
This folio/foot line uses horizontal rules to encase the information. The folio is set to match the combined height of the other elements, making it an easily managed unit at the bottom outer corners. *Pan Am Clipper*

**10.18**
The folio/foot line unit can be centered at the foot or the head of the page. This one is reversed from a 12-point black bar that hangs from a hairline box rule surrounding each page. *Interest*

**10.19**
The foot line is useful for readers who tear stories out for future reference. This publication, complete with recipes, certainly benefits its readers by running such information. The publication's title is set in a combination of condensed sans serif caps with italic serif lower-case to replicate the logo, an excellent connection between outside and inside. *Lose Weight Naturally*

10.20
The folio/foot line may be embellished with rules or bullets. The folio here is emphasized by having been set bold, which makes finding a page while flipping through the issue easier. *Southwest Spirit*

10.21
The format of this publication uses a narrow 8-pica column on the outside of each page. The folio/foot line, department headings, and captions are all that appear in it, making these elements extremely visible. The bold 4-point rule emphasizes the title. *Step-by-Step Electronic Design*

10.22
Folios and foot lines should be combined into a single element. This handsome centered unit is centered at the foot of each page. *Vis á Vis*

---

...into a company problem, and you delivered the report of your investigation in person, you would probably begin by saying something like this: "You asked me to check into the sales drop-off in Lubbock. Well, this is what I found out. . . ." The opening words of your communication would be clear, direct, straight to the point.

But many people, if asked to put the same report on paper, would communicate in a far different way. Believing that the tone of business writing must be formal and detached, they would

**20 SPIRIT**
MARCH 1991

...communications is to *communicate*—to transfer information from the mind of one person to another. You can best accomplish this objective, whether you are speaking or writing, by:
- Using plain language.
- Getting straight to the point.
- Avoiding a pretentious style.

Some communications experts insist we should write the same way we talk. I don't go quite that far. Verbal discourse tends to be laced with phrases ("See what I mean?" . . . "Listen to this" . . . "Hey, I'm telling you") that

And ...re are three ...ded people on the board-wiring line who complain the new soldering units are in an awkward location for them."

The general statement in the written report, about employee attitude, conveys an imprecise message. The real-life examples reveal the true picture. ●

*Howard Upton writes for business publications, including* The Wall Street Journal, *and lectures at the University of Wisconsin. His address: Upton Communications, P.O. Box 906117, Tulsa, Oklahoma 74112.*

10.20

---

be specified. The outer shape of the centermost blend became the inner shape of the next blend and so on until all the blends had been made ⑥. ☞ *A blend can be accomplished by selecting one, more or all points from each of the two shapes before choosing the blend tool. However, the transition between shapes will vary depending on which points are chosen. In general, the more similar the locations of the two points clicked with the blend tool, the smoother the transition.*

To accomplish the masking, Girard selected the lettering outline, chose Paint, chose None for both Stroke and Fill and clicked the Mask box to make the outline a clipping path. Then he completed the masking by choosing Send to Back from the Edit menu to put the clipping path in position behind the blend ⑥. ☞ *In Illustrator the mask must be behind the object to be masked.*

☞ *A grouped object cannot serve as a mask. If, instead of using a hand-drawn clipping path, you use an Illustrator primitive (a shape drawn with the rectangle or oval tool rather than with the pen) as a mask, you have to ungroup the shape first, because each primitive is really two objects grouped together — the outline and the center. After the object is ungrouped, choose the outline, assign it the characteristics of a mask through the Paint dialog box and choose Send to Back.*

Girard selected the clipping path and all blends and grouped them. Then he made another blended element (from white to light blue) and sent it to the back of the drawing to serve as the white of the eye. ☞ *Normally, a mask hides everything on the page except objects placed directly in front of it. But when a clipping (masking) path is grouped with other objects, only the objects grouped with the masking path are affected by the mask. Other objects on the page are not hidden.*

When masking was completed, Girard retrieved the unbridged lettering and moved it onto the blend-filled lettering. To complete the piece, he drew in the lettering for the words "of the" and then drew a background rectangle stroked with red and filled with process black. He used black again to draw filled rectangles to cover up the bridges between the letters (see page 1). Girard had found that even if the two lines that formed a bridge were directly on top of each other, the masked element would show through, so a patch was required to hide it.

☞ *When you create a complex clipping path in Illustrator 88, it's important to set Split Path Resolution in the Preferences dialog box to 0 to prevent the program from automatically breaking the path into smaller shapes in an attempt to reduce the complexity of the drawing. (In version 3.0 this is done by making sure that Split Long Paths On Save/Print is not selected.) Breaking the path in this way causes streaks of the masked element to show through just as bridging does. Although split-*

ting path was once important for efficient output of complex drawings, improvements in RIPs (raster image processors, the interpreters that tell the imagesetters where to place the PostScript dots for output) have reduced the need for it. To ensure that Linotronic output goes smoothly, you can specify RIP4.*

**TAVARUA**
Tavarua is a small Pacific island with a terrific surf break, as reflected in the logo for Tavarua Surf & Native Wear. Girard wanted a tapa cloth look for the logotype, so he used a technique he calls "Xerox distressing." He chose News Gothic Extra Condensed type from a book of type samples and enlarged it on a Xerox 1025 copier that the magazine staff purposely doesn't maintain beyond the minimum attention needed to keep it running ⑦. He scanned the result, opened it in Illustrator and autotraced it. ☞ *Placing control points by hand is a good way to construct the*

7 When the Tavarua logo was converted to Illustrator art, "Xerox-distressed" lettering was used as a template for tracing. When lettering from a sample book was enlarged on a photocopier, some of the irregularities resulted from enlargement; others (for example, the large "bite" in the top of the "D") were photocopier artifacts.

8 In the "Wild Blue Yonder" title art, hand-traced letters were arranged on ellipses. Portions of the ellipses were cut and used to replace the bottoms of the letters to ensure the right fit to the curves. Two masks were used — one for "Wild Blue" and one for "Yonder." Each mask was grouped with its blend.

Electronic Design    3

10.21

---

place. After a morning and afternoon of ploughing the fields, my brother and I often went for a ride on a four-wheel cart, which we had built from scratch, on the highway leading from Rio Piedras (our hometown) to San Juan—about a six-mile jaunt. The highway was almost empty in those days, so we had a great time pushing each other down the road. One afternoon we noticed a grassy hill that we thought would be exciting to ride down. So we did. When we got to the bottom, we were at the entrance of the exclu-

main reason I enlisted. As it turne... out, it was the best thing that could have happened to me, because I was able to devote myself to golf.

Back then we had maybe 400 or 500 golfers on the island. Now we have 10,000 or more. There are good reasons why they call Puerto Rico "Scotland in the Sun." We have nine 18-hole courses on the island. Four of these—which were designed by the maestro Robert Trent Jones, Sr.—belong to the sister resorts, the Hyatt Dorado Beach and the Hyatt Cerromar Beach, where I am the golf pro.
*Continued*

91
VIS a VIS
FEBRUARY 1991

10.22

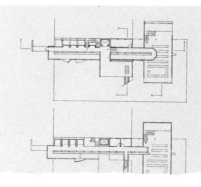

# NETWORK

December
1988

## NME to Construct First Comprehensive Specialty Hospital

## Two Hospitals Join PIA

National Medical Enterprises recently announced plans to construct the company's first comprehensive specialty hospital in Redding, Calif. The $13 million facility will comprise psychiatric, physical rehabilitation and substance abuse treatment services.

Norman A. Zober, Specialty Hospital

Redding," Zober said.

"Our new facility will eliminate a wait for admission to Redding Medical Center's physical rehabilitation and chemical dependency units, which currently operate at full capacity," explained Thomas J. Doherty, a Specialty Hospital Group executive vice president.

The new specialty hospital in North-

Psychiatric Institutes of America (PIA) opened a $9 million, 80-bed psychiatric facility near Palm Springs, Calif., in October, and acquired a 65-bed facility in Lafayette, La., in November.

The 54,000-square-foot Canyon Springs Hospital in Cathedral City will specialize in short-term psychiatric

10.23

Undergraduate Architecture
Elements of Architectural Design II

**103**

Spring 1989

The Photography
Library

Teemu Kurkela 1 4
Zeynep Celik, critic

Edward Kopel 2 3
Zeynep Celik, critic

10.24

for order. Then an elfin man stands, and the room grows quiet but for an insistent "shhhhhhh." Smiling shyly at the show of respect, Louis Devald speaks bluntly. He counters those like Rupke who argue that it is too risky to mortgage the Bradford Co-op's thriving chemical business to open a packing-house. "Look," says Devald, "even if it only breaks even, we all benefit if it moves our surpluses." A loud wave of consent swells around him. A voice calls for the vote. Others chorus, "Yeah."

Ten minutes later, when the vote is announced – "Seventy-five yes, twenty-five no" – there is a burst of applause and much scraping of chairs. Some bolt for the sagging food tables at the rear of the hall; others join the beer line at the bar. Shaking his head, Rupke strides out the door.

On the far side of the hall, under a huge mural of the marsh, Matthew Valk fans a fistful of photographs across a table. He has just returned from the American Northwest, where vegetables grow in Mount Saint Helens' backyard. "It's like the 1950s down there," he says, launching a tale of $20,000 houses, volcanic-ash soil that needs no fertilizer and a casual-labour rate of $3.50 per hour. "I told them we pay twice that, and they said, 'How do you do it?'" His work-weary listeners nod knowingly.

At 63, Valk is the marsh's guardian angel. Born in Rotterdam, this third-generation farmer has spent 42 years in the Holland Marsh, doing everything from "pulling carrots one by one" to managing farms. Valk says that cooperative marketing would solve a host of problems, but he doubts that it will ever happen. The memory of two bad years is all too easily erased by one good crop. A white-haired, blue-eyed man with an infectious laugh, Valk is now a consultant working out of a van equipped with a cellular telephone, a video camera and a weather radio. For 16 years, he headed the Muck Research Station, an experience about which he says, "Loved the job, hated the paperwork." Today, he stays in the field. "My wife says, 'What's this retirement all about? Now, you're working Saturdays and coming home at 8:00 at night.'"

As the meeting turns into a social gathering, several growers congratulate Devald on his speech. With but a few years of grade school behind him, Devald, 63, is a self-taught mechanical wizard. Eleven years ago, he welded together the first of two 12-metre-long dredges to clean silt from the canals, the first time he had ever built something that floated. Scant days before the launch of the first behemoth – 2 engines, 2 giant augers and 10 hydraulic pumps – consulting engineers were gleefully betting it would sink. It didn't.

Details of Devald's construction projects are hazy at best. He and his son-in-law Alex Makarenko never use drawings, just rough finger

sketches on the dusty shop floor. As Makarenko, 37, says, "Someone sweeps up, and there goes the blueprint." But they are known far and wide for making custom-built harvesters and planters for anyone who comes calling. They also build machinery for the 52-hectare onion and carrot farm run mainly by Devald's son Jack. Says Makarenko, "Jack breaks 'em; I fix 'em."

Born in Hungary's grape country, Devald has worked in the marsh

*Planting lettuce by hand, a Jamaican labourer kneels to his backbreaking task. The muck is tended by a wide range of nationalities, including migrant field hands flown in to work for minimum wage. Growers claim that unemployment insurance means locals do not need to sweat in the fields to earn a dollar.*

EQUINOX

10.25

## At the head of the page

10.23

When it is placed at the top of the page, a foot line is called a running head or header. The name of this publication, the date, and the pair of half-point rules are printed red. The initial caps that lead into the text are solid warm gray, and all else is black. *Network*

10.24

This elaborate system organizes several different kinds of information into a single element, united by hairline rules, creating an elegant tool for the transmission of content. *Abstract*

## Separated on the page

10.25

The folio and foot line can, of course, be separated. The folios here are located outside of the live area, in the upper outer corners. The foot line, in this case just the logo, is centered at the bottom of each page. This publication's simple, handsome layout and the consistent placement of the folio and foot line allow the elements to be separated without adding busyness. *Equinox*

10.26

The folio and foot line can be separated, one centered at the top and one at the bottom of the page. In this publication, the black backgrounds bleed to trim. This very unusual format is unique even for this publication: each issue of the quarterly is designed by a different designer. *Adeptations*

10.27

The folio is nearly halfway down the outside margin, and the foot line is placed just outside the live area at the bottom corner. These elements, which make use of extreme bold and light type and hairline rules, are in perfect keeping with this publication's design. *Sygeplejersken*

## In the outside margin

10.28

The folio/foot line can be in the outside margin, where the page-turning thumb goes. This treatment includes the title of the article or department above the folio, making it especially useful as a tab system. The type base lines hug the vertical rule, reading "up" on versos and "down" on rectos. *North Shore*

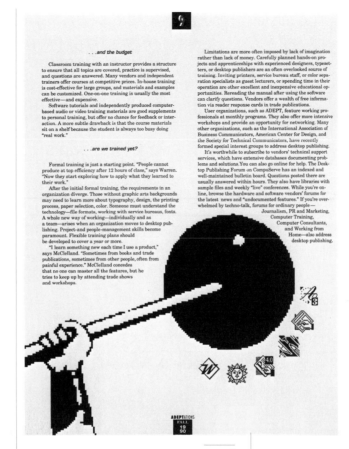

10.26

10.27

10.28

10.29

10.30

10.31

10.32

**10.29**

The folio/foot line can also go elsewhere in the outside margin. Notice the folio at the bottom is also stacked vertically. *Orientation '90*

### Aligned
### with a column

**10.30**

The folio can be aligned with the edge of a text column, looking eccentrically off-center. One column has an 8-pica measure and two have a 17-pica measure. The folio is aligned flush left with the first wide column. *The Trust Quarterly*

**10.31**

This folio is aligned with the outside edge of the center column and anchored to the page's perimeter. Knocked out of a blue-gray second color, it is asymmetrically positioned 18 picas from the outside trim. *interest NEWS*

### Other
### positions

**10.32**

This three-panel foldout publication uses migrating folios knocked out of 14-point black rules at the bottom of each page. The folio/rule unit is placed flush left on the left panel, centered on the center panel, and flush right on the right panel. *Potomac*

10.33
The folio's treatment can relate it to other typographic elements. A 12-point vertical bar is placed next to headlines and folios, creating a rhythmic pattern. *AmSouth Partners*

10.34
The folio/foot line can be placed in a shape. In this case it also appears in a different position on each page, printed with various screen tints and second colors. *Orientation '91*

10.35
It is not necessary to have a folio/foot line on every page. A blind folio/foot line is used on the recto of this opening spread. *Trump's*

10.36
The publication title and folio can be run on versos while the date and folio are run on rectos. These folio/foot line elements are positioned off-center, aligned flush right with the edge of the first column. *CA Magazine*

10.33

10.34

10.35

10.36

# 11

11.01

11.02

11.03

11.04

11.05

11.06

**For a very long time,** man could communicate only by making sounds. Direct knowledge lasted no longer than a single lifetime.

Humans began recording stories about the things around them by drawing on the walls of their caves. Paintings of objects became symbols, or **pictographs** (fig. 11.01). Pictographs show *things* and are highly representational: a drawing of a tree means a tree, a drawing of a cow means a cow. Essentially, language consisted entirely of nouns (people, places, and things), which made it very easy to learn. But as society developed and became more complex, symbols for things that could not be seen became necessary. Pictographs began to take on additional meanings. For example, a drawing of a cow could mean either a *cow* or *wealth,* since people used valuable cattle in trade. As pictographs were adapted into nonrepresentational symbols, it became necessary for people to learn their new meanings.

Many ideas required their own symbols, and these became the next step, called **ideographs** (fig. 11.02). Ideographs show *ideas* and *actions.* Though some ideographs were semirepresentational, as a group they required more learning to understand because they were essentially symbolic. This necessary learning separated societies into two groups: those who understood the written system and those who did not. A growing body of symbols developed, becoming increasingly difficult to learn. There was no connection between spoken and written language, so people had to learn two unrelated systems.

Eventually ideographs no longer satisfied the needs of the increasingly complex societies. A more flexible system was needed. Ideographs and pictographs evolved into new letter symbols that could be strung together into word clusters that were given meaning by those who had learned the system. For example, a *c* strung together with an *o* and a *w* became the symbol for an animal that was used for money and food. The new letterform system used smaller components that could be combined in many more ways but required much more learning to understand because they were not at all representational. The separation between those who knew how to write and those who did not continued to grow.

The Phoenicians, an extremely successful society of traders on the eastern shore of the Mediterranean Sea, developed a revolutionary new system in about 1800 B.C. that connected spoken sounds with writing. They identified twenty-two key sounds in their language and drew up twenty-two corresponding symbols, each representing one of the sounds (fig. 11.03). They logically reasoned that if the symbols were strung together as the sounds were, they could communicate with a greatly reduced vocabulary of symbols, and they could take advantage of the natural con-

abunt. Non fit impij nõ fic: fe
is que proijcit ventus a facie te
furgūt impij in iudicio: neœ pe
o iustor. Qm nouit dñs via i
r impior pibit. O ña pri, Of di
re fremuerūt getes : t ppli medita
nania, Afisterūt reges tre et pri

11.07

Nummus, et e pleno semper tollatur
Non unquam reputat, quanti sibi gau
unt quas eunuchi imbelles, ac molli:
Oscula delectent, et desperatio barbæ
t quod abortivo non est opus. Illa v
umma tamen, quod jam calida et m
nguina traduntur medicis, jam pecti

11.08

11.09

nection between verbal and written communication. Their invention – relating spoken and written sounds – is today called *phonetics*.

The Greeks adopted the Phoenician system around 1000 B.C., modifying it to their needs (fig. 11.04) by adding vowels and naming the letters.

The Romans took the Greek alphabet and made further changes, adding a *G* and *Z*, for twenty-three characters (fig. 11.05). Our modern alphabet subsequently gained three additional letters, the *J*, *U*, and *W*.

By writing quickly with pointers on wax tablets (which were easy to erase by smoothing over), Roman scribes, or writers, began joining letters together and, following the natural impulses of the human hand, introduced a slant to letters as well as ascenders and descenders, the parts of lower-case letters that extend beyond the main body of the characters (fig. 11.06).

After Rome's fall, the skill of writing was practiced in the western world almost exclusively in monasteries. With the exception of their illuminated manuscripts, not much written work was produced until the mid-fifteenth century, when movable type was invented.

Johannes Gutenberg (ca. 1397-1468) of Mainz, Germany, advanced the ability to communicate immeasurably by inventing an efficient system for attaching movable letters to a printing press. (There is some question about Gutenberg's having invented movable type. Ulrich Zell, a contemporary of Gutenberg's, wrote that a fellow named Laurens Coster of Haarlem, in the Netherlands, invented movable type in 1440, and that Gutenberg swiped the type and printed it in 1442. Two others, Pamfilo Castaldi of Italy and Procopius Waldfoghel of France, were also early movable-type printers. But Mainz seems to have become the center of printing, so Gutenberg gets the credit.)

Gutenberg, a goldsmith and craftsman capable of cutting punches – the molds into which molten metal was poured to make printable letters – invented movable type matrices and fit them to the printing press, which had been in use for centuries in China. His typeface was based on Textura,

the heavy black letters of handwritten manuscripts used at the time (fig. 11.07). His typeface has over three hundred letters, ligatures, and abbreviations, necessary for justification.

John Baskerville (1706-1775), a young and wealthy amateur, dedicated himself to perfecting the printing process. He set out to make his own paper, blend his own inks, and cut his own typefaces. Until then, paper was made on wire screens, which left a pronounced texture on the paper. Baskerville replaced the coarse screen with a fine mesh, which imparted a far smoother surface. Smoother paper allowed letters to be printed with greater detail and contrast between thicks and thins. So Baskerville designed a typeface, named for himself, that could take advantage of his new smoother paper. Baskerville is considered a transitional typeface, a major step forward from the preceding old-style faces (fig. 11.08).

More recently, typefaces have been developed to satisfy the needs and take advantage of modern technology. The 1938 ad in fig. 11.09 illustrates the aesthetic need for many typefaces. Stone, a typeface introduced in 1988, was designed specifically for digital reproduction.

The printed word has been in existence for only about 550 years. With it, millions of copies of a document can be made instantly; news and knowledge can be spread in minutes. Anyone can experience the culture and thought of past ages.

Today's use of type is based on centuries of typographic evolution, hundreds of improvements based on our need to record ideas in writing. Over the past centuries many improvements in the speed, accuracy, and precision of those written markings have evolved, from the development of the characters themselves to the technology of printing presses, paper, and inks. Each major step forward was driven by an improvement in available materials or by an opportunity to increase efficiency by speeding up some process.

The purpose of a printed document has always been to inform. The history of the written word's evolution is the history of the changing needs of society.

11.10

11.12

11.14

11.11

11.13

11.15

**B.C.**

**25,000**

Earliest known cave decorations drawn at Lascaux, France. This example is a tracing of a 27 -inch-long original (fig. 11.10).

**18,000**

Prehistoric handprints at Pech Merle cave in southern France are among the first recorded images consciously made by intelligent human beings (fig. 11.11).

**12,000**

First writing bones notched for counting.

**9000**

Mesopotamian clay tokens representing various livestock as well as quantities of goods.

**3100**

Earliest Egyptian hieroglyphics (Greek for "sacred carving"). *(See also* A.D. *1799)*

**3000**

Sumerian stone cylinder seals inscribed with names of individuals and organizations (fig. 11.12). • Sumerian pictograph writing (fig. 11.13).

**2800**

Sumerian cuneiform writing reads left to right.

**2500**

Egyptians write on dried pulp of papyrus, a giant swamp grass, and develop cursive script with reed pens. This drawing shows the harvesting of papyrus on the banks of the Nile (fig. 11.14).

**1600**

First alphabet developed in the Middle-East. Though it contains no vowels, its characters represent spoken sounds relating written and spoken communications for the first time.

**1500**

Chinese develop ideographs. This beautiful example means "tomorrow" and provides ample evidence for the belief that Oriental letterforms are works of art (fig. 11.15).

**1400**

Ten Commandments incised on stone tablets (fig. 11.16). • Egyptian Books of the Dead written on papyrus scrolls. Ability to make long rolls of papyrus allowed scribes to produce increasingly complex works (fig. 11.17) This example is from 600 B.C.

**950**

Phoenician traders bring alphabet to Greece.

**850**

Semites use first punctuation: vertical strokes separating phrases.

**800**

Greeks develop alphabet by adding vowels. They employ the boustrophedon ("as the ox plows") system, reading alternately left to right and right to left.

**625**

Babylonian cuneiform writing used wedge-shaped letters pressed into wet clay (fig. 11.18).

**600**

Earliest known dictionary written in central Mesopotamia, indicating need for various peoples to understand common words.

**585**

Torah, first five books of the Bible, written by exiles in Babylon to record history of the people of Israel.

**470**

First library created in Athens, though collections of religious texts existed since 3500 B.C. in some houses of worship.

**450**

Carrier pigeons used to speed Greek communication (fig. 11.19).

**402**

Aramaic script marriage contract (fig. 11.20).

**300**

Alexandria, the world's center of culture, has two libraries with 500,000 scroll books.

**256**

Chinese invent paintbrushes made of hair.

11.17

11.16

11.18

11.19

11.20

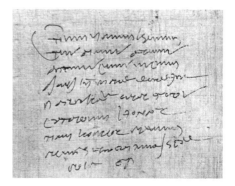

11.21

11.22

INGENTISTOLLEN
VERBERALENTAPA
SEDNONVELAMA
QVAMVENIREME
SIVEBOVMSIVEES

11.23

ERENSOSDOMITAREBOVES
ODERENONAFVGNEMELIOR
VITAADEOGELIDAMELIVSS
TICVMSOLENOVOTERRASI
OCTELEVESMELIVSSTIPVLA

11.24

Adinuicem dicen
uodest hocuerb
uia inpotestate e
imperat spiritib

11.25

**200**

Parchment developed in Pergamum, now beneath the modern city of Bergama, Greece, when papyrus supply from Egypt was temporarily interrupted.

**144**

Greek cursive script on papyrus (fig. 11.21).

**131**

*Acta diurna*, first newspapers, appear as official announcements hung in Roman streets.

**A.D.**

**48**

Roman soldiers invade Alexandria and destroy libraries.

**105**

Ts'ai Lun reports paper made from tree bark, cloth fiber, and fishnets in China.

**114**

Capital letters cut into Trajan's Column greatly influence letterform design (fig. 11.22).

**140**

Square capitals develop in Rome. Their squareness is dictated by the technique of stone carving, in which curves were more difficult to create than straight lines (fig. 11.23).

**150**

Books of folded parchment (a codex) begin replacing scrolls.

**300**

*Rustica*, simplified roman capitals, develop. They are slightly condensed to save valuable vellum (fig. 11.24).

**320**

Emperor Constantine has Bible copied into bound vellum books. It could take a single scribe years to duplicate one copy of the Testaments.

**350**

Uncials, rounded capital letters, develop in Rome (fig. 11.25).

**400**

Wood blocks used to print textiles in Egypt. • Black ink invented in China.

**450**

Half-uncials develop to ease writing with a pen on animal skin. The strokes become more rounded and easily rendered, introducing lower-case letters (fig. 11.26).

**476**

Monks illuminate hand-copied manuscripts as the early Middle Ages begin, developing dozens of character variations to make each line equal in length. This "justification," or evenness of column edges, is intended to please God with perfection (fig. 11.27).

**600**

Paper making spreads from China to Japan and west to Persia.

**770**

Japanese Empress Shotoku sanctions first printing on paper: a million prayers to ward off smallpox epidemic.

**800**

*Book of Kells,* Celtic illuminated masterpiece, completed.

**807**

"Flying money," money made of paper, used in China.

**814**

Arabs adopt Indian numerals, 0–9.

**850**

Carolingian script developed at court of Charlemagne: the Bible, Isaiah 58:1 on vellum (fig. 11.28).

**863**

Cyrillic alphabet, based on Greek, developed by missionaries to Moravia, now a part of Czechoslovakia.

**1000**

*Beowulf* manuscript written on vellum in Anglo-Saxon, a precursor to English language (fig. 11.29).

**1035**

First use of paper as packaging for vegetables and spices in Egypt. • Waste paper first recycled into new paper.

11.26

11.27

11.28

11.29

11.30

11.31

**1041**

Pi Sheng invents movable type made of baked clay and glue in China. The sculpted letters were glued onto a metal sheet, printed, and removed from the sheet for reuse. Carved wooden characters were developed about two hundred years later.

**1100**

Earliest use of paper in Sicily.

**1157**

Jean Montgolfier, one of first in Europe, begins making paper in Vidalon, France, after learning the trade in a Damascus paper mill as a prisoner.

**1200**

Textura, or Gothic, develops, so named because it produces the look of woven texture. Legibility was not the chief concern of this condensed handwriting style. Fitting many characters into a small space was. In fact, it fit about twice as many characters into the same space as its predecessor, Carolingian.

**1221**

Chinese develop movable type made of wood blocks.

**1250**

Goose quill first used for writing.

**1328**

*The Book of Hours of Jeanne d'Évreux* was a small personal prayer book created for the queen of France (fig. 11.30, shown larger than actual size). This is a text page of the Office of Saint Louis depicting a soldier, two musicians – one with bagpipes – and, at the bottom, a physician with his patient.

**1340**

The decorative initial becomes a feature on manuscripts. Initial caps are today's legacy. Shown, in order, are initials from the 14th century (Gothic), 16th century (Italian), and 19th century (French) (fig. 11.31).

**1350**

Humanistic cursive derives from Carolingian. The humanists contributed greatly to the evolution of the lower-case letters.

**1370**

Library of Merton College, Oxford University, founded.

**1380**

John Wycliffe's English translation of the Bible (fig. 11.32).

**1390**

First German paper mill started by Ulman Stromer at Nuremberg (fig. 11.33).

**1400**

Medieval manuscripts are scribed by reed or quill on parchment made from the skin of sheep (fig. 11.34), or on vellum, a calfskin rubbed with lime and pumice. A single Florentine bookseller employs up to 50 scribes at a time.

**1418**

First European wood engraving.

**1445**

Chinese develop copper type.

**1448**

Johannes Gutenberg of Mainz invents movable type matrices and fits them to the printing press. His wooden typeface resembles Textura, the heavy black letter of handwritten manuscripts used in Germany at the time. His typeface has over 300 letters, ligatures, and abbreviations, necessary for justification.

**1450–1500**

Incunabula, Latin meaning "cradles," is the name for books printed in this 50-year period. The development of typecasting allowed 35,000 works to be printed in these first 50 years, for a total of 8 to 12 million copies. Printing spread very quickly: there were more than 1,000 printers in some 200 locations in Europe during this period.

**1455**

Gutenberg's 42-line-per-page Bible is first book printed from movable type. Until now, monks sometimes spent their entire lives writing a single book (fig. 11.35).

**1460**

Albrecht Pfister of Bamberg produces first book including both woodcut illustrations and text.

11.32

11.33

11.34

11.35

nic̨e has abigunt rubrica ac pice liqu
o iuxta in unū locum congregant:au
i & has & talpas amurca necant.Con
s felle cacumina tági iubét.Priuatim
uliere icitati mensis nudis pedibus r
rpat frondé fimo boum diluto aspar
luitur ita uirus medicaminis. Mira
auerti grandines carmine credát pler

11.36

And here begynnyth her tale +
I In olde dayes of kyng Artur
Of Whiche britons spekith gret honour
Al Was this lond ful filled of fayrye
The elf quene With her ioly companye
Daunced ful ofte in many a grene mede
This Was the olde opinion as I rede
I speke of many an hundred yeris a goo

11.38

11.37

11.39

E ffigiem'q; toro locat haud ignara futuri.
S tant aræ circum,et crines effusa sacerdos
T er centum tonat ore deos,Herebum'q; Chaos'q;
T er gemnam'q; Hecaten·tria Virginis ora Dianæ.
S parserat et latices simulatos fontis Auerni,
F alcibus et messæ ad lunam quæruntur ahenis
P ubentes herbæ nigri cum lacte ueneni,
Q uæritur et nascentis equi de fronte reuulsus,
E t matri præreptus amor·

11.40

1469
Johannes de Spira (a transplanted German originally named Johann von Speyer) opens the first printery in Venice and produces the first roman typeface. It is based on humanistic manuscripts produced in the area (fig. 11.36). • The gradual shift away from Gothic to humanistic or roman typefaces begins in Europe.

1470
Nicolas Jenson produces his roman typeface in Venice. His goal is to create an even color, rather than to perfect the beauty of individual characters. • A page from a blockbook showing the gospels looks much like a modern comic book (fig. 11.37).

1478
A year after producing the first book printed in England, William Caxton produces Chaucer's *Canterbury Tales* (fig. 11.38). Nearly all of Caxton's books are in English, a sharp departure from the rest of Europe, which publishes almost exclusively in Latin. Caxton, a merchant and diplomat, learned the art of printing in Cologne, then set up his press in his retirement. At the time, each area in England had its own spelling variations. Caxton adopted the spellings of the London area. These spellings, being the earliest printed versions, spread and are still in use today. For example, he gave us *right* instead of the then-common *richt*.

1493
A page from Hartmann Schedel's *World Chronicle*, the first important illustrated work in Europe (fig. 11.39).

1494
John Tate establishes first English paper mill in Hertfordshire.

1500
First use of black lead pencils in England.

1501
Aldus Manutius hires Francesco Griffo to produce first italic typeface, based on slanted handwriting. His typeface, which fit more characters into a given space than any roman typeface of the day, is ideal for the small, portable pocket books Manutius prints (fig. 11.40, shown actual size).

**1507**

Oldest known drawing of printing press (fig. 11.41).

**1513**

First illustrated English news pamphlet, *True Encounter*, gives eyewitness account of the Battle of Flodden (fig. 11.42). • News-letters develop as early form of newspaper to advertise trading house prices.

**1535**

First printing in New World by Esteban Martin and Juan Pablos in Mexico. • Claude Garamont produces Garamond typeface (the spelling of his name was changed on a Frankfurt specimen sheet in 1592) in France. Printers became their own type designers when they had to cut their own fonts (fig. 11.43).

**1550**

Folios, or page numbers, are introduced.

**1569**

Christophe Plantin of Antwerp begins Polyglot Bible, showing simultaneous translations in Latin, Greek, Hebrew, Aramaic, and Syriac, side by side. The finished work is published in 1572 (fig. 11.44).

**1592**

First known typeface "showing," or sampler, printed in Frankfurt.

**1605**

First public library founded in Rome.

**1609**

First weekly newspaper appears in Strasbourg: *Avisa Relation Oder Zeitung*.

**1611**

King James Version of the Bible completed. It had two issues, the "He Bible" and the "She Bible," due to a typo in Ruth 3: 15 (fig. 11.45).

**1620**

Blaeu press improves on Gutenberg's press. Early presses made uneven impressions, so letters could have little contrast between thick and thin strokes. The Blaeu press permits greater letterform contrast.

11.41

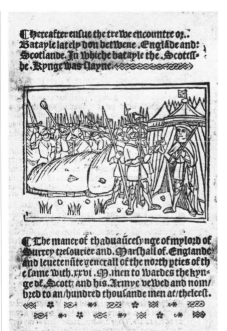

11.42

uilísque prudentiæ, Mediolani principem locum te-nuerunt.Incidit Galuanius in id tempus quo Medio-lanum à Federico AEnobarbo deletū eſt, vir ſumma rerum geſtarum gloria , & quod in fatis fuit, inſigni calamitate memorabilis . Captus enim , & ad trium-phum in Germaniam ductus fuiſſe traditur: ſed non multo póſt carceris catenas fregit, ingentíque animi

11.43

11.44

11.45

11.46

The Daily Courant.

Numb.

Wednesday, March 11. 1702.

11.47

11.48

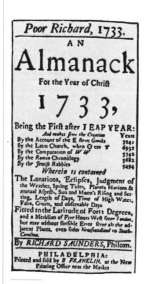

11.49

Quoufque tandem al
tientia noſtra ?quam
ror iſte tuus eudet? c
ſe effrenata jactabit a
noſturnum præfidiu
bis vigiliæ, nihil timo
ABCDEFGHIJ

11.49

11.50

Poor Richard, 1733.
AN
Almanack
For the Year of Chriſt
1733,

11.51

1631

*La Gazette de France*, first major French periodical, founded.

1639

Stephen Daye begins first North American printing press in Cambridge, Massachusetts.

1653

Boston public library opens.

1662

London is home to 60 publishers.

1663

Bible translated into Algonquin and printed in Boston (fig. 11.46).

1685

William Bradford begins printing in Philadelphia.

1690

First American paper mill founded in Philadelphia.

1702

*Daily Courant*, London's first daily newspaper, founded (fig. 11.47).

1704

*The Boston News-Letter*, first news weekly in America, founded.

1714

Englishman Henry Mill receives patent on typewriter. • Typical papermaking press used in the eighteenth century (fig. 11.48).

1720

William Caslon produces Caslon typeface. It is still in wide use today, attesting to its classic proportions and balance (fig. 11.49). Shown are original letterforms and Caslon 540 digital characters.

1721

Newspapers often depicted the city in which they were published near the title (fig. 11.50).

1723

Benjamin Franklin begins printing in Philadelphia. This example (fig. 11.51) was printed in 1733, using imported type made by Franklin's contemporary, William Caslon.

**1757**

John Baskerville, amateur Birmingham printer, develops three major innovations: his typeface Baskerville, which has pronounced thicks and thins, wove paper (for the first time, paper did not have an uneven surface created by the wire mesh that helps drain water in the paper-making process) that accepts thin character strokes better, and improved printing ink, which is smoother and denser (fig. 11.52).

**1764**

Englishman George Cummings receives patent for coating paper, allowing letterforms to develop thinner strokes.

**1766**

Pierre-Simon Fournier invents the point system, publishes *Manuel Typographique*, which begins the transition from old-style to modern typefaces (fig. 11.53, shown actual size).

**1780**

First steel-nib pen.

**1788**

John Bell of London is the first type designer to discontinue using the long *s*, which looks like a lower-case *f* in this typeface (fig. 11.54).

**1796**

Alois Senefelder of Munich invents lithography, using oily ink on smooth stone for printing.

**1798**

Senefelder's lithographed page of Mozart's *Die Zauberflöte* (Magic Flute) for quartet, written seven years previously (fig. 11.55).

**1799**

One of Napoléon's officers discovers the Rosetta Stone, which, after 40 years of decoding, reveals that Egyptian hieroglyphics is a two-tier alphabet, with some characters also representing ideas and objects. The Rosetta Stone is used to translate all other hieroglyphics (fig. 11.56).

**1800**

The London *Times* switches from wood to Stanhope presses, prints 250 sheets per hour, circulation 2,500.

*BIRMINGHAMIAE:*

Typis JOHANNIS BASKERVILLE.

MDCCLVII.

11.52

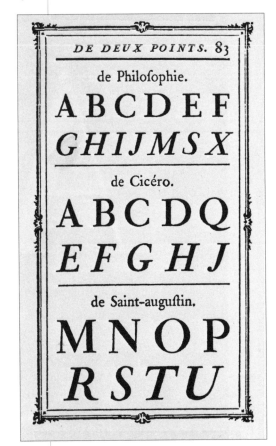

11.53

Quousque tandem abutere, Catilina, patientia noſtra? quamdiu nos etiam furor iſte tuus eludet? quem ad finem sese effrenata jaĉtabit audacia? nihilne te noĉturnum præsidium palatii, nihil urbis vigiliæ, nihil timor populi, *Quousque tandem abutere, Catilina, patientia noſtra? quamdiu nos etiam furor iſte tuus eludet? quem ad finem sese effrenata jaĉtabit audacia? nihilne te noĉturnum præsidium pala-*

11.54

11.55

11.56

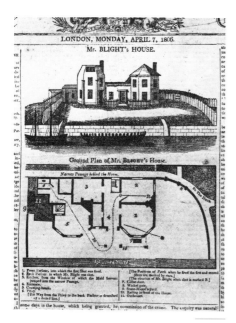

11.57

11.62

ABCDEFGHIJ
KLMNOPQRST

11.58

# LETTER

11.59

tête, Catilina, patientiâ
nostrâ? quamdiu etiam
furor iste tuus nos elu-
det? quem ad finem sese
*effrenata jactabit auda-*
*cia? nihilne te nocturnum*

11.60

**ABCDEFGH**
**a b c d e f g h**
**ABCDEFGH**
**a b c d e f g h**

11.61

11.63

**1806**
Robert's paper-making machine improved in England by Gamble and Donkin with financial help from Fourdrinier brothers, producing paper in continuous sheets. • The London *Times*'s first cover illustration shows the path of a murderer (fig. 11.57).

**1815**
Vincent Figgins designs Egyptian typeface unique with its heavy slab serifs, so named because Egyptian culture and artifacts were extremely popular at the time. Called a "typographical monstrosity" at first; later called "the most brilliant typographic invention of the 19th century" (fig. 11.58).

**1816**
First sans serif typeface introduced by William Caslon IV (fig. 11.59).

**1818**
Giambattista Bodoni's widow publishes *Manuale Tipografico* to Bodoni's specifications five years after his death (fig. 11.60). Bodoni cut about 300 fonts during his lifetime, all showing marked contrast of thicks and thins.

**1820**
"Fat Faces" introduced. Advertising typefaces are identifiable by their exaggerated thick and thin contrast. This, one of the earliest, was named Modern Canon (top, fig. 11.61). Today's Poster Bodoni, among others, carries on this tradition (bottom).

**1822**
Sans serif, or "grotesque," typefaces introduced in display sizes only. • French physicist Nicéphore Niepce (fig. 11.62) makes first photographic copy. The photograph, "Table Laid for a Meal," took 14 hours to expose. • J. L. Pouchée introduces typecasting machine that purports to make 200 characters at a time, thereby saving 12 percent on type manufacture. Though used for years in France, it was never adopted elsewhere and was ultimately a failure; Pouchée himself "took it out to sea and threw it overboard" (fig. 11.63).

**1835**
*New York Herald* founded: 4 pages for a penny.

1839
First use of daguerreotypes (early photographs) in European journals.

1851
*Daily Times* founded in New York City (renamed *The New York Times* in 1857).

1858
The London *Times* installs two huge 10-cylinder Hoe presses, which print 20,000 sheets per hour on two sides, circulation 57,000 (fig. 11.64).

1868
Octavius Dearing introduces the California typecase in San Francisco, a wooden box that organizes characters, making hand-setting type quicker and easier (fig. 11.65). • Christopher Sholes invents typewriter that is as fast as handwriting.

1872
Firmin Gillot of Paris perfects system for photoengraving from line drawings.

1873
The London *Times* installs Kastenbein's typesetting machine. First London daily to be typeset mechanically.

1880s
Elaborate, highly visible advertising typefaces proliferate This printer's composing stick illustrates how type was typically set (fig. 11.66).

1880
Stephen H. Horgan perfects halftone for use in newspapers.

1884
Lewis E. Waterman of New York invents the fountain-pen ink storage system. • Example of metal type (fig. 11.67).

1885
Ottmar Mergenthaler invents Linotype typesetting machine. Until now, all type was hand set one letter at a time, a method essentially unchanged since Gutenberg's invention in 1448 (fig. 11.68).

11.64

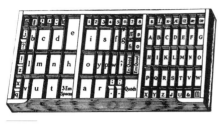

11.65

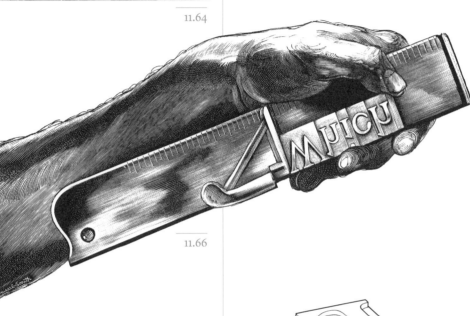

11.66

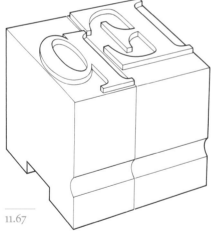

11.67

11.68

11.69

11.70

ABCDEFGHIJKLMNO
abcdefghijklmnopqrstu

11.71

ABCDEFGHIJKLMNC
abcdefghijklmnopqrstuvwxy

11.72

ABCDEFGHIJKLMNOPQRSTU
abcdefghijklmnopqrstuvwxyz

11.74

11.75

IN THE BEGINNING
GOD CREATED THE HEAVEN AND THE EARTH. ❧ AND
THE EARTH WAS WITHOUT FORM, AND VOID; AND
DARKNESS WAS UPON THE FACE OF THE DEEP, & THE
SPIRIT OF GOD MOVED UPON THE FACE OF THE WATERS.
❧ And God said, Let there be light: & there was light.
that it was good: & God divided the light from the darkness. And God called
the light Day, and the darkness he called Night. And the evening and the
morning were the first day. ❧ And God said, Let there be a firmament in the
midst of the waters, & let it divide the waters from the waters. And God made
the firmament, and divided the waters which were under the firmament from
the waters which were above the firmament: & it was so. And God called the
firmament Heaven. And the evening & the morning were the second day.
❧ And God said, Let the waters under the heaven be gathered together unto
one place, and let the dry land appear: and it was so. And God called the dry
land Earth; and the gathering together of the waters called he Seas: and God
saw that it was good. And God said, Let the earth bring forth grass, the herb
yielding seed, and the fruit tree yielding fruit after his kind, whose seed is in
itself, upon the earth: & it was so. And the earth brought forth grass, & herb
yielding seed after his kind, & the tree yielding fruit, whose seed was in itself,
after his kind: and God saw that it was good. And the evening & the morning
were the third day. ❧ And God said, Let there be lights in the firmament of
the heaven to divide the day from the night; and let them be for signs, and for
seasons, and for days, & years: and let them be for lights in the firmament of
the heaven to give light upon the earth: & it was so. And God made two great
lights; the greater light to rule the day, and the lesser light to rule the night: he
made the stars also. And God set them in the firmament of the heaven to give
light upon the earth, and to rule over the day and over the night, & to divide
the light from the darkness: and God saw that it was good. And the evening
and the morning were the fourth day. ❧ And God said, Let the waters bring
forth abundantly the moving creature that hath life, and fowl that may fly
above the earth in the open firmament of heaven. And God created great
whales, & every living creature that moveth, which the waters brought forth
abundantly, after their kind, & every winged fowl after his kind: & God saw
that it was good. And God blessed them, saying, Be fruitful, & multiply, and
fill the waters in the seas, and let fowl multiply in the earth. And the evening
& the morning were the fifth day. ❧ And God said, Let the earth bring forth
the living creature after his kind, cattle, and creeping thing, and beast of the
earth after his kind: and it was so. And God made the beast of the earth after
his kind, and cattle after their kind, and every thing that creepeth upon the
27

11.73

1886
Merganthaler's Linotype machine first used commercially by New York *Tribune*. The Linotype's speed allows newspapers to set late-breaking news closer to printing deadlines (fig. 11.69). Each line of type, called a slug, could now be created at once and the letters immediately recycled for continued use, thanks to an ingenious keylike matrix that guided each letter to its correct slot (fig. 11.70). • Pica measuring system adopted in English-speaking countries.

1887
Tolbert Lanston invents Monotype typesetting machine, introduced commercially three years later.

1894
Linn Boyd Benton and Theodore L. DeVinne design Century typeface (fig. 11.71).

1896
Bertram G. Goodhue designs Cheltenham typeface (fig. 11.72).

1905
Offset lithography printing developed by Ira Rubel, who introduces a flexible metal printing plate, speeding up the printing process. • An exquisite example of a privately printed English Bible, produced in limited edition (fig. 11.73).

1906
Ludlow typecasting machine for headlines introduced.

1908
Morris Fuller Benton designs News Gothic typeface (fig. 11.74).

1910
Cubism, a semiabstract style using geometric shapes, created in France. This example is by Juan Gris (fig. 11.75). • 24 million copies of 2,433 newspapers printed daily in U.S.

1911
Frederic W. Goudy designs Goudy Old Style typeface, based on Italian Renaissance designs. Goudy, out of work and broke at 33, designed over 100 typefaces before his death at 82.

1916

Dadaism, a movement that rejected conventional artistic values, created in Zurich and New York. Max Ernst's 1924 cover of *The Little Review* (fig. 11.76) explores new ideas of what a layout "ought" to be.

1917

De Stijl ("the style") movement created in Holland as a refinement of cubism. This example is by Theo van Doesburg (fig. 11.77).

1918

Constructivism, an abstract, geometric style that used modern industrial materials, created in Russia. El Lissitzky, the most famous constructivist, emphasized simplicity, shape, and tension between art and type in Amsterdam's 1922 *Wendingen* cover (fig. 11.78).

1919

Bauhaus founded in Weimar by architect Walter Gropius. The basic tenet was that art and industry should be joined in education. This example, by László Moholy-Nagy, is from a Bauhaus prospectus designed in 1923 (fig. 11.79). • Futurism, a movement that embraced dynamic rhythms and energy, created in Italy.

1920

Morris Fuller Benton reworks Century type as Century Schoolbook.

1926

Paul Renner designs Futura typeface.

1928

Jan Tschichold's *Die Neue Typographie* published, describing his radical theory of page organization, including asymmetrical, importance-based positioning of type and increased attention to white space. • Eric Gill designs Gill Sans typeface.

1930

Four-color offset lithography press developed. • Innes Alphabets introduced, making headline setting easier. A forerunner to rub-on lettering, the Innes letters were printed on gummed paper, cut apart, and stuck in position by the artist (fig. 11.80).

11.76

11.77

11.78

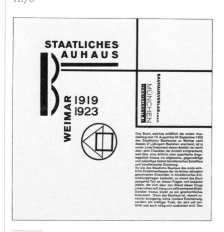

11.79

11.80

11.81

11.82

THIS IS
A PRINTING OFFICE

☙

CROSSROADS OF CIVILIZATION

REFUGE OF ALL THE ARTS
AGAINST THE RAVAGES OF TIME

ARMOURY OF FEARLESS TRUTH
AGAINST WHISPERING RUMOUR

INCESSANT TRUMPET OF TRADE

FROM THIS PLACE WORDS MAY FLY ABROAD
NOT TO PERISH ON WAVES OF SOUND
NOT TO VARY WITH THE WRITER'S HAND
BUT FIXED IN TIME HAVING BEEN VERIFIED IN PROOF

FRIEND YOU STAND ON SACRED GROUND

THIS IS A PRINTING OFFICE

11.83

VOGUE

3 Hours
Reading Time

FIRST
AUTUMN
FASHIONS

The Big Four in Furs
Ascending Hats
Transition Dresses
New Accessory Trio

15 Articles by
Marjorie Kinnan Rawlings
Glenn L. Martin
Elliot Paul
Ilka Chase
Ivy Low
Moss Hart
Major George Fielding Eliot
Frank Crowninshield
Wilfred Fleisher
Sheila Hibben
Irwin Edman
André Maurois
Sir Thomas Beecham ... and others

JULY 15, 1943 · PRICE 35 CENTS

11.84

The Wiltshire Gazette
News ⚜ Chronicle   Daily ⚜ Record
The Staffordshire Chronicle.
HAMPSHIRE ⚜ CHRONICLE
THE SCOTSMAN
THE WEST CUMBERLAND NEWS
FINANCIAL TIMES

11.85

**1932**
Stanley Morison designs Times New Roman for the London *Times* (fig. 11.81). The redesign takes three years to plan after Morison is hired in 1929 as an adviser. • Brush lettering becomes popular, a trend that continues through the mid-1950s. • Typesetting by teletype tape introduced.

**1938**
Chester Carlson invents xerographic process; another 22 years will pass before it is applied in a readily installed office machine. • One of A. M. Cassandre's *Harper's Bazaar* covers, an excellent example of combining surrealism, cubism, and constructivism (fig. 11.82).

**1940**
Beatrice Warde writes *Inscription for a Printing Office*. It has since been translated into 28 languages and cast in bronze for the entrance to the U.S. Government Printing Office in Washington (fig. 11.83). A renowned typophile, Warde is perhaps best remembered for her "crystal goblet" metaphor, given at an address to the British Typographers' Guild in 1932: "Shimmering crimson wine (is best) served in a crystal clear goblet, because everything about it is calculated to *reveal* rather than to hide the beautiful thing which it was meant to *contain*. ... So good typography helps the mental eye to see *through* type and not *upon* it."

**1942**
Alexander Liberman's *Vogue* cover (fig. 11.84) is an early example of placing subject listings on the cover.

**1946**
A sampling of English newspaper title-pieces shows that, seven hundred years after its design, Gothic – or Textura – is still used because of its suggestion of tradition and stature. Many other newspapers have switched to non-Gothic title-pieces, using such types as Baskerville Bold Titling and Perpetua Bold Titling (fig. 11.85).

**1947**
Phototypesetting, invented in 1890s, is improved to point where it can be practical.

**1948**
Offset litho becomes printing standard. Letterpress, invented by Gutenberg, required printer to make all final design decisions as he "locked up" design in chase. Offset puts design control into the hands of the designer, as it uses "mechanicals" that are photographically reproduced.

**1950**
Hermann Zapf designs Palatino typeface, an updated Italian Renaissance design (fig. 11.86).

**1954**
Monotype's Monophoto typesetting equipment introduced. • Mergenthaler Linotype's Linofilm typesetting machine introduced.

**1955**
Adrian Frutiger designs Univers typeface, the first to be designed in a wide range of weights and widths (fig. 11.87).

**1957**
Max Miedinger designs Helvetica typeface (fig. 11.88). • Letraset dry-transfer lettering introduced.

**1958**
Hermann Zapf completes six-year design of Optima typeface, a classic roman sans serif face (fig. 11.89). • One of Henry Wolf's many glorious covers for *Harper's Bazaar* (fig. 11.90). Wolf's work is recognizable for its conceptual ingenuity. • Bradbury Thompson mixes steel engravings and layered elements with classical typography, most notably in a series of 60 issues of *Westvaco Inspirations*. The 23-year series under his design supervision is now completed (fig. 11.91).

abcdefghijklmnopqrst
ABCDEFGHIJKLMN

11.86

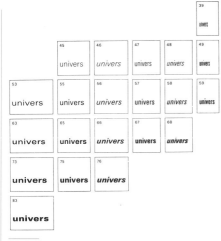

11.87

Roman
*Italic*
**Bold**
***Bold Italic***
Light
*Light Italic*
Condensed
**Bold Condensed**

11.88

Optima
*Optima Oblique*
**Optima Bold**
***Optima Bold Oblique***

11.89

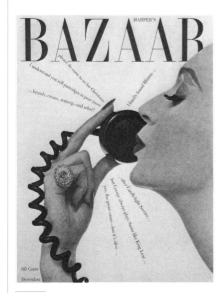

11.90

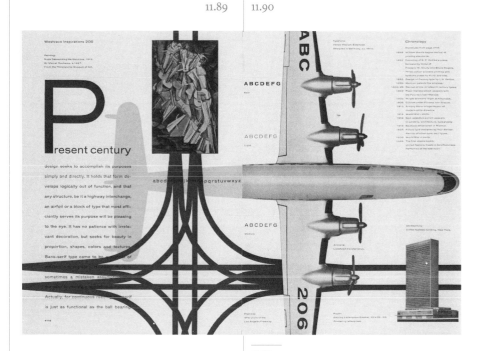

11.91

11.92

AVANT GARDE 13

PORTRAITS OF THE AMERICAN PEOPLE A MONUMENTAL PORTFOLIO OF PHOTOGRAPHS

11.93

**1960**
Xerox 914 is first production-line automatic office copier (fig. 11.92). It puts the power to disseminate information into the hands of anyone. When copies were laboriously made by hand, knowledge was easily controlled. Photocopiers are everywhere: at the library, at the pharmacy, at the quick-print shop, at one of the many chains of photocopy shops that have sprung up across the country. All it takes is a few cents to make a near-perfect reproduction. Inexpensive, high-quality copiers are marketed for personal use. Now literally anyone can be a printer (or at least a reproducer of printed information).

**1961**
IBM Selectric, the "golf-ball" typewriter, introduced.

**1962**
London's *Sunday Times* publishes first color supplement.

**1963**
First application of mouse as pointing device. • OCR (optical character recognition) faces designed.

**1964**
First word processor: IBM Magnetic Tape Selectric Typewriter.

**1969**
Mergenthaler Linotype installs first digital typesetting machine, the Linotron 1010, in the country's largest printing facility, the U.S. Government Printing Office. It can set both Old and New Testaments in just 18 minutes.

**1970**
Scanner reproduction introduced • Herb Lubalin and Tom Carnase design Avant Garde Gothic typeface for *Avant Garde* magazine (fig. 11.93). It is later adapted as a display typeface, and later still as a text face. America's greatest graphic designer through the 1950s and 1960s, Lubalin said, "The best typography never gets noticed." • London *Times* first British newspaper to use photocomposition.

**1971**

Rudy de Harak's record cover describes asymmetry in both type and imagery (fig. 11.94).

**1972**

Color xerography introduced.

**1977**

Laser typesetting machine introduced.

**1979**

A page of the first book whose text and imagery were composed at a single work-station, harkening back to the comprehensive work of the scribes some six hundred years earlier (fig. 11.95).

**1981**

First integrated type, photo, and layout system introduced by Scitex (fig. 11.96).

**1984**

Apple introduces Macintosh computer. The first model has a black and white screen, a single 400k disk drive, and only 128k of RAM. This modest beginning nevertheless marks the birth of affordable single-station publishing.

**1986**

Four-color laserwriter introduced.

**1987**

Seymour Chwast's poster integrates type and imagery using Chwast's own illustrative style. Notice the c is an ear and the 3 and 4 are set into the lion's eyes (fig. 11.97).

**1988**

Rick Valicenti's brochure spread employs unexpected and playful typographic mixing so the type becomes its own illustration (fig. 11.98).

**1990**

A spread from an annual report by Frankfurt Gips Balkind (fig. 11.99). The pages are cut in half, allowing the reader to mix the messages in a myriad of combinations.

11.94

11.95

11.96

34 Festival
International du Film
Publicitaire
Cinéma et Télévision
American Premiere
21 October 1987
Lincoln Center

11.97

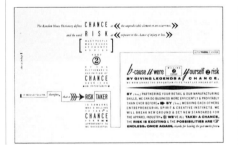

11.98

11.99

# GLOSSARY

**ALPHABET LENGTH** The measurement, in points or picas, of the lower-case alphabet of a specific typeface and size.

**AMPERSAND** A symbol (*&*) developed from the Latin *et*, meaning "and."

**ARTICLE** A story or textual composition that is part of a publication.

**ASCENDER** The part of a lower-case letter that extends above the mean line, or top of the x-height.

**ASCII** Unformatted computer files lacking typeface, typesize, and style information. Used to exchange information between computer systems, such as Macintosh and MS-DOS.

**ASYMMETRICAL** A design arrangement in which the space is unequally divided.

**BALLOT** A square bullet, so named because, being square, it is sometimes used to receive a check-marked vote.

**BASE LINE** The imaginary line on which letters rest. Descenders hang below the base line.

**BIO** Short for biography; an author's credentials or affiliation.

**BIT MAP** A digital interpretation of a letter or image in which each unit will either print or not print. Bit-mapped images are jagged.

**BLEED** Type or imagery that extends to the trim edge of a page.

**BLURB** A brief statement accompanying a headline that summarizes an article.

**BODY TYPE** Type of 6 to 14 points, used for lengthy text composition; also called text type.

**BOLDFACE** A heavier version of the normal weight of a typeface.

**BOX RULE** A rectangle made of lines. Box rules can be made more interesting by giving one of the lines greater weight.

**BREAKING FOR SENSE** Breaking display type into segments so the meaning is clear, rather than breaking them when the measure is filled.

**BREAKOUT** An excerpted section of an article presented as display type to catch a reader's attention.

**BULLET** A dot, which can be any size, used as a decorative or organizing device.

**BYLINE** Author's credit line.

**CALLOUT** *See* Breakout.

**CAP HEIGHT** The height of a capital letter from the base line to the top of the letter.

**CAPTION** The explanatory text accompanying a photo or illustration; usually set smaller than the text. Also called a legend or cut line.

**CENTERED** A typographic arrangement in which the left and right edges of the copy are mirror images of each other. Also, when an element appears in the center of a defined space.

**CHARACTER COUNT** The total number of characters, including word spaces, in a piece of copy.

**CHARACTERS** Individual letters, numerals, punctuation, and so on.

**CHARACTERS PER PICA** The average number of characters in a given size of a typeface that will fit into 1 pica of space. Used as a means of determining the length of copy when set in type.

**CLIP ART** Previously created illustrations and typographic compositions, available as line art or on disk, for copyright-free use by anyone.

**COLOR** The relative lightness or darkness of an area of type.

**COLUMN INCH** A newspaper measurement designating space that is one column wide by 1 inch deep.

**COLUMN WIDTH** The measurement from the left to the right edge of a group of lines of set type.

**CONDENSED** A narrower version of the normal width of a typeface.

**CONTENTS** A listing of the subject matter and its location (page number) in a document.

**COPY** In design and typesetting, manuscript type; in printing, all material to be printed (type, illustrations, photos).

**COPYFITTING** The process of estimating the amount of space typewritten copy will occupy when it is set in type.

**CROP** To eliminate portions of an image.

**DECK** A subhead appearing just beneath or near the headline.

**DEPARTMENT HEAD** A standing head on regular pages in a publication.

**DESCENDER** The part of a lower-case letter that hangs below the base line, or base of the x-height.

**DIGITAL TYPESETTING/COMPOSITION** The printing of characters and artwork from electronic originals.

*DINGBAT* An ornamental symbol or design used to get attention.

*DISPLAY TYPE* Type intended to catch attention and generate viewer reaction. Generally larger than 18 points.

*DOTS PER INCH (DPI)* Measurement describing resolution of laser printers and typesetters.

*DOWNLOADABLE FONT* A font that can be temporarily stored in a printer's memory.

*DROP CAP* An enlarged initial letter that extends below the first base line of body text. A drop cap should be base aligned with one of the text's base lines.

*EM* A square of the point size of the type being used. Used in indentions and word spacing, an em in 6-point type is 6 points wide by 6 points high; whereas an em in 8-point type is 8 points wide by 8 points high.

*EN* Half the width of an em. An em in 6-point type is 3 points wide by 6 points high.

*EXPANDED* A wider version of the normal width of a typeface.

*EXPORT* To send files from one program to another.

*EXTRACT* A lengthy quote taken from another source. It is usually set across a narrower column and in a smaller type size than the surrounding text.

*FACING PAGES* Two pages that face each other in a multipage document, also called a spread. Some publications have more than two facing pages, for example a trifold brochure.

*FLUSH* Even, or aligned, on one edge. This term can be applied to the alignment of any elements in a design, although it most often is used in reference to lines of type.

*FOLIO* A page number. Odd numbers are right-hand pages; even numbers are left-hand pages.

*FONT* One size and design of a given type style, including caps and lower-case letters, numerals, fractions, accented characters, punctuation, bullets, and symbols.

*FONT EDITOR* A software program that allows changes in existing letters. Particularly useful for customizing nameplates, logos, and department headings.

*FOOT LINE* A publication's name and publication date, placed at the foot of the page.

*FOOT MARGIN* The white space at the bottom of a page.

*FORMAT* (1) A series of instructions that are retained by the computer for standardized applications, such as text or headline treatments. (2) A standardized layout for a publication.

*FOUNTAIN EFFECT* Smooth gradation from light to dark in a halftone screen.

*GRID* A matrix of nonprinting lines that guide the placement of elements on the page.

*GROTESQUE* European term for sans serif or Gothic.

*GROUPING* Locking adjacent text and graphics together so they can be moved, saved, or resized as a single element.

*GUTTER* The white space extending from where two pages of a publication join at the binding edge to each page's live area — the inside margin.

*HAIRLINE RULE* A ¼-point rule.

*HANGING INDENT* An indention in which the first line of type extends beyond the left edge of the body copy that follows.

*HANGING INITIAL* An initial placed in the margin, to the left of the text.

*HEADER* Recurring copy at the top (or head) of the page that helps orient the reader. It can include such information as title, issue date, and page number.

*HEADLINE* Prominent display type, intended to summarize the accompanying copy and attract attention.

*HEAD MARGIN* The white space at the top of a page.

*HIGH-RESOLUTION OUTPUT* Artwork produced on image setters with a resolution of more than 1,200 DPI.

*HUNG PUNCTUATION* Punctuation set in the margin to achieve an optically flush edge.

*IMAGE SCANNER* A hardware accessory that converts reflective copy into an electronic file.

*IMPORT FILTER* A filter that allows page layout programs to accommodate various word processing programs.

*INDENTION* The space inserted at the beginning of a line of type. In text it is used to indicate the beginning of a new paragraph.

*INITIAL CAP* An enlarged letter at the beginning of a block of text or display type.

*ITALIC* Type in which the letters are slanted to the right and drawn to suggest handwriting. True italic fonts are most frequently drawn to accompany serif typefaces. *See* Oblique.

*JUMP LINE* A short phrase at the end of a page of text indicating the continuation of the text on another page, for example, "Continued on page 34."

*JUSTIFIED TYPE* Lines of type that are flush on both the left and right edges.

*KERN* To tighten up the space between two letters for optically consistent letter-spacing.

*KNOCKOUT* Any element that appears in white on a darker background; also called a dropout.

*LANDSCAPE ORIENTATION* Horizontal.

*LAYOUT* The arrangement of text and graphics on a page.

*LEADERS* Dots or dashes used to lead the eye across space, for example, from title to page number on the contents page.

**LEAD-IN** The first few words of copy set in italic, boldface, or all caps.

**LEADING** Also written as *ledding*. *See* Line spacing.

**LETTERSPACING** The spacing between individual letters.

**LIFTOUT** *See* Breakout.

**LIGATURE** Two or three characters linked to create a single letterform, for example, ff, fi, ffi, ffl.

**LIGHTFACE** A lighter version of a normal weight of any given typeface.

**LINE FOR LINE** A spec that indicates copy is to be set so that the lines break as they are typed or marked; the line breaks can thus be predetermined by the designer. This is necessary to "break for sense" (divide the copy into meaningful segments).

**LINE SPACING** The spacing between the bottoms of the descenders and the tops of the ascenders in lines of type. Also known as leading.

**LINING FIGURES** Numerals that are the same height as capital letters and align on the base line. *See also* Old-style figures.

**LINKING** Connecting columns in a story so the text flows continuously but the columns may be moved.

**LIVE AREA** The printing area of the page contained within the margins.

**LOWER-CASE** The small letters, or minuscules, of a type alphabet. When type was set in metal, these letters were stored in a drawer literally below the capital letters, or "upper case." Specified as *lc* or by marking a slash through the letters to be set in lower-case.

**MARGINS** The nonprinting areas surrounding the live area.

**MASTER PAGES** Left- and right-hand page elements that are automatically applied throughout a document.

**MASTHEAD** The listing of staff, address, and subscription information in a publication.

**MEAN LINE** The implied line at the top of the x-height.

**MEASURE** The length of typeset lines; the width of the column.

**MINUS LEADING** Setting type with less space from base line to base line than the type's size; the ascenders and descenders can overlap. An example of a spec for minus leading is 12/10.

**MINUS LETTERSPACING** Reducing the normal spacing between characters in a word.

**MODEM** A hardware accessory that connects a computer to phone lines.

**MS-DOS (MICROSOFT DISK OPERATING SYSTEM)** A system that governs how IBM PC-compatible computers process and store information.

**MUGSHOT** A very ordinary head-and-shoulder portrait photo, usually starkly lit and lacking composition, much like a police photo taken at the time of arrest.

**NAMEPLATE** A newsletter's title, usually appearing at the head of the first page. Also called a banner or logo.

**OBLIQUE** A slanted font in which the letters retain their roman characteristics (unlike italic). Most frequently found in sans serif faces.

**OLD-STYLE FIGURES** Numerals having ascenders and descenders. The body matches the x-height of the face. *See also* Lining figures.

**OPTICAL ALIGNMENT** Adjustment of letters and other elements so that they *appear* to be correctly aligned with one another.

**OUTLINE FONT** A typeface alphabet stored as a series of lines and arcs that are scaled to size at the time of printing. Outline fonts require less disk space and are more flexible than bit-mapped fonts.

**OVERSCORE** A rule or line set above type. *See also* Underscore.

**PAGE VIEW** A function that enables you to view a page layout at various sizes, for example, 50, 75, 100, and 200 percent.

**PHOTOTYPESETTING** A typesetting method in which light-sensitive paper is exposed to negative letterforms on film, creating black characters on a white background.

**PICA** A unit of measurement equaling 12 points, or approximately 1/6 inch. *See also* Point.

**PI CHARACTERS** Reference marks and symbols designed to match any other faces. Assembled in pi fonts.

**PICT FILES** Object-oriented files containing only black and white. *See also* TIFF files.

**PIXEL** Short for picture element; a dot that is the smallest unit displayed on a computer screen.

**POINT** The basic increment of typographic measurement. There are 12 points in a pica, 72 points in an inch.

**POINT SIZE** The size of type measured from the top of the ascenders to the bottom of the descenders, not, as is so often mistakenly thought, the height of the capital letters alone.

**PORTRAIT ORIENTATION** Vertical.

**POSTSCRIPT** A language developed by Adobe Systems to describe pages of scalable text and graphics.

**POSTURE** The angle of stress of a typeface: roman (vertical), italic (oblique), back slant (oblique to the left).

**PRINTER FONT** Scalable outlines for a given character set that enable a printer to print characters as clearly as possible.

**PULL QUOTE** A quote or statement extracted from an article and reset in display type to attract readers.

**RAGGED** Multiple lines of type set with either the left or right edge uneven. Word spacing remains constant in ragged setting.

**RANDOM ACCESS MEMORY (RAM)** Temporary memory storage in a computer or printer. The data disappear when the device is turned off.

**READ-ONLY MEMORY (ROM)** Permanent memory that stores data shared by all programs in a computer or printer.

**RECTO** A right-hand page, odd-numbered. *See also* Verso.

**RESIDENT FONT** A typeface built into a printer.

**RESOLUTION** The number of dots per inch (DPI) displayed on a computer screen or used by a laser printer or digital typesetter. Higher resolution – more dots per inch – provides clearer and smoother imagery.

**ROMAN** Type that has a vertical emphasis, unlike italic, cursive, or oblique, which are all slanted.

**ROUGH RAG** Ragged type set without hyphenation. Words that cannot fit on a line are carried down to the next, creating a very ragged edge. *See also* Tight rag.

**RULE** A typographic line whose thickness is specified in points.

**RUNAROUND** Type set to fit around another typographic or illustrative element, reflecting its contour. Also called wraparound.

**SANS SERIF** Type without serifs.

**SCALING** Resizing images to fit a layout.

**SCALLOPED COLUMNS** Page design with columns of unequal length. Scalloped columns should be aligned at the tops to make the page look organized, but the bottoms hang unfilled, making page layout much easier.

**SCANNER** A device that reads text or information from a photo or other artwork and converts it into digital data that can be placed electronically into a page layout program.

**SCHOLAR'S MARGINS** White space added to the outside margins of each page. Named for the extra-wide margins provided in scholarly texts for writing notes.

**SCREEN FONTS** Bit-mapped characters that appear on a computer screen.

**SERIFS** Small strokes at the ends of the main strokes of letters.

**SIDEBAR** A short article related and placed next to the main article.

**SMALL CAPS** Capital letters designed to be about the same size and color as the x-height of lower-case letters. Part of a complete text-type font.

**SPREAD** Facing pages in a publication.

**STANDING HEAD** Distinctive display type that announces a recurring department.

**STICK-UP CAP** An enlarged initial letter that extends above the top of body text, usually base aligned with the text's first line.

**STORY** *See* Article.

**STRESS** The direction of thickening in a curved stroke.

**STYLE** Electronic file containing typeface, size, style, letterspacing, alignment, and indention. Allows rapid typographic changes when preparing page layout.

**SUBHEAD** A secondary level of display type, usually located between the headline (primary typographic element) and the text.

**SUBSCRIPT** A character that prints below the base line of the type.

**SUPERSCRIPT** A character that prints above the mean line of the type.

**SURPRINT** Line copy superimposed over screened copy on the same printing plate. Not to be confused with overprinting, which involves two printing plates.

**SWASH CHARACTER** A character with flourishes.

**TEMPLATE** A page layout file containing formatting instructions.

**TERMINAL** The end of a letter's stroke when not ended with a serif.

**TEXT** Copy that is smaller than display type. *See also* Body type.

**TIFF (TAGGED IMAGE FILE FORMAT) FILES** A file format that describes scanned photos containing grays.

**TIGHT RAG** Ragged type set with hyphens. Words that cannot fit on a line are broken by hyphenation and continued on the next line, creating a smoother edge than in rough rag. *See also* Rough rag.

**TILING** Printing documents larger than the maximum paper size on a PostScript laser printer. The document is printed in sections, which must then be pasted together.

**TRACKING** Uniform letterspacing in type.

**TURNOVERS** The second and all subsequent lines of headlines and bulleted items, indented a similar distance to the right of the bullet.

**TYPEFACE** A named type design, such as Bodoni, Cheltenham, Futura.

**TYPE FAMILY** All the variations of a typeface designed with similar characteristics. Type families usually consist of the basic roman, italic, and bold variations. Enlarged type families include condensed, expanded, shaded, outline, and combinations of the above.

**U/LC** The abbreviation for upper- and lower-case, a typesetting designation.

**UNDERSCORE** A rule or line set below the type. *See also* Overscore.

**UPPER-CASE** Capital letters, or majuscules, of a type alphabet. Specified as *UC* or *all caps* or by underscoring the words to be set in caps with three lines. *See also* Lower-case.

**VERSO** A left-hand page, even-numbered. *See also* Recto.

**WEIGHT** A letter's amount of blackness, relative to the space within it.

**WHITE SPACE** The blank areas of the page. Good design requires deliberate use of white space.

**WIDOW** A very short line at the end of a paragraph.

**WORD SPACING** The space between words.

**X-HEIGHT** The height of lower-case letters excluding ascenders and descenders. It is limited by the base line and the mean line.

# BIBLIOGRAPHY

In addition to the following excellent books, I recommend these publications: The American Institute of Graphic Arts' *ANNUALS; COMMUNICATION ARTS* magazine; *IN-HOUSE GRAPHICS; PRINT* magazine; *PUBLISH* magazine; *STEP-BY-STEP GRAPHICS* magazine; and The Type Directors Club's *ANNUALS.*

Aldrich-Ruenzel, Nancy, and John Fennell, *DESIGNER'S GUIDE TO TYPOGRAPHY.* New York: Watson-Guptill Publications, 1991.

Baudin, Fernand. *HOW TYPOGRAPHY WORKS.* New York: Design Press, 1989.

Beach, Mark, and Polly Pattison. *OUTSTANDING NEWSLETTER DESIGNS.* Portland, Oregon: Coast to Coast Publishing, 1990.

Bigelow, Charles, Paul Hayden Duensing, and Linnea Gentry. *FINE PRINT ON TYPE: THE BEST OF FINE PRINT MAGAZINE ON TYPE AND TYPOGRAPHY.* San Francisco: Bedford Arts Publications, 1988.

Blumenthal, Joseph. *ART OF THE PRINTED BOOK 1455–1955.* Boston: David R. Godine, 1973.

Burns, Aaron. *TYPOGRAPHY.* New York: Reinhold, 1961.

Carter, Rob, Ben Day, and Philip Meggs. *TYPOGRAPHIC DESIGN: FORM AND COMMUNICATION.* New York: Van Nostrand Reinhold, 1985.

Chappell, Warren. *A SHORT HISTORY OF THE PRINTED WORD.* New York: Knopf, 1970.

Dair, Carl. *DESIGN WITH TYPE.* Toronto: University of Toronto Press, 1985.

Fabre, Maurice. *A HISTORY OF COMMUNICATIONS.* New York: Hawthorn Books, 1963.

Goudy, Frederic W. *THE ALPHABET AND ELEMENTS OF LETTERING.* New York: Dover Publications, 1963.

Haley, Allan. *PHOTOTYPOGRAPHY: A GUIDE FOR IN-HOUSE TYPESETTING.* New York: Charles Scribner's Sons, 1980.

Hutchinson, James. *LETTERS.* New York: Van Nostrand Reinhold, 1983.

Kepes, Gyorgy. *LANGUAGE OF VISION.* Chicago: Paul Theobald, 1945.

Koren, Leonard, and R. Wippo Meckler. *GRAPHIC DESIGN COOKBOOK.* San Francisco: Chronicle, 1989.

Korger, Hildegard. *HANDBOOK OF TYPE AND LETTERING.* New York: Design Press, 1992.

Kvern, Olav Martin, and Stephen Roth. *REAL WORLD PAGEMAKER 4.* New York: Bantam Books, 1990.

Logan, Robert K. *THE ALPHABET EFFECT: THE IMPACT OF THE PHONETIC ALPHABET ON THE DEVELOPMENT OF WESTERN CIVILIZATION.* New York: William Morrow, 1986.

McCrum, Robert, William Cran, and Robert MacNeil. *THE STORY OF ENGLISH.* New York: Elisabeth Sifton Books/Viking, 1986.

Meggs, Philip B. *A HISTORY OF GRAPHIC DESIGN.* New York: Van Nostrand Reinhold, 1983.

Müller-Brockmann, Josef. *GRID SYSTEMS IN GRAPHIC DESIGN: A VISUAL COMMUNICATIONS MANUAL.* Niederteufen, Switzerland: Arthur Niggli Ltd., 1981.

Owen, William. *MODERN MAGAZINE DESIGN.* Dubuque, Iowa: Wm. C. Brown Publishers, 1992.

Parker, Roger C. *NEWSLETTERS FROM THE DESKTOP.* Chapel Hill, North Carolina: Ventana Press, 1990.

Quark, Inc. *QUARK XPRESS TIPS.* Denver: Quark, Inc., 1989.

Ruder, Emil. *TYPOGRAPHY: A MANUAL OF DESIGN.* Teufen, Switzerland: Arthur Niggli Ltd., 1967.

Snyder, Gertrude and Alan Peckolick. *HERB LUBALIN: ART DIRECTOR, GRAPHIC DESIGNER AND TYPOGRAPHER.* New York: American Showcase, 1985.

Spencer, Herbert. *PIONEERS OF MODERN TYPOGRAPHY.* Cambridge, Massachusetts: The MIT Press, 1983.

Spiekermann, Erik. *RHYME AND REASON: A TYPOGRAPHIC NOVEL.* Berlin, Germany: H. Berthold AG, 1987.

Tschichold, Jan. *ASYMMETRIC TYPOGRAPHY.* New York: Reinhold, 1967.

_____ . *TREASURY OF ALPHABETS AND LETTERING.* New York: Design Press, 1992.

White, Alex. *HOW TO SPEC TYPE.* New York: Watson-Guptill Publications, 1987.

White, Jan V. *GRAPHIC DESIGN FOR THE ELECTRONIC AGE.* New York: Watson-Guptill Publications, 1988.

_____ . *GREAT PAGES: A COMMON SENSE APPROACH TO EFFECTIVE DESKTOP DESIGN.* El Segundo, California: Serif Publishing, 1990.

Williams, Robin. *THE MAC IS NOT A TYPEWRITER.* Berkeley, California: Peachpit Press, 1990.

Wingler, Hans M. *THE BAUHAUS.* Cambridge, Massachusetts: The MIT Press, 1969.

Zapf, Herman. *ABOUT ALPHABETS.* Cambridge, Massachusetts: The MIT Press, 1970.

# DESIGNER CREDITS

hanks to each of the following for permission to use their work in this book: **1.16** UC SANTA CRUZ REVIEW *Jim MacKenzie, AD* **1.17** THE WASHINGTON POST MAGAZINE *Brian*
*›yes, AD* **1.18** MEMPHIS *Murry Keith, AD* **1.19** CARING *Karen Kephart, Editor; Geer Design, AD* **1.20** PACIFIC NORTHWEST *Shauna Wolf Narciso, AD* **1.21** NEW ENGLAND BUSINESS *Judy Dombrowski, AD* **1.22** BRAKE & FRONT
D *Linda Pyle, AD* **1.23** AUTOMOBILE MAGAZINE *Larry Crane, AD* **1.24** PSYCHOLOGY TODAY *Fo Wilson, AD* **1.25** THE DIAMOND *W.N. "Buff" Silveria, Editor* **1.26** EUROPEAN TRAVEL & LIFE *Jeanne Dzienciol, AD* **1.27** TEXTILE
NTAL *Charlotte E. Caffrey & Nancy J. Ashmore, Editors* **1.28** SAN FRANCISCO FOCUS *Matthew Drace, AD* **1.29** SHAPE *Sonya Weiss, EAD; Garry Tosti, DD* **1.30** NEW YORK WOMAN *Ann Kwong, AD* **1.31** TIME *Rudolph C. Hoglund,*
*) (Copyright © 1989, The Time Inc. Magazine Company. Reprinted by permission.)* **1.32** EDISON NEWS *Jack O'Brien, Editor* **1.33** NORMAL *Paul Davis, AD* **1.34** EAST WEST *Betsy Woldman, AD* **1.35** CONTINENTAL PROFILES
*b Cato, GD* **1.36** ALL ABOUT US *Victoria A. Randle, Editor* **1.37** HIPPOCRATES *Jane Palecek, AD* **1.38** WIGWAG *Paul Davis, AD* **1.39** CONNECTICUT LIFESTYLES *Faye Griffiths, Editor; Leslie Woodward, GD* **1.40** CHILDREN'S
SINESS *S. Ashley VanSlyck, AD* **1.41** ART NEW ENGLAND *Meg Birnbaum, AD; Design = i* **1.42** NEW MIAMI *Kevin Jolliffe, AD* **1.43** THE FACE *Phil Bicker, AD* **1.44** TAMPA BAY LIFE *Alfred Zelcer, DD* **1.45** BANDWAGON *Peterson*
*Company, Design* **1.46** PSYCHOLOGY TODAY *Fo Wilson, AD* **1.47** BRAKE & FRONT END *Linda Pyle, AD* **2.16** THE TREASURY PRO *Ken L. Parkinson & Joyce R. Ochs, Publishers* **2.17** SALES & MANAGEMENT *Ken Surabian,*
*)* **2.18** DIMENSIONS *Weisz Yang Dunkelberger Inc., Design* **2.19** LODESTAR *Don Weller, AD* **2.20** AUDIO *Cathy Cacchione, AD* **2.21** GOLDEN YEARS *Carol B. Hittner, Editor in Chief* **2.22** PERSONAL COMPUTING *Nancy Gordon,*
*)* **2.23** AMERICAN WAY *Connatser & Company, AD* **2.24** BLOCKBUSTER *Scott Kelley, AD* **2.25** COLUMBIA *Florence Keller, AD* **2.26** LODESTAR *Don Weller, AD* **2.27** GP GROWTH *Carole Siracusa, Editor; InHouse Design Associates,*
*esign (© 1990 Georgia-Pacific Corporation. All rights reserved.)* **2.28** INTERFACE *Kate S. Neessen, Editor; Eric Hanson & Cynthia Rykken, AD* **2.29** BP AMERICA SCENE *Brian Apelt, Editor; The NorthShore Group, DD* **2.30**
EDICAL ECONOMICS *John Newcomb, DD* **2.31** ARCHITECTURAL RECORD *Alberto Bucchianeri, DD; Anna Egger-Schlesinger, Senior Associate AD* **2.32** CARING *Karen Kephart, Editor; Geer Design, AD* **2.33** USCEA INFO *Robert*
*vingston, Editor* **2.34** UCLA MAGAZINE *Juliet Beynon, AD* **2.35** PERSONNEL JOURNAL *Susan Overstreet, DD* **2.36** NEW YORK WOMAN *Ann Kwong, AD* **2.37** AT&T FOCUS *Deutsch Design, Inc., DD* **2.38** INTERVIEW *Jamie Hartwell,*
*litor* **2.39** CARING *Karen Kephart, Editor; Geer Design, AD* **2.40** PACIFIC NORTHWEST *Shauna Wolf Narciso, AD* **2.41** NEW ENGLAND MONTHLY *Hans Teensma, DD* **2.42** KCET MAGAZINE *Lisa Wrigley, AD* **2.43** CHILDREN'S
SINESS *S. Ashley VanSlyck, AD* **2.44** FLEET NORSTAR DIRECTIONS *Tribich Design Associates, DD* **2.45** FLORIDA BUSINESS SOUTHWEST *Eleanor K. Sommer, Publisher; Ken Gooderham, Editor* **2.46** AMERICAN WAY *Alisann*
*ixon, AD* **2.47** LIFE ASSOCIATION NEWS *Dee Cohen, AD* **2.48** FLEET NORSTAR DIRECTIONS *Tribich Design Associates, DD* **2.49** WIGWAG *Paul Davis, AD* **2.50** HAMILTON SPIRIT *Kim Shank, Editor* **2.51** PASSWORD *Warren*
*Dana & David T. Marko & M. Lynn Reno, Editors; BD&E, Design* **2.52** NEW YORK *Robert Best, DD* **3.11** VOLKSWAGEN WORLD *Marlene Goldsmith, Editor; Richard Fish, AD* **3.12** UC SANTA CRUZ REVIEW *Jim MacKenzie,*
*D* **3.13** NEW ENGLAND MONTHLY *Hans Teensma, DD* **3.14** TAMPA BAY LIFE *Wendy McMillan, AD* **3.15** OUTSIDE *John Askwith, DD (Reprinted by permission from Outside magazine. Copyright © 1989, Mariah Publications*
*rporation.)* **3.16** CHILDREN'S BUSINESS *S. Ashley VanSlyck, AD* **3.17** LODESTAR *Don Weller, AD* **3.18** AMERICAN WAY *Connatser & Company, AD* **3.19** CLEVELAND MAGAZINE *Gary Sluzewski, DD* **3.20** USAIR *David McClure,*
*D* **3.21** HIPPOCRATES *Jane Palecek, AD* **3.22** INSIGHT ON THE NEWS *Roberta Morcone, DD (Reprinted with permission from Insight. All rights reserved.)* **3.23** BESTWAYS *Dennis K. Mead, AD* **3.24** PUBLIC RELATIONS JOURNAL
*san Yip, AD* **3.25** THE FACE *Phil Bicker, AD* **3.26** SPY *B.W. Honeycutt, AD* **3.27** ROLLING STONE *Fred Woodward, AD* **3.28** NEW YORK WOMAN *Ann Kwong, AD* **3.29** FLEET NORSTAR DIRECTIONS *Tribich Design Associates,*
*D* **3.30** BP AMERICA SCENE *Brian Apelt, Editor; The NorthShore Group, DD* **3.31** CONNECTICUT'S FINEST *Bett McLean, DD* **3.32** MEDICAL ECONOMICS *John Newcomb, DD* **3.33** WORLD MONITOR *Laura N. Frank, AD* **3.34**
EMICAL PROCESSING *Karen L. Kramer, Editor* **3.35** ELECTRONIC MUSICIAN *Kathy Marty, AD; Bob O'Donnell, Editor* **3.36** M *Dennis Freedman, AD* **3.37** SYRACUSE UNIVERSITY MAGAZINE *Christopher O. Purcell, DD* **3.38**
OSSIER *David Whitmore, AD* **3.39** UCLA MAGAZINE *Juliet Beynon, AD* **3.40** INVENTION & TECHNOLOGY *Theodore Kalomirakis, AD* **3.41** RESTAURANT BUSINESS *Lisa Powers & Charli Ornett, Art Direction* **3.42** NOTRE DAME
AGAZINE *Walton R. Collins, Editor; Don Nelson, AD* **3.43** L'EXPANSION *Josyanne Challeton, AD* **3.44** NEW ENGLAND MONTHLY *Hans Teensma, DD* **3.45** INSIDE ALBANY *Wendy Berninger, Editor* **4.19** MEDICAL ECONOMICS
*hn Newcomb, DD* **4.20** SYRACUSE UNIVERSITY MAGAZINE *Christopher O. Purcell, DD* **4.21** NEW YORK *Robert Best, DD* **4.22** TAMPA BAY LIFE *Alfred Zelcer, AD* **4.23** USAIR *David McClure, AD* **4.24** PACIFIC TIDINGS *Susan*
*itt, Editor; Darrell Cassidy, DD* **4.25** NEW ENGLAND MONTHLY *Hans Teensma, DD* **4.26** SSR-TIDNINGEN *Per Olof Kristenson, Editor; Jonas Söderström, AD* **4.27** SPY *B.W. Honeycutt, AD* **4.28** CA MAGAZINE *Judy Margolis,*
*litor & Art Director; John Shardalow, Typographer* **4.29** AUDIO *Cathy Cacchione, AD* **4.30** HIPPOCRATES *Jane Palecek, AD* **4.31** NIBBLE *David A. Krathwohl, Editor* **4.32** CONNECTICUT'S FINEST *Bett McLean, DD* **4.33** NEW
AMI *Kevin Jolliffe, AD* **4.34** TREASURY PRO *Ken L. Parkinson & Joyce R. Ochs, Publishers* **4.35** OUTSIDE *John Askwith, DD (Reprinted by permission from Outside magazine. Copyright © 1989, Mariah Publications Corporation.)*
**36** BECKMAN LIFE *Jeanie Herbert, Editor; Artworks Advertising, Design* **4.37** APPRISE *Jeanne Euker, AD* **4.38** NEW YORK WOMAN *Ann Kwong, AD* **4.39** AMERICAN WAY *Connatser & Company, AD* **4.40** CA MAGAZINE *Judy*
*argolis, Editor & Art Director; John Shardalow, Typographer* **4.41** KCET MAGAZINE *Lisa Wrigley, AD* **4.42** BUSINESS WEEK *Malcolm Frouman, AD* **4.43** INTERCHANGE *Joanne Kitsos, Editor* **4.44** SALES & MARKETING
ANAGEMENT *Ken Surabian, AD* **4.45** ATHENEUM *Guthrie Sayen, Editor; Peter Good, DD* **4.46** PERSONAL COMPUTING *Nancy Gordon, AD* **4.47** LDS HOSPITAL PROGRESS *Richard Nash, Editor; Easton Design Group, DD* **4.48**
ARING *Karen Kephart, Editor; Geer Design, AD* **4.49** SYRACUSE UNIVERSITY MAGAZINE *Christopher O. Purcell, DD* **4.50** INSIDE ALBANY *Wendy Berninger, Editor* **4.51** INSIGHT *Sheila Kaufman & Susan Mead, Editors* **4.52**
ARING *Karen Kephart, Editor; Geer Design, AD* **4.53** CELLULAR MARKETING *Judy L. Rudrud, Publisher* **4.54** CFO *Barbara D. Savinar, AD* **4.55** M *Dennis Freedman, AD* **4.56** D *David Harris, AD* **4.57** UC SANTA CRUZ REVIEW
*n MacKenzie, AD* **4.58** GULF COAST *Linda L. Titus, AD* **4.59** NEW ENGLAND MONTHLY *Hans Teensma, DD* **4.60** BUSINESS WEEK *Malcolm Frouman, AD* **5.19** AMERICAN PHOTO *Mark Gartland, AD (Reprinted with*
*ermission of American Photo, Diamandis Communications Inc., a wholly-owned subsidiary of Hachette Publications Inc.)* **5.20** INSTITUTIONAL INVESTOR *Chel S. Dong, AD* **5.21** M *Dennis Freedman, AD* **5.22** CHILDREN'S
USINESS *S. Ashley VanSlyck, AD* **5.23** THE EDGE *Kristin Frantz, AD* **5.24** CIPS NEWS *Debby Brasel, Editor* **5.25** SCANORAMA *Tommy Säflund, AD* **5.26** ESSENCE *Susan L. Taylor, Editor-in-Chief* **5.27** TRUSTCORP VISTAS *Public*
*ffairs Department, Editors* **5.28** D *David Harris, AD* **5.29** NEW YORK *Robert Best, DD* **5.30** SPORTS ILLUSTRATED *Steven Hoffman, DD (The example is reprinted courtesy of Sports Illustrated from the November 14, 1988 issue.*
*opyright © 1988, The Time Inc. Magazine Company. All Rights Reserved.)* **5.31** SNOW COUNTRY *Julie Curtis & Nancy Graham, AD* **5.32** RESTAURANT BUSINESS *Lisa Powers & Charli Ornett, Art Direction* **5.33** FLEET NORSTAR
IRECTIONS *Tribich Design Associates, DD* **5.34** IN HOUSE GRAPHICS *Ronnie Lipton, Editor* **5.35** NATURAL HISTORY *Thomas Page, DD* **5.36** OUTSIDE *John Askwith, DD (Reprinted by permission from Outside magazine. Copyright*
*1989, Mariah Publications Corporation.)* **5.37** PASSWORD *Warren B. Dana & David T. Marko & M. Lynn Reno, Editors; BD&E, Design* **5.38** PACIFIC NORTHWEST *Shauna Wolf Narciso, AD* **5.39** PARENTS *Clifford M. Gardiner,*
*D; Richard Loretoni, AD* **5.40** CLEVELAND MAGAZINE *Gary Sluzewski, DD* **5.41** MIDWEST LIVING *Richard Michels, AD* **5.42** ELECTRICAL CONTRACTOR *Larry C. Osius, Editor & Publisher; Gerry Quinn, Graphics* **5.43** AMERICAN
AY *Connatser & Company, AD* **5.44** M. *Karen Kephart, Editor* **5.45** INTERCHANGE *Joanne Kitsos, Editor* **5.46** FREUNDIN *Andreas Danch, Editor* **5.47** AMSOUTH PARTNERS *Roger Ellenburg, AD; Carol Vaezi, Typography; Andi*
*ampbell, Editor; Debra Windham, Publications Manager* **5.48** NEW ENGLAND MONTHLY *Hans Teensma, DD* **5.49** SPORTS ILLUSTRATED *Steven Hoffman, DD (The example is reprinted courtesy of Sports Illustrated from the*
*arch 5, 1990 issue. Copyright © 1990, The Time Inc. Magazine Company. All Rights Reserved.)* **5.50** WIGWAG *Paul Davis, AD* **5.51** TAMPA BAY LIFE *Alfred Zelcer, DD* **5.52** PEBBLE BEACH *Karen Hunter, Editor (Reprinted by*
*ermission from Pebble Beach – The Magazine.)* **5.53** USAIR *David McClure, AD* **6.07** TEXTILE RENTAL *Charlotte E. Caffrey & Nancy J. Ashmore, Editors* **6.08** HISPANIC *Alberto Insúa, AD (Reprinted with permission from*
*ispanic Magazine.)* **6.09** FAMILY CIRCLE *Nancy Clark, Deputy Editor* **6.10** VIRGINIA LEADER *Dawn Steward, Editor* **6.11** ELLE DEUTSCH *Sylvia Monteiro, AD* **6.12** SARA LEE INTERCHANGE *Joanne Kitsos, Editor* **6.13** VIEW *Douglas*
*eay, AD* **6.14** GLAMOUR *Kati Korpijaakko, AD* **6.15** DOMAIN *Jody Halton, AD* **6.16** PHOTOMETHODS *Debbie Todd, AD* **6.17** STEP-BY-STEP *Michael J. Hammer, AD* **6.18** NATIONAL GEOGRAPHIC TRAVELER *Suez B. Kehl, AD*
**19** SANTA BARBARA MAGAZINE *Kimberly Kavish, AD* **6.20** WASHINGTON FLYER *Rebecca Seely, Publisher* **6.21** SPORTS AFIELD *Gary Gretter, DD* **6.22** TRUMP'S *Bernard Scharf, AD; David Doty, Editor* **6.23** WASTE AGE *Jerry*
*chwartz, Publisher* **6.24** LIFE ASSOCIATION NEWS *Dee Cohen, AD* **6.25** TAMPA BAY LIFE *Alfred Zelcer, DD* **6.26** DOWN EAST *Davis Thomas, Editor; D. Timothy Seymour, AD* **6.27** ONLINE TODAY *Thom Misiak, AD* **6.28** MODERN
ATURITY *James H. Richardson, AD* **6.29** AMSOUTH PARTNERS *Roger Ellenburg, AD; Carol Vaezi, Typography; Andi Campbell, Editor; Debra Windham, Publications Manager* **6.30** TAPPI JOURNAL *Steven A. Yeager, AD* **6.31**
NNAPOLITAN *Janine Orr, DD* **6.32** ABA JOURNAL *David P. Jendras, DD* **6.33** EDUCATIONAL LEADERSHIP *Al Way, AD* **6.34** CASE CURRENTS *Craig Neil McCausland, Designer* **6.35** INSIDE SPORTS *Scott F. Kelly, AD* **6.36** SPORT
*ony Fox, AD* **6.37** CA MAGAZINE *John Shardalow, Typographer* **6.38** FOOD & WINE *Elizabeth Woodson, AD* **6.39** GOLDEN YEARS *Debbie Billington, AD* **6.40** EXECUTIVE EDGE *Frank M. Milloni, AD; Lisa Umlauf-Roese, Designer*
**.41** DH HEADLINES *Karin Bumgardner, Editor* **6.42** AIA MEMO *Pam del Canto & Tony Dyson, ADs* **6.43** AM RICAS *John Isely, DD* **6.44** INTERCOM *Diana Losch, Designer* **6.45** SYRACUSE UNIVERSITY MAGAZINE *Christopher*
*. Purcell, DD* **6.46** THE STREET *Dan Peyton, Designer* **6.47** CV MAGAZINE *Frierson + Mee, AD* **6.48** AMERICAN CITY & COUNTY *Brian Buxton, AD* **6.49** CARIBBEAN TRAVEL AND LIFE *John Isely & Liz Clark, Design* **6.50** CHILDREN'S
OSPITAL OF PITTSBURGH PULSE *Geyer & Geyer Graphic Design, Design* **6.51** BN NEWS *David Beard, GD* **6.52** CURRENT *Gerri Winchell Design, Design* **6.53** ADEPTATIONS *Aaron Kramer, AD* **6.54** VELONEWS *Dan Wildhirt,*
*D* **6.55** KANSAS TELEPHONE TIMES *Linda A. Laughlin, Editor* **6.56** VIEW *Douglas Deay, AD* **6.57** NEW ENGLAND MONTHLY *Hans Teensma, DD* **6.58** TRAVEL LIFE *Ken Smith, DD* **6.59** JACKSONVILLE TODAY *Mary Fisher Sellers,*
*D* **6.60** WIGWAG *Paul Davis, AD* **7.16** TIMESTALK *Louise E. Frank, Editor* **7.17** FOCUS ON HEALTHCARE *Jeff Anderson & Roy Miller, Editors* **7.18** TELLER *Terri Moyer, Editor* **7.19** TEXTILE RENTAL *Nancy Ashmore, Editor*
**.20** WIGWAG *Paul Davis, AD* **7.21** UPDATE *Jeff Anderson & Roy Miller, Editors* **7.22** CIPS NEWS *Debby Brasel, Editor* **7.23** THE PULSE *Judi Norkiewicz, Editor* **7.24** TRUMP'S *Bernard Scharf, AD; David Doty, Editor* **7.25** DIALOGUE
*he Agency Graphic Design, DD* **7.26** DOMAIN *Jody Halton, AD* **7.27** PACIFIC TIDINGS *Susan Stitt, Editor; Darrell Cassidy, DD* **7.28** HARTFORD MONTHLY *Sara A. Barbaris, DD; Christine Koch, AD* **7.29** INSIDE NORWALK HOSPITAL
*anet B. Kroll, Editor* **7.30** NEWSLINE *Stephen Perrella, Editor/DD* **7.31** ADEPTATIONS *Michael Waitsman, Editor; Greg Thompson, Cover Design* **7.32** ENTERPRISE *Nancy J. Daigler, Editor* **7.33** DEP TODAY *Ford Folios, DD* **7.34**
APERAGE *Jack O'Brien, Editor & Publisher* **7.35** NATION'S BUSINESS *Hans A. Baum, AD* **7.36** BRAKE & FRONT END *Linda Pyle, AD* **7.37** ISLANDS *Albert Chiang, AD* **7.38** VIS VIS *Kevin Fisher, AD* **7.39** AUTOMOTIVE REBUILDER
*inda Pyle, AD* **7.40** TEXAS MONTHLY *D. J. Stout, AD* **7.41** NEW PERSPECTIVES QUARTERLY *Steven Rachwal, DD* **7.42** MEDICAL ECONOMICS *John Newcomb, DD* **7.43** I-D *Stephen Male, AD* **7.44** AM RICAS *Edgardo C. Reis,*
*ditor; John Isely, DD* **7.45** TRAVEL HOLIDAY *Wendy Palitz, AD* **7.46** INTERCITY MAGAZINE *Tony Quinn, Editor; Rami Lippa, AD* **7.47** PEBBLE BEACH *Karen A. Hunter, Editor; Musgrave & Friends, Design* **7.48** INTEREST *Untel*
*& Untel inc, Design* **7.49** EYE ON LSSI *Julie A. Bokser, Editor* **7.50** NETWORK NEWSLETTER *Lori A. McDonough, Manager; Thomas A. Popp, Editor* **7.51** THE ALAN REVIEW *Leila Christenbury & Robert C. Small, Jr., Editors; Tucker*
*Conley, AD* **7.52** FOLIO: *Lowry Thompson, DD* **8.08** PC NEWS *Tom Starner, Editor* **8.09** EXECUTIVE UPDATE *Roy Miller, Editor; Fiegenschue Design, DD* **8.10** STEP-BY-STEP ELECTRONIC DESIGN *John Odam, DD* **8.11**
DEPTATIONS *Michael Waitsman & Kathy McClelland, Editors* **8.12** JOURNAL OF CASH MANAGEMENT *Ken Parkinson & Joyce Ochs, Editors* **8.13** ELLE DEUTSCH *Sylvia Monteiro, AD* **8.14** GIFT REPORTER *Jean Fujisaki, AD* **8.15**
IEW *Douglas Deay, AD* **8.16** PHOENIX HOME & GARDEN *Barbara Glynn Denney, AD* **8.17** AMERICA *Ken Smith, DD; Brad Zucroff, AD* **8.18** NEW YORK ALIVE *John L. Moore, AD* **8.19** THE AMERICAN SCHOOL BOARD JOURNAL
*Gregg W. Downey, Editor* **8.20** HI FI & ELECTRONIK *Torry Lindstrøm, Editor; Lisa Høyrup, AD* **8.21** CASA CLAUDIA *Carlos Henrique S. Barros, AD* **8.22** VARIAN MAGAZINE *Martha Kelley Rees, Editor; Arias & Sarraille Design*
*Group, Design* **8.23** THE BOTTOM LINE *Camille Gutmore, Publications Manager; Ruth Moraga, Graphics Specialist* **8.24** AM RICAS *Edgardo Reis, Director; John Isely, DD* **8.25** TRAVEL & LEISURE *Bob Ciano, AD* **8.26** CLASSIC
D *Dean Wilson, AD* **8.27** MEN'S FITNESS *Jeff Byers, AD* **8.28** ENTERTAINMENT WEEKLY *Michael Grossman, DD; Mark Michaelson, Sr AD* **8.29** ¾TNAIZER *Louise M. Axelson, Editor; Steve Smith, AD; Harry Rich Associates,*
*Design* **8.30** CONTINENTAL PROFILES *Janine H. Gevas, AD; David Doty, VP Editorial & Art* **8.31** PERSONNEL JOURNAL *Susan Overstreet, DD* **8.32** LOOK AT FINLAND *Martti Mykkanen, AD* **8.33** CONNECTICUT'S FINEST *Bett*
*McLean, DD; Lawrence Woodhull, AD* **8.34** U.S. NEWS & WORLD REPORT *Rob Covey, AD* **8.35** HIPPOCRATES *Jane Palacek, AD* **8.36** NATIONAL GEOGRAPHIC *William Graves, Editor; Gerard A. Valerio, Design; David Doubilet,*
*Photo* **9.12** DISCOVER *Conrad Warre, AD* **9.13** TEXAS MONTHLY *D.J. Stout, AD* **9.14** PULSE! *Tom Fillebrown, AD* **9.15** MEN'S HEALTH *Mike McGrath, Editor (Reprinted by permission of Men's Health Newsletter. © 1991,*
*Rodale Press, Inc. All rights reserved.)* **9.16** JOURNAL OF THE INSTITUTE OF NUCLEAR MATERIALS MANAGEMENT *Gregory L. Schultz, Editor; Innovative Design & Graphics, Design* **9.17** COMPUTERTALK *Neil R. Bauman, Editor*
**.18** MODERN MATURITY *James H. Richardson, AD* **9.19** TEXAS MONTHLY *D.J. Stout, AD* **9.20** AM RICAS *John Isely, DD* **9.21** SPORTS ILLUSTRATED *Steven Hoffman, DD (The example is reprinted courtesy of Sports Illustrated.*
*Copyright © 1989, The Time Inc. Magazine Company. All Rights Reserved.)* **9.22** ARQUITETURA & CONSTRUC O *Carlos Henrique S. Barros, AD* **9.23** FORTUNE MAGAZINE *Margery Peters, AD* **9.24** CHICAGO *Barbara Solowan,*
*DD* **9.25** AMERICAN HERITAGE *Peter Morance, AD* **9.26** MIRABELLA *John Tennant, CD* **9.27** SYRACUSE UNIVERSITY MAGAZINE *Christopher O. Purcell, AD* **9.28** SIERRA *Martha Geering, AD* **9.29** ARCHAEOLOGY *Alexander*
*sely, AD* **9.30** AMERICAN PRINTER *Jill Roth, Editorial Director* **9.31** BLITZ *Christophe Gowans, AD* **9.32** YOUR PERSONAL BEST *Frank M. Milloni & Lisa Umlauf-Roese, Designers* **9.33** HG *Dania Martinez Davey, AD* **9.34** MACGUIDE
MAGAZINE *Dino Philip Offenhauser, AD* **9.35** XPLORATION *Mike Salisbury Communications, Inc., AD* **9.36** SPORTS ILLUSTRATED *Steven Hoffman, DD (The example is reprinted courtesy of Sports Illustrated from the March*
*27, 1989 issue. Copyright © 1989, The Time Inc. Magazine Company. All Rights Reserved.)* **10.16** BODY BULLETIN *Frank M. Milloni, AD* **10.17** PAN AM CLIPPER *John Hair, AD; David Doty, VP Editorial & Art* **10.18** INTEREST
*Untel & Untel inc, Design* **10.19** LOSE WEIGHT NATURALLY *Lisa Umlauf-Roese, AD (Reprinted by permission of Lose Weight Naturally. © 1991, Rodale Press, Inc. All rights reserved.)* **10.20** SOUTHWEST SPIRIT *Michele Oumano,*
*AD; David Doty, VP Editorial & Art* **10.21** STEP-BY-STEP ELECTRONIC DESIGN *John Odam, DD* **10.22** VIS VIS *Kevin Fisher, AD; David Doty, VP Editorial & Art* **10.23** NETWORK *Madelaine King, Corporate DD; Sandy Wills,*
*Graphics Coordinator; Tom Lombardi, Design Consultant* **10.24** ABSTRACT *Willi Kunz Associates, Design* **10.25** EQUINOX *Ulrike Bender, AD* **10.26** ADEPTATIONS *Michael Waitsman & Kathy McClelland, Editors* **10.27**
YGEPLEJERSKEN *Peter Skeel Hjorth, Editor* **10.28** NORTH SHORE *Ken Ovryn, AD* **10.29** ORIENTATION '90 *Bret D. Haines, AD; Terri J. Hiers, Editor* **10.30** THE TRUST QUARTERLY *Juliette Hayes, Editor; John Massey, Design*
*Consultant* **10.31** INTEREST NEWS *Le Mot Dessiné Inc., Design; Rosemary Collins, Editor* **10.32** POTOMAC *Victoria A. Lamb, Editor* **10.33** AMSOUTH PARTNERS *Roger Ellenburg, AD; Carol Vaezi, Typography; Andi Campbell,*
*Editor; Debra Windham, Publications Manager* **10.34** ORIENTATION '91 *Bret D. Haines, AD; Terri J. Hiers, Editor* **10.35** TRUMP'S *Bernard Scharf, AD; David Doty, Editor* **10.36** CA MAGAZINE *Judy Margolis, AD*

# INDEX

# COLOPHON

This book, designed by the author, was written and composed on a Macintosh SE/30 with one meg RAM upgrade, using MacWrite II, Aldus PageMaker 4.01, and Aldus FreeHand 3.0. The text is Adobe Minion and Minion Expert, set 10/13 by 13½ picas.

Preliminary laser copies were printed on a Texas Instruments microLaser Plus with two meg RAM upgrade. The film was output on an L300 by Kingsport Press. Halftones and line art were shot conventionally by Jay's Publisher's Service.

Text paper is 80-pound Glatfelter Offset, smooth eggshell finish. The book was printed and bound by Kingsport Press in Kingsport, Tennessee.